Cambridge English

Complete
IELTS

Bands 4–5

Teacher's Book

**Guy Brook-Hart and Vanessa Jakeman
with David Jay**

CAMBRIDGE

CAMBRIDGE UNIVERSITY PRESS
Cambridge, New York, Melbourne, Madrid, Cape Town,
Singapore, São Paulo, Delhi, Tokyo, Mexico City

Cambridge University Press
The Edinburgh Building, Cambridge CB2 8RU, UK

www.cambridge.org
Information on this title: www.cambridge.org/9780521185158

First published 2012

Printed in the United Kingdom at the University Press, Cambridge

A catalogue record for this publication is available from the British Library.

ISBN 978-0-521-17956-0 Student's Book with Answers with CD-ROM
ISBN 978-0-521-17957-7 Student's Book without Answers with CD-ROM
ISBN 978-0-521-18515-8 Teacher's Book
ISBN 978-0521-17958-4 Class Audio CDs (2)
ISBN 978-0521-17960-7 Student's Book Pack (Student's Book with Answers
with CD-ROM and Class Audio CDs (2))
ISBN 978-1107-60245-8 Workbook with Answers with Audio CD
ISBN 978-1107-60244-1 Workbook without Answers with Audio CD

Contents

Introduction

Who Complete IELTS Bands 4–5 is for

Complete IELTS Bands 4–5 is an enjoyable and motivating topic-based course designed to help students with a B1 level of English to achieve their best score at IELTS. It starts with short, simple tasks and gradually builds up students' abilities to deal confidently with full-length IELTS tasks by the end of the course.

It offers:

- comprehensive analysis and practice of the **task types** used in IELTS Reading, Listening, Speaking and Writing papers.

- a step-by-step approach to **writing tasks** using models as guidance and sample answers.

- a systematic approach to **speaking tasks** with model answers and a focus on pronunciation.

- stimulating authentic reading texts that provide training in the skills and strategies needed to deal with exam **reading tasks**.

- listening activities that provide training in the skills and strategies needed to deal with exam **listening tasks**.

- coverage of major **grammar** and **vocabulary** areas which are known to be essential for success in IELTS. These are supported by work on correcting common mistakes as revealed in the Cambridge Learner Corpus.

- coverage of features of spelling where IELTS students at this level have problems.

- motivating **pair-work** and **group-work** exercises.

What the Student's Book contains

- **Ten topic-based units of nine pages** each covering topic areas frequently encountered in IELTS.

- Each unit covers tasks from each of the four papers in the exam, so all units contain work on **Listening**, **Reading**, **Writing** and **Speaking**. The units also cover **essential IELTS-related grammar and vocabulary**.

- Each exam task type is integrated into a range of classroom activities designed to equip students with the **strategies and approaches** needed to deal with the demands of IELTS.

- Practice for each part of the test is accompanied by **detailed information and advice** about what the task involves and how best to approach it.

- **Ten unit reviews** that provide additional exercises on the grammar and vocabulary encountered in each unit.

- **Writing and Speaking Reference sections** containing detailed advice to students on how to approach writing and speaking tasks in the exam, complete with exercises and model answers.

- A **Language Reference section** giving clear and detailed explanations of the grammar covered in each unit.

- **Ten Word Lists** containing lexical items encountered in the Student's Book units or recording scripts. We suggest that the best time to use these lists is towards the end of the unit, perhaps before doing the Speaking or the Writing sections. Students may use these lists for self-study and reinforcement of lexis encountered in the unit. Here are some suggestions as to how students can use them which you can discuss with them.

  - Students should use the page reference given to find the items in the unit and study how the words/ phrases are used in context.

  - They can use a learner's dictionary (such as the *Cambridge Learner's Dictionary*) to compare the dictionary definitions with the definitions given in the word list. In many cases, the definitions will coincide, but they will be able to study further examples in the dictionary.

  - Students can annotate the word lists themselves or copy items to their notebooks for further study.

  - You can suggest to students that they should not try to memorise all the items, but they should select a number of words and phrases that seem most useful to them and try to use them when doing speaking and writing tasks.

- A **full IELTS Practice Test**.

- A **CD-ROM intended for self-study** which provides further exercises to prepare students for IELTS.

The Cambridge Learner Corpus (CLC) ⊘

The Cambridge Learner Corpus (CLC) is a large collection of exam scripts written by students taking Cambridge ESOL English exams around the world. It contains over 200,000 scripts and is growing all the time. It forms part of the Cambridge International Corpus (CIC) and it has been built up by Cambridge University Press and Cambridge ESOL. The CLC contains scripts from:

- 200,000 students.
- 100 different first languages.
- 180 different countries.

Exercises in the Student's Book which are based on the CLC are indicated by the following icon. ⊙

What the Workbook contains

- **Ten units designed for homework and self-study**. Each unit contains full exam practice of **IELTS Reading** and **Listening tasks**.
- **IELTS writing tasks** with model answers.
- Further practice in the **grammar** and **vocabulary** taught in the Student's Book.
- An **audio CD** containing all the listening material for the Workbook.

What the Teacher's Book contains

- **Detailed notes** for the ten units in the Student's Book which:
  - state the **objectives** of each unit.
  - give **step-by-step advice** on how to treat each part of each Student's Book unit.
  - give **supporting information** to teachers and students about IELTS tasks.
  - offer suggestions for **alternative treatments** of the materials in the Student's Book.
  - offer a wide range of ideas for **extension activities** to follow up Student's Book activities.
  - contain **comprehensive answer keys** for each activity and exercise, including suggested answers where appropriate.
- **Ten photocopiable activities**, one for each unit, designed to provide enjoyable recycling of work done in the Student's Book unit, but without a specific exam focus. All photocopiable activities are accompanied by teacher's notes outlining:
  - the objectives of the activity.

  - a suggested procedure for handling the activity in the classroom.

- **Five photocopiable Progress Tests**, one for every two units, to test grammar and vocabulary taught in the units.
- **Ten photocopiable Vocabulary Extension word lists.**

The words and phrases in the photocopiable Vocabulary Extension word lists have been selected using the Cambridge International Corpus and relate to the topics of the unit. They are intended to provide students with extra vocabulary when doing IELTS tasks. We suggest that you hand these lists out near the beginning of the unit. Most of the words and phrases do not occur in the units themselves, but students may be able to use some of them during the speaking or writing activities in the unit.

Here are some suggestions on how these word lists can be used:

- Ask students to go through the word lists in conjunction with a good learner's dictionary such as the *Cambridge Advanced Learner's Dictionary* and check how the words/phrases are used in the examples (many of the definitions will be the same).

- Ask students to select 5–10 items which they would like to be able to use themselves and ask them to write their own sentences using the items.

- Encourage students to copy the items they find most useful to their notebooks.

- Ask students to refer to these word lists before doing speaking or writing tasks in the units. Give students time to look at the relevant list and think (and discuss with you) how they can use words/phrases before they do the task itself.

- When students do the tasks, pay particular attention to any use they make of items from the lists and give them feedback on how correctly they have used an item.

What the Class Audio CDs contain

There are **two audio CDs** containing **listening and speaking material** for the ten units of the Student's Book plus the Listening Practice Test. The listening and speaking materials are indicated by different coloured icons for each of the CDs.

Unit 1 Great places to be

Unit objectives

- **Reading:** introduction to scanning; introduction to table-completion and note-completion tasks; looking for synonyms and paraphrases; introduction to key ideas

- **Listening:** introduction to form-completion tasks; spelling and numbers; identifying the type of information required

- **Vocabulary:** features of attractive cities (*excellent shopping, lively festivals*, etc.); good and bad aspects of cities (*fast public transport, high crime rate*, etc.); things which contribute to happiness (*earning money, having plenty of free time*, etc.); collocations and prepositional phrases; locations (*in the mountains, near the desert*, etc.); phrases expressing likes/dislikes; *percent* or *percentage*

- **Speaking Part 1:** introduction to Part 1 questions; giving details; expressing likes and dislikes

- **Pronunciation:** sentence stress – stressing words which answer the question or give main information

- **Grammar:** present simple and continuous – forms and uses

- **Writing Task 1:** understanding and analysing pie charts and bar charts; writing simple summaries with introductions and overviews

- **Spelling:** spelling changes when making nouns plural

Starting off

❶ *As a warmer* For students to get to know each other, with books closed, draw this table on the board.

	a place	a type of food	an activity
I like ...			
I dislike ...			

- Ask students to work alone and quickly copy and complete the table with their own ideas. To get them started, you can give them an example of a place you like and a place you dislike.

- Tell students to work in small groups (of three or four) and take turns to say what they like and dislike and give a reason for each. The other students in the group should say if they feel the same.

- When they have finished, ask students to change groups. Write these two prompts on the board:
  - *Students in my group generally like/dislike ... because ...*
  - *One student in my group likes/dislikes ... because ...*

- Elicit when they should use *like/dislike* and when they should use *likes/dislikes* (i.e. third-person singular, present simple).

- Tell students to take turns to report what they discussed to their new group, using the prompts you have written on the board. They should each speak for about a minute.

- Finally, round up with the whole class.

> **Answers**
> **1** New York **2** Rio de Janeiro **3** Dubai **4** Amsterdam **5** Shanghai **6** Sydney

❷ Before students do this exercise:

- write the following on the board.
  I'd like to visit New York because
  – *it has excellent shopping.*
  – *the shopping is excellent.*

- elicit a few similar sentences using the ideas in the Student's Book. Point out that with *lots to do*, we need to say ... *because* <u>there is</u> lots to do.

- tell students they can add their own ideas to the ones in the Student's Book.

When students have finished discussing the exercise in pairs, round up with the whole class.

Extension idea Ask students: *Which of these cities have you already visited? What is it like? What did you like about it? What did you dislike?*

Reading 1 Table completion

❶ *As a warmer* Tell students to look at the Starting off section again.

- Tell them: *Scientists have studied the cities in Starting off. They have found that one of the cities is the friendliest city in the world. Which one do you think it is? Why?*

- Ask students to work in small groups to discuss this.

Before students do the exercise, elicit from the whole class why *friendly inhabitants* is good. Ask students to suggest what *inhabitants* means (*answer*: the people who live in a particular place, the citizens). Encourage students to guess the meanings of other words they don't know when they do the exercise.

> **Suggested answers**
> **2** fast public transport G **3** crowded streets B
> **4** a high crime rate B **5** people in a hurry B
> **6** a relaxed lifestyle G

Extension idea Ask students: *Which are aspects of your home town or city?*

❷ When students have finished, round up with the whole class and write their ideas on the board.

❸ This is a scanning exercise. Scanning is moving your eyes quickly over the passage to locate a particular word or phrase that you may then need to read around more carefully.

- Tell students that it is easier to scan for names of people or places, because they start with a capital letter and usually stand out on the page.
- Tell students that one of the things they will have to do in the IELTS test is read very quickly to find where answers are located. There are many exercises in the course to develop their speed-reading skills.
- At the same time, they will need to be able to pick out the <u>key ideas</u> in questions – these ideas tell them what information they need to find.

Before students read, and perhaps with the passage covered, elicit the key idea in each question (*answers*: 1 four cities 2 friendliest). Tell students they should not try to read the whole passage carefully or try to understand everything. They should:

- pass their eyes over the passage till they recognise the names of the cities;
- underline them;
- read what is said about each city more carefully to answer question 2.

Give students two minutes to answer the questions, and be strict about the time limit.

> **Answers**
> **1** Rio de Janeiro, Lilongwe, Amsterdam, New York
> **2** Rio de Janeiro

❹ This is another scanning exercise but this time it is a little harder as students are scanning for phrases.

- Tell students to look at the good and bad aspects in Exercise 1 again before they start reading.
- Give them two minutes to scan the passage. Again, be strict about the time limit.

- Warn students that they won't find the exact phrases in the passage, but phrases which mean the same.

Students from traditional educational backgrounds may find speed-reading techniques hard to master. Do not expect immediate results; students require repeated practice in order to learn to scan.

> **Answers**
> friendly inhabitants, a high crime rate,
> a relaxed lifestyle, people in a hurry

❺ Table completion is an IELTS Reading task. It tests students' ability to scan for information using words already in the table to help locate answers.

Tell students:

- it is important to look at the task to see what parts of the passage they need to read again in order to answer the questions – they don't always need to read the whole passage again.
- they should use names of the cities which they scanned for in Exercise 3 to help them find the answers in the passage.
- they should make the connection with the words in italics in the table and words in the passage which express the same meaning.
- in the live exam, words will not be in italics. It has been done here to help them.

Don't set a time limit. If students wish, they can work in pairs to do this task.

> **Answers**
> inhabitants – populations
> lifestyle – way of life
> don't have so much – have less
> reputation for – known for
> have little – be short of
> don't pay attention to – ignore

❻ Ask students:

- *Should you write your own answers, or should you copy a word from the passage for each answer?* (copy)
- *How many words can you write for each answer?* (one)
- *What happens if you write two words?* (the answer is wrong)

> **Answers**
> **1** relaxed **2** money **3** crime **4** time **5** strangers

Alternative treatment When you round up, write the answers on the board, but write *mony* and *estrangers* (i.e. *money* and *strangers* spelled wrongly). Tell students there are some mistakes and ask them to identify them. Point out that answers are only correct if they are copied exactly from the passage.

Draw students' attention to the Exam advice. Go through it and point out when they did each of the things advised.

❼ Alternative treatment To give students a chance to express their own views on ideas in the passage, you can ask:

- *What methods did the psychologists use to find out how friendly people were?* (*answer*: Dropping a pen, pretending to be blind. Since these two points were not focused on when students were answering the questions, they may need to check again.)

- *What would people in your city do in these situations?*

- *What would you do?*

Listening Form completion

❶ 🎧 Alternative treatment Before they listen, ask students to look at the words and numbers and say if there are any names of letters or numbers that they don't know how to say in English.

Answers
2 ✗ 3 ✓ 4 ✗ 5 ✓ 6 ✗ 7 ✓ 8 ✗

Extension idea 1 Many students have difficulty hearing the difference between *fifty* and *fifteen*, especially as the final *n* of *fifteen* is lightly pronounced and hard to hear. You can tell students that the difference is in the stress and the short and long i (*fifty – fifteen*). Read out others they may confuse, such as *forty* and *fourteen*, *ninety* and *nineteen*, and ask students to write down the ones you say. They can then practise doing this in pairs, here or after exercise 2.

Extension idea 2 Point out different ways of saying:

- double letters (*L–L* or *double L*);
- 0 (*zero*, which is what they will hear in the exam, *O* or *nought*);
- ordinal numbers: *first, second, fifth*, etc.

❷ 🎧 Extension idea Ask students to work in pairs and take turns to spell their names, addresses, telephone numbers and email addresses while their partner writes them down. They then show each other their answers to check if they are correct.

❸ As a warmer With books closed, ask students to work in small groups and list as many different types of holiday accommodation as they can. Give them three minutes to do this.

- Round up with the whole class and write their ideas on the board.

Extension idea

- Elicit one advantage and one disadvantage of staying in a hotel when on holiday (e.g. *advantage – no cooking or cleaning; disadvantage – expensive*). Write these on the board.

- Ask students to work in small groups and write as many ideas as possible in their notebooks.

- When they have finished, ask them to change groups and each take a minute or two to present their ideas to their new group.

- Finally, ask one of your more confident students to present the advantages and disadvantages of staying in a hotel, and another student to present the advantages and disadvantages of staying in an apartment. When they have finished, ask other students to add any other advantages or disadvantages which were not mentioned, or say which they prefer – a hotel or an apartment – and why.

❹ Draw students' attention to the Exam overview on page 7. Point out that in the IELTS exam, they hear each part once only, so it's important to know what to expect before listening and to use the preparation time for each section well.

Form-completion tasks are typical Listening Part 1 tasks. They test students' ability to listen for specific details: it's important to know what details they should listen for beforehand, hence this exercise where they analyse as far as they can what type of information is required for each gap. Point out that some words in a form may be spelled out and students have to write them down.

Answers
1 a 3, 4, 6 **b** 1, 2 **c** 5
2 7 something in the apartment
8 something you can see from the apartment
9 something about the air conditioning
10 something for a car

❺ 🎧 Use the following procedure.

- Tell students to look at the instructions. Ask:
  - *Must you write two words, or should you sometimes write one word?* (sometimes one)
  - *Must you write either words or a number, or can you write words and a number?* (words and a number)

- *What happens if you write three words?* (the answer will be wrong)

- Tell students to write their answers while they listen and play the recording once as in the exam.

- After listening, give them a little time to complete their answers and then compare them with a partner.

- Play the recording a second time for students to check and complete their answers.
- Tell students to look at the recording script to make sure their answers are correct.
- Round up answers with the whole class, asking students to spell them out and for you to write on the board. If any are misspelled, ask students to check in the recording script and correct them.

Answers
1 Leo Blucher   **2** Blumengasse   **3** 4312 11057
4 1st   **5** nine/9 days   **6** two hundred / 200
7 kitchen   **8** (the) beach   **9** quiet
10 parking space / parking / space

Extension idea 1 Go through the Exam advice with your students to reinforce the procedure for doing form-completion tasks which they have just followed.

Extension idea 2 To activate the language and skills they have been practising, ask students to change partners and work with someone they haven't worked with in this lesson. They should do the simple photocopiable role-play on this page. Before they start:

- tell each pair if they are pair A or pair B (they will later have to work with people from the other pair);
- hand out their role-play cards and give them five minutes to prepare.

When they are ready, give them about five minutes to do the role-play itself.

❻ This is similar to a Speaking Part 2 task, which is covered in more detail in Unit 3. The activity here is intended, like others in this unit, to get students used to speaking at length.

- Give students a minute or two to prepare. Meanwhile, go round the class helping individual students with what they want to say.
- When they work in pairs, tell them that the person who is not speaking should just listen and ask questions when their partner has finished.
- Round up with the whole class by asking: *Which places sounded really nice? Why?*

Reading 2 Note completion

❶ *As a warmer and with books closed* If appropriate for your class, write these questions on the board:

- *Why are people in some countries happier than in others?*
- *What can governments do to try to make people happier?*
- Elicit some ideas for each question from the whole class (e.g. people are happier in countries with good health services; governments can make people happier by providing good schools).

❶ Work in pairs. Your teacher will tell you if you are pair A or pair B. Read the information below and follow the instructions for your pair.

Pair A
You work for an agency which rents out holiday apartments. Someone from pair B is going to phone you to ask about holiday apartments. Decide what questions you need to ask in order to get the details on the form below.

Pair B
You are thinking of renting a holiday apartment in London. Decide what you would say to someone who is completing the form. For example, your maximum price, what special requirements you need, etc.

Chelsea Apartments, London
Name: ....
Address: ....
....
Telephone number: ....
Email address: ....
Number of people: ....
Starting date: ....
Length of stay: ....
Price: maximum ....
Other requirements:
....
....

❷ Work with someone from the other pair. Ask and answer questions to complete the form.

- Tell students to work in small groups and think of as many ideas for each question as they can.
- When they have finished, ask them to change groups and report their ideas to their new group.

With books open, ask which ideas are reflected in the photos.

Extension idea Ask students: *What photos would you choose to show people's happiness in your country?* They can discuss this question in pairs or small groups.

❷ This is a scanning task which requires students to find names in the passage and then read around the names to find information associated with them.

- Give students one minute to do this.
- When they have finished, point out to students that the information they need may come before or after the name of the person.

> **Answers**
> 1 a Costa Rican economics professor
> 2 a researcher

Extension idea To give more practice scanning:
- give students one minute to underline the following numbers (you should write them on the board): *1, 3, 143* and *2008*.
- when they have finished, ask them to work in pairs and say what each number refers to (1 – Costa Rica's position on the index; 3 – the number of measurements; 143 – the number of countries on the index; 2008 – when the index was created).

❸ Note-completion tasks test students' abilities to scan the passage for specific information. They reflect the type of reading activity that might be required on an undergraduate course of study. The words in the notes will be synonymous with words in the passage, so students will have to process the meaning of both to find the correct words to complete the notes. In other words, the task is more challenging than the ones students did in Exercise 2.

Students should use the title of the notes to find the right parts of the passage (this is scanning).

Words have been italicised in the notes to help students find corresponding meanings in the passage – though you can point out that this help is not given in the exam.

You should ask the following questions.

– *Is it necessary to read the whole passage carefully in order to complete the notes?* (no)

– *Why not?* (the notes are about the 'Happy Planet Index' – you needn't read parts which don't deal with that)

– *Do you need to spend time understanding parts of the passage which don't give answers to the questions?* (no)

Students can do this exercise in pairs to give them more confidence.

> **Answers**
> 1 The Happy Planet Index (this is dealt with in the last two sentences of paragraph 1 and in paragraph 3)
> 2 started – created
>   lists – ranking/ranks
>   effect – impact
>   the quantity – how much
>   uses – consumes
>   population – citizens

❹ Ask students to focus on the instructions. Ask:

– *How many words or numbers can you use?* (one)

– *Can you use a word and a number?* (no – if you could, the instructions would say 'and/or a number')

When they have finished, tell students to check their answers in pairs. They should make sure they have copied them exactly from the passage.

Round up by writing students' answers on the board. Ask them to spell their answers to you when you write them.

Alternative treatment In order to reinforce the idea that they don't need to read and understand the whole passage to deal with the task, ask students to cover paragraph 2 while they are completing the notes.

> **Answers**
> 1 2008 2 143 3 environment 4 resources
> 5 health 6 citizens

Extension idea To reinforce the idea of scanning rather than reading the whole passage carefully from the outset, ask students the following questions.

– *Did you need to read the whole passage carefully to find the answers, or did you read some parts quite quickly and other parts more carefully?*

– *Were there any words in the passage which you didn't understand? Did you need to understand all these words in order to complete the notes?*

❺ **Alternative treatment** Ask students to work in groups and rank each idea in order of importance. Tell them they can add other things to the list. When they have finished, ask them to change groups and report their decisions to their new group.

Vocabulary Collocations and prepositional phrases

❶ As a warmer With books closed, ask students to work alone and think of three or four things they can say to describe the area where they live, e.g. *I live in a busy street near the city centre.* When they are ready, ask them to work in small groups and describe the area where they live to each other.

With books open, draw their attention to the introduction on adjective–noun collocations. Write *relaxing long journey* and *holiday* on the board. Ask students which adjective is usually found with each noun (*long journey, relaxing holiday*). Ask if it's possible to say *long holiday* and *relaxing journey* (yes). Tell them that collocations are words that are often found together and which make your English sound more natural, but that they are not fixed expressions.

Alternative treatment If your students all speak the same language, ask them to suggest adjective–noun (or noun–adjective) collocations in their own language.

> **Answers**
> 2 main   3 pretty   4 tall   5 large   6 industrial
> 7 quiet   8 suburban   9 tiny

❷
> **Answers**
> 1 by / near   2 in / near   3 in   4 by / in / near
> 5 in / near   6 on   7 by / near   8 in

❸ Ask students to change groups from their group in Exercise 1. Give them a minute or two to think and plan before they speak.

Extension idea Round up by asking students:
- *Who lives in the nicest place?*
- *Which of the places would you like to visit?*

Speaking Part 1

❶ 🎧 As a warmer With books closed, ask students to work in pairs, perhaps with someone they haven't worked with previously in class. Say to them: *When you meet someone for the first time, what questions do you normally ask?* To get them going, you can elicit one or two, such as: *Where do you come from? What do you do?* Ask them to think of four or five questions and write them down. Round up with the whole class and write the questions on the board. Then ask students to ask each other the questions.

Alternative treatment Before students listen, tell them that the questions are typical Speaking Part 1 questions. Ask them:

- *Do you think you should answer each question with just a few words or should you try to give longer answers? Why?* (In general they should try to give longer answers – these show the student's ability to speak fluently, use a range of grammar and vocabulary and construct sentences. Answering with one or two words shows little language ability and tends to shut conversations down.)

Refer students to the Exam overview on page 7. Elicit answers to these questions:

- *How long does the Speaking test last?* (about 14 minutes)
- *How many parts does the test have?* (three)
- *How many examiners and candidates are there in the Speaking exam?* (there is one examiner and one candidate only)

After students have listened to the candidates, ask if they think the candidates did well (they gave longish answers, used a range of vocabulary, spoke fluently, and answered the questions exactly).

	occupation	where from	where located	words used to describe place
Hanan	student, studying medicine	Muttrah, Oman	by the sea, near the mountains	large, beautiful, old, hot, very pleasant, important
Kwan	student, studying economics	village in Korea	near Chonju, in mountains	small, friendly people, good place to live

Note: This is a good moment to do the work in the Pronunciation section on sentence stress on page 13 which is based on Hanan and Kwan's answers.

❷ Give students time to prepare their answers. Help them with any vocabulary they need.

Extension idea Students often learn a lot from listening to how their partners do a speaking activity and having a chance to do things better a second time. When they have finished doing the speaking activity, ask them to change partners and repeat the task.

❸ Alternative treatment with books closed Write *I like* and *I don't like* on the board. Ask students to suggest phrases which mean the same.

Tell students that questions about what they don't like are quite common in Speaking Part 1 and often give candidates problems because they don't expect them.

Answers
a 1, 2, 4, 7 **b** 3, 5, 6, 8

4 Answers
Hanan: 2, 4, 5, 6 **Kwan**: 1, 3, 7, 8

5 *Alternative treatment* Ask students to work in pairs and complete the table from memory before they listen again. They then listen to check and complete their answers.

	likes	dislikes	how changing
Hanan	sea, the part of the city by the sea, shopping, buying clothes	the hot weather, hot wind from the desert	building more houses and roads, getting busier
Kwan	walking in the mountains, the people	busy main road, traffic	more traffic, village is becoming noisier, young people leaving, not so lively

Note: This is a good moment to do the Key grammar section on the present simple and present continuous.

6 Again, give students time to think about their answers and help them with vocabulary where necessary. Encourage them to prepare answers of two or three sentences where possible.

Extension idea 1 When they have finished, ask students to discuss how they could improve their answers to each question. Then ask them to change partners and repeat.

Extension idea 2 Write on the board:

- *What do you like about …?*

- *What don't you like about …?*

- Ask students in pairs to think of three topics for these questions (e.g. *What do you like about studying English? What don't you like?*)

- Ask students to change partners and then take turns to ask and answer their questions.

- Finally, round up with the whole class.

Pronunciation Sentence stress 1

1 Point out that Pronunciation counts for a quarter of the IELTS Speaking score. This means that in addition to listening to their grammar, vocabulary and fluency, examiners also note how easily they can understand the candidate. Those who speak clearly and at the correct pace will do better.

Explain that there are recognised features of pronunciation, and examiners want to see how well candidates can use and control these. Tell students that candidates with good pronunciation will get higher marks.

As a warmer with books closed In order to teach students what sentence stress is, play the recording of Hanan answering the two questions. Ask:

- *Does Hanan say all the words equally quickly, or does she say some words more slowly and clearly?*

- *Which words does she say more slowly and clearly? Listen again and note them down.* (see answers for exercise 2)

Tell students this is called 'stress'. Play the extract again and ask: *Does she speak louder on the words she stresses?* (no)

Alternative treatment The way sentences are stressed in English may be different to the way they are stressed in the students' languages. If you all speak the same language, discuss how stress is different between English and the students' language.

2

Answers
Hanan stresses: *student, medicine, doctor, Muttrah, Oman*
Kwan stresses: *student, economics, Chonju University, small village, Chonju, Korea*

3 Tell students they should say the words which are not stressed quite quickly, but spend more time saying the stressed words. They shouldn't say them louder.

4 Tell students it is important to stress the words which carry the main information of the sentence. If they stress other words, the listener may not understand, or may understand something different.

5 *Extension idea* Ask confident students to do this activity in front of the whole class. When they've finished, give them feedback. Then ask the whole class to change partners and do the activity again.

Key grammar
Present simple and present continuous

1 In the IELTS test, Grammar is awarded a separate band score in both the Speaking and Writing modules. Candidates are assessed on their ability to use correct and appropriate grammar and on the range of sentence types that they produce. Even simple sentences need to be written accurately but in order to raise their score above Band 4, they also need to be able to show that they can use some complex sentence types and have an understanding of the relevant tenses and structures.

Answers

2 *come* (present simple)   3 *find* (present simple)
4 *are leaving* (present continuous)

❷ | **Answers** | | |
|---|---|---|
| present continuous | to talk about something happening now | *At the moment I'm studying English.* |
| present simple | to express what someone feels or thinks | *I find the traffic very unpleasant.* |
| present continuous | to talk about something which is changing | *Young people are leaving the village.* |
| present simple | to talk about something which is always true | *I come from Muttrah in Oman.* |

After they've finished the exercise, go through the Language reference on page 120 of the Student's Book.

Extension idea Ask students to work in pairs and write their own sentences as examples for each use of the tenses. When they've finished, ask them to read them out to the whole class.

❸ **Answers**

1 is/'s visiting   2 am/'m studying; want
3 does not / doesn't like; rains
4 is improving; is building   5 do; like

❹ Exercises in the Student's Book which have this icon ◉ are based on research carried out in the Cambridge Learner Corpus (CLC). This is a huge database containing what candidates have written in Cambridge exams. In this book, specific examples are included of what candidates who achieved a Band 4 or 5 wrote in the IELTS test.

By using the CLC, the authors can:

- analyse how candidates perform in specific tasks and where they need to improve;
- pinpoint the language areas where large numbers of candidates from a range of language backgrounds have problems (with grammar, vocabulary, spelling and punctuation) and design exercises to remedy those problems;
- include error-correction exercises (such as the one here) based on actual errors made by students in the exam and reflecting the most frequent ones.

Use the example in question 1. Elicit what the error is and what the rule from the Language reference is.

Students do the rest of the exercise. They can then work in pairs and compare their answers. Finally, round up with the whole class and elicit why each sentence is incorrect (i.e. relate it to the rules in the Language reference).

Answers

2 ~~grow up~~ are growing up
3 ~~bringing is~~ bringing / brings
4 ~~are encourage~~ encourage / are encouraging
5 ~~become~~ are becoming
6 ~~are believing~~ believe

Writing Task 1

This section introduces students to some simple pie and bar charts and starts to build up their confidence in dealing with graphic data. A step-by-step approach is taken to analysing the information and summarising it in writing.

❶ ***As a warmer with books closed*** Ask students to work in small groups and brainstorm as many reasons as possible for visiting a foreign country, for example, *for a holiday.*

- Students then change groups and compare ideas.
- Tell students to open their books and look at the pie chart. Ask: *What are the main reasons for visiting New Zealand?*
- Elicit from students what pie charts in general show (*answer*: how a total amount is divided into different parts).
- Ask: *If you add all the percentages in a pie chart, what is the result?* (100%)

Answers

1 for a holiday   2 29%   3 the number of people who go to New Zealand on business
4 other reasons   5 for pleasure

Extension idea Ask students to draw a similar pie chart for international visitors to their country. They can base the chart on one of the following:

- statistics they look for on the internet
- their local knowledge
- their imagination.

The point is to get students to think about how pie charts are constructed and the information which goes into them. When they have finished, ask them to work in small groups and present the information to each other. If you think it is beneficial, this extension idea can be used at different stages of this section with other charts.

② Tell students that the sample summary in this exercise is much shorter than the one they will have to write themselves in the exam, but that it is intended as an easy introduction. You can also point out that students should:

- as far as possible, use their own words when writing the summary, not lift words and phrases from the question.
- order the information in a logical way (e.g. like here from largest to smallest).
- include an overview of the main points of the information given.

Alternative treatment Especially if your students' writing skills are weak, ask them to write out the summary in full, not just copy the missing words into the gaps. When they have finished, ask them to work in pairs and check each other's answers to make sure they have copied accurately.

> **Answers**
> 1 go to New Zealand   2 The largest percentage
> 3 see friends and family   4 13 percent
> 5 other reasons   6 for pleasure

Extension idea Ask students:

- *What is the purpose of the first sentence?* (to introduce the subject)
- *Does the summary contain all the main information from the chart, including numbers?* (yes)
- *Is the information presented in a logical way (e.g. from the highest figures through to the lowest)?* (yes)
- *What is the purpose of the final sentence?* (to give a general overview of the main features of the information)

To focus on the need for students to use their own words, ask them to look at the first sentence. Ask: *Which words express the idea of …?*

- *international visitors* (= people from other countries);
- *reason* (*why*).

③ Encourage students to answer the questions using their own words where possible. You can elicit alternative phrases for *Country of origin* (e.g. *Where the visitors are from / the country they come from*).

> **Suggested answers**
> 1 The chart shows where visitors to New Zealand come from.   2 Australian   3 UK: 12 percent, US: 9 percent   4 12 percent   5 Yes, the 'other' countries. 6 They come from English-speaking countries.

④ *Alternative treatment* Ask students to work in pairs and find the five false facts together.

- Elicit why the first sentence is false (the chart shows where people come from, but doesn't show how many people go to New Zealand).
- When students rewrite the summary, ask them to write it out in full.

> **Answers**
> ~~third~~ second; ~~go to~~ come from; ~~other European countries~~ other countries; ~~70 percent~~ 60 percent

⑤ **Answers**
> 1 percent   2 percentage

⑥ Elicit why *percent* is not correct in question 1. Students can do the rest of the exercise in pairs.

> **Answers**
> 2 ~~percentage~~ percent   3 ~~percent~~ percentage
> 4 ~~percentage~~ percent   5 ~~The ten percent~~ Ten percent
> 6 ~~percent population~~ percent of the population
> 7 ~~percentage~~ percent (x2)
> 8 ~~percent people~~ percentage of people

⑦ *Alternative treatment* Especially if your students need help with this, ask them:

- *How is the bar chart different from a pie chart?* (it shows comparative figures, but not out of a total of 100% for all categories)
- *Do the percentages all add up to 100%?* (no)
- *Do visitors do one main activity or more than one main activity?* (more than one)
- *Which two are most popular?* (walking, sightseeing)
- *Which two are least popular?* (visiting volcanoes and visiting museums)
- *Which activities are indoor activities and which are outdoor activities?* (all are outdoor activities except visiting museums)

> **Suggested answers**
> 1 what international visitors to New Zealand do when they are on holiday   2 85 percent
> 3 go to see places of interest / go sightseeing
> 4 45 percent   5 50 percent   6 40 percent
> 7 going to museums   8 people

⑧ **Suggested answers**
> 1 The chart shows how people visiting New Zealand travel while they are in the country.
> 2 cars, nearly 70 percent
> 3 planes and coaches, more than 30 percent
> 4 train, just over 20 percent
> 5 boat, about 6 percent   6 public transport

❾ Sample answer

The chart gives information on the means of transport used by overseas visitors to travel in New Zealand.

Nearly 70 percent of visitors travel around in New Zealand by car, which is the commonest mode of transport. The second and third most common ways of travelling in the country are by plane or coach, and just over 30 percent of visitors use each of these. By comparison, just over 20 percent of visitors use trains and the least popular method of travel is by boat, which six percent of travellers use.

Overall the chart shows that although cars are the most popular means of transport, more people use public transport than private transport.

Spelling Making nouns plural

❶ Tell students that correct spelling is extremely important in IELTS and is assessed in three parts of the test. Students at this level lose many marks by:

- spelling words wrongly in the listening paper, even when they have understood the listening;
- copying words wrongly in the reading paper, even when the words they need are in the passage they are reading;
- spelling words inaccurately in the writing tasks.

Answers
2 bosses   3 boys   4 feet   5 men   6 matches
7 parties   8 wives

Extension idea Ask students to work in pairs and think of one extra example for each of the rules. To reinforce them, go through the rules in the Language reference on page 120 with your students.

❷ Research from the CLC reveals that many of the words in this exercise are spelled wrongly by IELTS candidates in the exam. When students have finished, ask them to compare their answers in pairs.

Answers
2 children   3 countries   4 cities   5 lives
6 families   7 watches   8 potatoes   9 activities
10 crashes

Extension idea Ask students to dictate the correct spelling of each word while you (or another student) write the word on the board.

Unit 1 photocopiable activity: Class statistics   Time: 40-50 minutes

Objectives

- To practise present simple and present continuous
- To practise writing short summaries with introductions and overviews
- To practise the correct use of *percent* and *percentage*
- To practise giving extra details in answers

Before class

You will need one photocopy of page 16 for each student.

❶ Tell students to look at sentence a and ask why *come* is correct (it talks about something which is always true). Ask them to look at sentences b–g and circle the correct form of the verbs.

Answers
b are studying   **c** think   **d** is getting   **e** like
f are earning   **g** have   **h** is improving

❷ Explain to students that they are going to conduct a survey to find out information for statements a–g. Before they start, they need to think of questions for each statement. For example, for sentence a, *Do you think the traffic in your town is getting worse?* Ask students to work in pairs and write questions.

❸ Ask students to mingle, interviewing each of the other class members in turn. Remind them that when answering, it is important to give extra information, rather than just one or two words. For example, when answering statement a, they should say *No, I'm from a big city / small town*, etc. rather than just *No*. They should use the table to keep a record of the answers. After collecting the information, students sit with their original partner and calculate the percentages of how many people answered 'yes' or 'no' for each statement. Then go through statements a–g with the whole class, and ask students to say what information can go in the gaps. Encourage language such as *less than, more than, the majority of students*, as well as precise figures such as *20%, 50%*, etc.

❹ Ask the class to look at statement a. Tell them to complete the pie chart using the information they gathered. If they need help with this, do it as a whole class. Then, write the following outline on the board:

The chart shows … The majority of the students … However, … Overall, …

They should work in pairs to copy and complete the outline with a brief summary of the pie chart. Once they have finished, ask them to check their work, paying particular attention to the use of *percent* and *percentage*.

Class statistics

❶ Circle the correct options.

In our class …

a .... *come* / *are coming* from a big city.

b .... *are studying* / *study* only one language at the moment.

c .... *are thinking* / *think* that the people in their home town are unfriendly.

d .... think that the traffic in their town *gets* / *is getting* worse.

e .... *are liking* / *like* to keep fit.

f .... *are earning* / *earn* money from a job at the moment.

g .... *are having* / *have* plenty of free time.

h .... think that public transport in their country *is improving* / *improves*.

❷ Write questions to find out about sentences a–g.

a *Do you* .... ?

b .... ?

c .... ?

d .... ?

e .... ?

f .... ?

g .... ?

h .... ?

❸ Interview other students in the class. Make notes on the answers.

	How many answer 'yes'? (✔) What other information did they give?	How many answer 'no'? (✘) What other information did they give?
a		
b		
c		
d		
e		
f		
g		
h		

❹ Complete this pie chart for a statement.

☐ from the countryside

■ from a big city

▨ from a town

⊠ other

Vocabulary extension

Unit 1

Abbreviations: n/sln/pln = noun / single noun / plural noun; v = verb; adj = adjective; adv = adverb; p = phrase; pv = phrasal verb; T/I = transitive/intransitive; C/U = countable/uncountable

affluent *adj* having a lot of money

architecture *n* [U] the design and style of buildings

border *n* [C] the line that separates two countries or states

building *n* [C] a structure with walls and a roof, such as a house, school, etc.

capital *n* [C] the most important city in a country or state, where the government is based

coast *n* [C/U] the land beside the sea

community *n* [C] the people living in a particular area

council *n* [C] the group of people elected to govern a particular area, town or city, and organise services for it

the countryside *n* [U] land that is not in towns or cities and has farms, fields, forests, etc.

explore *v* [I/T] to go around a place where you have never been in order to find out what is there

farming *n* [U] working on a farm or organising the work there

housing estate *n* [C] an area with a large number of houses that were built at the same time

immigrant *n* [C] someone who comes to live in a different country

inner city *n* [C] the part of a city that is closest to the centre, often where buildings are in a bad condition and there are social problems

middle class *n* [C] a social group that consists of well-educated people, such as doctors, lawyers and teachers, who have good jobs and are neither very rich nor very poor

neighbourhood *n* [C] an area of a town or city that people live in

the outskirts *pln* [U] the outer area of a city, town or village

province *n* [C] one of the large areas which some countries are divided into because of the type of government they have

rent *v* [T] to pay money to use something for a short time

resident *n* [C] someone who lives in a particular place

rough (neighbourhood) *adj* dangerous or violent

run-down *adj* Run-down buildings or areas are in very bad condition.

safe *adj* not dangerous or not likely to cause harm

the seaside *n* [U] the area near the sea, especially where people spend their holidays and enjoy themselves

suburb *n* [C] an area where people live outside the centre of a city

surroundings *pln* the place where someone or something is and the things that are in it

trendy *adj* fashionable at the moment

woodland *n* [C/U] an area of land with a lot of trees

working class *n* [C] the social class of people who have little money and who usually do physical work

Unit 2 People's lives

Starting off

❶ *As a warmer* Ask students to work in small groups. Ask them to say which person in their family they most admire and why.

With books open, tell students they should guess what each of the people did.

Extension idea Ask students if they know about any of the people in the photos. If they do, ask them to tell the rest of the class about them.

❷ *Extension idea* Ask students to think of one other famous person who they admire and what they did/have done. They then work in pairs and exchange information and ideas.

Reading 1
Flow-chart completion; short-answer questions

❶ *Extension idea* Ask students to take turns to tell each other about someone they know who has travelled a lot.

❷ Explain to students that the purpose of this question is to practise skimming the passage to get a general

idea of the contents before reading it more carefully. Skimming is reading quickly and superficially to get a general idea of the contents and the structure of a passage without trying to understand in detail or deal with difficult vocabulary or concepts.

- Tell students they should skim IELTS passages before dealing with the tasks.

- Give them two minutes for this. It's a good idea to watch your students while they do speed-reading activities, especially to start with. You will notice the students who follow the passage word-for-word with their finger or with a pencil. You should point out that this is not reading quickly – they should pass their eyes over the sentences, picking out the words which carry meaning, and form a general impression. If they have difficulty with this, illustrate what you mean by highlighting *explorer* and *Middle East* in the first two sentences.

- Tell students who don't finish the passage in two minutes that they're reading too slowly. In the exam, they will have to skim a much longer passage in about the same amount of time before dealing with the exam tasks.

> **Answer**
> her life

❸ The purpose of this exercise is to practise scanning. Give students 90 seconds to do this.

Alternative treatment Before they read, ask students where Stark travelled most – in Africa and America or in Europe and the Middle East (*answer*: Europe and the Middle East). With books closed, ask students to work in small groups and brainstorm what languages she might need to speak when she travelled in these regions.

> **Answers**
> French, German, Italian, Persian, Russian, Turkish, Arabic

❹ Flow-chart completion tests students' ability to scan a passage to locate specific information using words on the chart to help them.

Ask students to look at the flow chart and say what a flow chart is (*answer*: a diagram which shows the stages in a process). Ask what this flow chart shows (*answer*: stages in Freya Stark's life).

Alternative treatment Elicit the key ideas in each stage of the flow chart. You can tell students that key ideas are the main idea or the words which express the central meaning of each phrase or sentence (e.g. *born* in the first stage).

Ask students to number the stages A–H and to write these letters in the margin opposite where each stage is mentioned in the passage (e.g. A at the beginning of the second paragraph, etc.).

Suggested answers
1 a school/college, etc. 2 a job 3 something you learn - a skill or a language 4 a form of transport
5 a prize 6 a length of time

5 Ask students:

– *Must you write two words or can you write one word?* (you can write one or two words)

– *Must you write words and a number or can you write words or a number?* (you can write just words, just a number, or words and a number)

When they have finished, ask students to work in pairs and compare their answers.

Alternative treatment Especially with a weak class, or one which lacks confidence, you can work through the questions with your students to show them how completion tasks work.

- Elicit the connection between *First formal education* in the question and *no formal education as a child* in the passage, which will take students on to the answer in the next sentence. Elicit what *formal education* means (*answer*: at an educational institution).

- Ask students to scan to find *Italy* in the passage and then elicit what job is mentioned (*nurse*).

- Ask students to scan for *Lebanon* in the passage and then ask for the paraphrase of *learned* used in the passage (*studied*).

- Ask how *Syrian mountains* is expressed in the passage (*mountainous area in Syria*).

- Elicit what word is used in the passage to express the idea of *won* (*awarded*).

- Elicit what phrase carries the idea of *a further* in the passage (*the next*).

Answers
1 London University 2 nurse 3 Arabic 4 donkey
5 Gold Medal 6 12/twelve years

6 Short-answer questions test students' ability to scan the passage for specific information.

Tell students that: it's important to be sure that they understand exactly what the question is asking before they try to answer it; the key ideas are the words which say what answer is required (e.g. *What word ... to describe explorers*).

Suggested answers
2 What historical event
3 What did Stark produce / Iran
4 What group of people / research / Iran

7 To ensure students understand the instructions, ask:

– *Can you use two words and a number, or must you use two words or a number?* (you can use two words and a number)

– *Should you use your own words, or should you copy words from the passage?* (copy words from the passage)

– *Do you think you will see exactly the same words in the passage as in the questions, or will you see different words in the passage which express the key ideas in the questions?* (answer: different words which express the key ideas)

Tell students to scan till they find each key idea expressed in the passage, and then to read that part carefully. Tell them to underline the words which they need in the passage and to copy them exactly.

When they have finished, students can compare their answers with a partner.

Answers
1 heroes 2 World War 1 3 (a) map
4 (the) Assassins

Extension idea 1 When you round up, write the answers your students give you on the board, but write *World War One* and *asasins*. Ask students what mistakes you have made (*answer*: they should copy exactly – *World War 1*, which is two words and a number – and be careful with double letters). Note that candidates do not lose marks in the exam for omitting to write capital letters.

Extension idea 2 Go through the Exam advice to reinforce good exam technique.

8 *Extension idea 1* If you think they are suitable for your students, ask these extra questions:

– *Which do you find more interesting when you travel: the people or the places? Why?*

– *Which do you prefer: travelling to places or seeing them on television? Why? What are the advantages of each?*

Extension idea 2 Refer students back to Freya Stark's flow chart. Ask them to work alone and draw a flow chart which describes the main stages in their life. Tell them it needn't have so many stages as Stark's. When they have finished, they should work with a partner and explain the information in their chart.

Listening Note completion

❶ *As a warmer* Ask students: *When do people ask you when you were born, your address and other details like this?* (*Suggested answer*: when completing a form.) Ask them to think of typical questions people ask when completing a form with your details.

Tell students that the questions are typical of questions they will hear people asking in Part 1 of the Listening exam. The gapped answers are typical of the task they will have to complete.

Answers
2 h   3 g   4 a   5 f   6 c   7 e   8 d

❷ **Answers**
1 a, c   **2** b, e, f, g, h   **3** d

❸ ∩ Ask students: *What is the relationship between the speakers in each case?* Elicit that the first one is between a customer and a travel agent or airline-booking clerk. Elicit what word(s) gave the answer (*answer*: *flight*). (*Suggested answers* 2 opticians (*glasses*) 3 driving instructor and learner (*driving lessons*) 4 students (*maths class*))

Answers
Conversation 1: (h) Mobile: 07816 038924
Conversation 2: (g) Price $349
Conversation 3: (a) October 12th
Conversation 4: (f) at 4.30 p.m.

Extension idea Ask students to work in pairs.

- They choose two more questions and answers from the exercise and write their own short dialogues.
- They then work with another pair and take turns to read their dialogues, and complete answers by writing words and/or numbers in the gaps.
- Round up by asking two or three pairs to read out their dialogues to the whole class.

❹ *Extension idea* When they have finished the exercise in the book, ask your students: *Have any of you been on a difficult journey, or read about one? What qualities/things were important?*

❺ Remind students that in the IELTS test, they will perform better if they are clear about what they are being asked to write before they listen.

Suggested answers
a 2   **b** 1, 5   **c** 4, 5   **d** 6, 7, 8   **e** 9, 10   **f** 3

❻ Point out that the words used in the recording are often not the same as the words used in the questions/notes.

Answers
1 e   2 g   3 i   4 a   5 h   6 f   7 d   8 b   9/10 c

❼ Note-completion tasks test students' ability to understand specific information and details, and particularly facts rather than ideas or opinions.

∩ After students have listened once, ask them to compare their answers in pairs, but don't round up with the whole class.

- Play the recording again for students to check their answers, reminding them that in the exam they'll only hear the recording once.
- If you, or your students wish, play the recording a third time, but with students following the recording script. Tell them to check their partners' answers when they listen.
- Remind them that many students at their level lose marks in the listening paper because they spell answers wrongly. When you round up, check spelling with them, particularly of *office*, *languages* and *media studies*.

Answers
1 Dubashi   2 27/twenty-seven   3 office worker
4 (Central) Africa   5 Elbrus   6 first aid   7 five languages   8 media studies   9 fishing   10 fit

❽ **Answers**
1 c   2 a   3 d   4 b

Extension idea Ask students to suggest other endings for 1–4 (e.g. *I can operate a washing machine*). Then ask them to suggest sentences with other verbs – you can suggest the verbs (e.g. *make, do, speak*).

❾ **Answers**
1 1 and 4   2 2 and 3

❿ *Alternative treatment* Ask students to work in small groups. They do this exercise and decide in the end who they have most in common with.

Speaking Part 1

❶ *As a warmer* With books closed, tell students they are going to work on Speaking Part 1 again. Tell them to think of good advice for doing Speaking Part 1. You can start them off by asking: *Should you answer questions with one word or one or two sentences?* (*answer*: one or two sentences). Ask them to suggest other advice.

- When students do the exercise in the book, ask them to give reasons for their choices.

Suggested answers
Students should tick 2, 3 and 6, in both columns.

You can tell students that:

- where possible they should give longish answers because this shows ability to construct longer sentences, use correct grammar, show their fluency, use good pronunciation and a range of vocabulary;

- correcting mistakes shows they are thinking about the language and what they are saying, and also tells the examiner that they are monitoring what they say and making an effort to improve;

- it's important to answer relevantly; if they don't understand, they should ask the examiner to repeat the question.

Extension idea Ask students to rewrite 1, 4 and 5 so that they become good advice.

(*Suggested answers:* 1 Give quite long answers of one or two sentences. 4 If you don't understand the question, ask the examiner to repeat it. 5 Try using more advanced vocabulary. If you can't think of a word, explain what you mean using other words.)

❷

> **Answers**
> 2, 3 and 6

❸ Tell students that they are not expected to speak English perfectly when they do the Speaking test. Examiners will expect them to make mistakes, but they will make a better impression if they can sometimes correct themselves. They will also improve their score if they show they are trying to express ideas even though they find the language difficult. Draw your students' attention to Hussein saying 'not large or small' as a way of expressing himself when he doesn't know the word. Tell students they should not avoid trying to say things, but should make an effort to try to express themselves.

> **Answers**
> 1 *I'm sorry, could you repeat, please?*
> 2 He uses *middle* instead of *medium-sized* and *am* instead of *have*
> 3 *sorry*

❹ *Alternative treatment* Students have already listened to Hussein. Ask them to work in pairs and try to complete the sentences from memory. They then listen to check their answers.

> **Answers**
> 1 we enjoyed doing the same
> 2 I love doing sports
> 3 I did those in my free
> 4 because she explained things
> 5 so we learned a lot

❺ Younger students especially may be unused to talking to adults and unused to speaking at length to adults. They may also be shy and nervous. All these things may reduce the amount they are comfortable saying in the Speaking test. These problems are only really overcome with practice and with encouragement from the teacher. Tell them that it is essential to speak at some length, that the examiner wants to hear them speaking and is interested in what they say.

> **Answers**
> 1 1, 2 and 4 give reasons
> 2 3 and 5 explain results or consequences

Extension idea Elicit other ways of making answers longer (by giving examples, adding extra information).

Note: Now is a good moment to do the Key grammar section on the past simple and, immediately afterwards, the Pronunciation section on verbs + -ed.

❻ Give students time to think about their answers and make a few notes, but don't help them with vocabulary. Tell them they should try to express ideas even if they don't know the exact word.

❼ *Alternative treatment* Before they do the exercise, elicit the following points from Exercise 1 (ask: *Should you give short answers to the questions?*):

- Give quite long answers of two or three sentences.
- Give some extra details when you answer.
- Correct your mistakes when you can.
- If you don't understand the question, ask the examiner to repeat it.
- If you can't think of a word, explain what you mean using other words.

While students listen to their partners, they should think about what their partner does and, at the end, give them feedback.

Key grammar Past simple

❶
> **Answers**
>
> | infinitive | past | infinitive | past |
> |---|---|---|---|
> | be | was / were | go | went |
> | spend | spent | watch | watched |
> | look | looked | do | did |
> | play | played | like | liked |
> | start | started | explain | explained |
> | make | made | learn | learned / learnt |
> | enjoy | enjoyed | miss | missed |

❷ Go through the Language reference section on page 121 with students.

Extension idea Ask students to work in pairs. Ask students to:

- say which of the verbs in Exercise 1 are irregular (*be, spend, go* and *do*);
- add the base forms of ten other irregular verbs to the list. They then exchange lists with another pair and each pair completes their new list with the past forms.

❸ Ask students to check their answers by looking at the list of irregular verbs in the Language reference on page 121.

> **Answers**
> 1 left   2 got; forgot   3 gave; rode   4 drove; bought
> 5 caught   6 wrote; put

❹ Use the example: elicit why *is* is wrong and why the past simple is necessary (*answer*: because a time is given in the past).

> **Answers**
> 2 ~~want~~ wanted   3 ~~were reached~~ reached
> 4 ~~has dropped~~ dropped   5 ~~was risen~~ rose

Pronunciation Verbs + -ed

❶ 🎧 Elicit how each *-ed* ending is pronounced before you play the recording. Afterwards, ask students to work in pairs and repeat each verb.

> **Answers**
> 1 b   2 c   3 a

❷ 🎧

> **Answers**
>
> | /t/ | /ɪd/ | /d/ |
> |---|---|---|
> | asked, finished, hoped, liked, looked, watched, wished | ended, invented, needed, started, wanted | appeared, enjoyed, improved, occurred, played, remembered |

Extension idea Before going through the Language reference on page 121, ask students to work in pairs and see if they can spot any rule or pattern for when the three different pronunciations are used.

❸ Tell the student who is listening to listen carefully and correct any mispronunciations their partner makes.

Extension idea Point out to students that there are many adjectives which express how people feel which also end in *-ed*.

- You can write two or three on the board, e.g. *surprised, excited, depressed*.
- Ask students to suggest others to add to the list.
- Tell them the same pronunciation rules apply. Ask them to decide how the adjectives are pronounced.

❹ ***Extension idea 1*** Ask students to write two more sentences of their own using verbs from Exercise 2. They then read them to a partner who says if they are true for them and if not, corrects them.

Extension idea 2 Ask students to change partners and report what their previous partner told them.

Reading 2 True / False / Not Given

❶ *As a warmer* With books closed, ask students to work in small groups. Tell them: *Imagine you are going on a long journey to somewhere you've never been before. What problems do you think you might have?* Ask them to make a list.

Alternative treatment Don't explain words in the exercise to them that they don't know. If possible, elicit the meanings, e.g. *missing*: *If your family and friends don't come with you, how will you feel?*

Extension idea Ask students to add one or two more problems to the list.

❷ Both these questions practise skimming skills. Give students a maximum of two minutes and be strict about the time limit. When they finish, ask them to compare their answers with a partner.

> **Answers**
> 1 if it was possible for seafarers in the past to sail from Hawaii to Tahiti without navigational instruments
> 2 he started to teach his skills

Extension idea You can go back to the subheading and say to students: *Read the passage again in your own time. What traditional methods did Mau use?* This is quite a challenging task, so allow students to do this in their own time (*answers*: a traditional boat, no navigational instruments, using the stars, the feel of the wind and the look of the sea, no compass or charts).

❸ ❹ Tell students that the True / False / Not Given (TFNG) task is designed to see if they can decide whether the information in a statement is expressed in the passage or not.

- Point out that this exercise illustrates the difference between the three options. Ask students to do the exercise in the book and then discuss their answers in pairs.

- Elicit reasons for each answer by asking students to quote from the passage.

> **Answers**
> 1 False (to find out if seafarers in the distant past could have found their way from one island to the other without navigational instruments)
> 2 True (see above)
> 3 Not Given (the expedition was organised by the Polynesian Voyaging Society, but it does not say they owned the boat)

It is often difficult to decide if a question is False or Not Given. Students should choose False when the information in the passage contradicts the statement. They should choose Not Given when there is no information about the statement in the passage. Point out that there should still be words in a 'not given' statement that they can use to find a place in the passage.

❺ For each question in the set, this task tests students' ability to:

- scan the passage to locate the right place (scanning is when you read quickly to locate specific information in a passage); and then

- read that part of the passage in detail to find the answer.

In a full-length IELTS passage, scanning skills are key.

- Tell students that the questions in True / False / Not Given tasks usually contain a word or phrase which is the same as or similar to a word or phrase in the passage. This is to help them locate the part of the passage which relates to the statement, even when detailed reading shows the answer to be Not Given. In this particular exercise, which is an introduction to the task, the underlined words are the same. In the exam, they may be similar, but not the same.

- When students have answered the questions, elicit the evidence in the passage which gives them their answers (given in brackets in the answers).

> **Answers**
> 1 True (Mau was the only man alive who knew how to navigate just by observing the stars, the wind and the sea ...)
> 2 False (he had never before sailed to Tahiti ...)
> 3 Not Given (The passage says he did it without a compass or chart, but not what he thought of them.)
> 4 Not Given (The passage says his grandfather began the task of teaching him, but doesn't say he was his only teacher ...)
> 5 True (Later Mau used a circle of stones to memorise the positions of the stars ...)
> 6 Not Given (The passage says Hawaii's first inhabitants navigated by reading the sea and the stars, but not that they could read or write.)
> 7 False (He allowed them to write things down because he knew they would never be able to remember everything ...)

❻ Students may find the first question challenging.

- Elicit names for family relations to remind students: aunt, uncle, cousin, grandfather, grandmother, etc. You can ask students to brainstorm a list of relations before they start.

- Tell students that in the IELTS speaking test, the Examiner cannot help them with words they don't know, so before they answer these questions, they should think how they can explain their family's traditional skills when they don't know the words. Also they should take a moment to think about which skills they will find easiest to explain and avoid any that are just too difficult to express in the exam.

- Give students time to think and prepare their answers on their own before they speak.

Vocabulary
Working out the meanings of words

❶ *As a warmer* Ask students: *When you're reading a passage and you come to a word you don't understand, what can you do?* They should suggest these:

- guess the meaning from the context;
- use a dictionary (this is not possible in the exam);
- look at the shape of the word; or
- ignore it if it's not essential for a question.

Don't round up with the exact meanings of these words, as this is the aim of Exercise 2, which follows.

Alternative treatment Tell students there are various techniques for guessing the meaning of words they don't know. They can try the following techniques.

- Look at the shape of the word: ask them to look at *seafarers*. Ask: *Is there a word inside that word which you recognise?* You can elicit *sea*. Ask: *What does '-er' often mean?* Give examples such as *runner* or *helper*. This should give them enough of the meaning: people connected with the sea.

- Think of the meaning of a word that they know (e.g. *chart* meaning diagram). Ask them if this fits the context in the passage (no), so what might it mean? They can do the same for *pools*, especially as they will know *swimming pool*.

- With irregular verbs, they should think of the base form: *lay*. Ask them if they know other uses of *lay*, e.g. *to lay the table*. This should lead to a close approximation to the meaning.

Remind students that whatever they decide the word means, they must look at it in the context. Does the meaning they think the word has fit the context?

 Answers

| 1 b | 2 a | 3 b | 4 a | 5 a | 6 b |

Extension idea Ask students if there were other words in the passage which they didn't understand. Write them on the board. Then, ask students to look at the context and guess the meanings.

Point out that in the exam itself passages are longer than this one and they are not expected to understand all the vocabulary in them. Tell them to focus on the important words: those that help them understand the main ideas and help them answer the questions. Other words that are not essential can be 'skimmed over'.

❸ Answers

1 someone who does research

2 a device for opening bottles

3 someone who is/was standing nearby

4 someone who communicates

Extension idea Write these two words on the board and ask students to guess what they mean: *theatre goer, weight-watcher* (*theatre goer* – someone who goes/is going to the theatre; *weight-watcher* – someone who is watching their weight, i.e. being careful about how much they eat).

Ask students to work in pairs and think of two or three more words ending in *-er* or *-or*. They then say the words to another pair of students, who have to say what they mean.

 Before students do this exercise, go through the Language reference on page 121 with them.

Answers

1 *cyclists* – people who ride bicycles;
  motorists – people who drive cars
2 *likeable* – can be liked, easy to like
3 *liquefying* – making into a liquid
4 *undoubtedly* – certainly;
  prehistoric voyagers – people who travelled by sea before historical times
5 *navigable* – possible to navigate
6 *remade* – made again
7 *informants* – people who give information;
  simplify – make more simple
8 *impassable* – can not be passed along

Writing Task 2

❶ *As a warmer* With books closed, ask students to compare family life now and family life in their grandparents' time. Ask about:

- size of families;
- if both parents work;
- if grandparents, etc. live with the family;
- who does what household tasks;
- how much freedom children have, etc.

Before working on this section, refer students to the Exam overview, so that they realise what Writing Task 2 involves. In this unit they are focusing on a writing task where they have to discuss the advantages and disadvantages of a situation or circumstance.

When students read the writing task, tell them:

- to underline the things they must deal with while they're reading the task (e.g. *being part of a large family in the past*).
- they should always do this with Writing tasks as they will lose marks if they don't answer the question exactly.

Students will not score above Band 5 for Task Response (content) if they only answer part of the question; and if they misunderstand the topic (write a tangential response) they will score Band 4 or below for this criterion. (Losing marks in this way for content can also affect marks for the other criteria. Vocabulary, for example, is rated according to its relevance to the prompt.)

This exercise is intended to give students practice in analysing the question so that they will answer it as accurately and relevantly as possible.

Answers

| 2 F | 3 F | 4 T | 5 T | 6 T |

Extension idea 1 Ask students to work in small groups and brainstorm a list of advantages and disadvantages of being part of a large family. When they have finished, ask students to change groups and put their ideas together with students from other groups.

Extension idea 2 Read the following statements to the whole class. After you have read each statement, students must say whether it is an advantage (A) or a disadvantage (D).

1 Children always had other children to play with, so childhood was more enjoyable. (A)

2 Children could share looking after their parents when they were old. (A)

3 The family home was more crowded. (D)

4 Having many people in the family meant tasks were shared among more people. (A)

5 The family had less money because the father or mother stayed at home to look after so many children. (D)

6 Families could not afford so many things. (D)

7 Children learned social skills by living with a lot of other children in the same house. (A)

8 There was less money for the education of each child. (D)

9 With many children, parents gave less attention to each child. (D)

10 People in large families were never lonely. (A)

➋ | **Answers**
1 **Advantages:** other children to play with, learned social skills, learned to defend themselves, helped in the house and became more responsible, learned from different generations and older brothers and sisters, supported family members, looked after old people, never lonely.

Disadvantages: children quarrelled, one parent had to stay at home, so family earned less, less money for children's education, less attention for individual children.

2 students' own answers

➌ Tell students they should:

- make a quick plan before they start writing. This will help them to organise their ideas and structure their essay. Explain that they just need two or three key ideas on either side of the topic.

- organise their notes (and essay) in paragraphs. Many candidates write just one long paragraph. Others start a new paragraph with every sentence. Both these approaches will lose them marks.

- write a balanced answer. Many candidates spend too long writing about one side of the topic (e.g. the advantages) and don't leave enough time or have enough to say about the other side. This will also reduce their mark.

Alternative treatment Before students do this exercise, ask them:

- *What are paragraphs?* (a part of a text that contains at least one sentence and starts on a new line)

- *When should you start a new paragraph?* (when you are going to talk about a new aspect of the topic)

- *Why is it important to write in paragraphs?* (Because it gives your answer a clear, logical, well-organised structure. It helps the reader to follow what you are saying.)

Ask them to read the essay again and say what the main topic of each paragraph is in one to three words (*answer*: paragraph 1: introduction; paragraph 2: advantages; paragraph 3: disadvantages; paragraph 4: conclusion and opinion / writer's opinion).

Answers
2 f 3 d 4 e 5 b 6 a 7 h 8 g

➍ Exercises 4 and 5 work on ways of:

- linking information and ideas to make the essay more cohesive

- writing more complex sentences.

Students will achieve a higher band score if they can do these things.

When students have done the exercise, go through the Language reference on page 121 with them.

Answers
2 but 3 and 4 Also 5 and 6 However
7 but 8 Also

➎ | **Answers**
1 *also* and *however* 2 *but* and *and*

➏ Tell students that their first paragraph should be a short introduction to the essay containing perhaps one to three sentences. They will score higher marks if they express the topic using their own words rather than repeating the words in the question exactly.

- A typical opening sentence says how things have changed and/or why the topic is an important one to discuss. The second sentence may state what the writer is going to write about and may sometimes include a brief statement of opinion.

- When students answer question 2, tell them that if they are not sure how to begin a paragraph, write a short sentence saying what the paragraph is about. Then complete the paragraph with the ideas or information they have said they are going to write about.

- When they answer question 3, tell them that they must express their opinion when answering the question and their opinion must be clear to the reader. Some students may find expressing a definite opinion unfamiliar or uncomfortable if they come from educational cultures where individual opinions are not encouraged or valued. Impress upon them the fact that they are not marked for their opinions (there are no right or wrong opinions); they are marked for their language and the relevance of their opinion to the topic and their argument.

Answers
1 a two   b the first   c the second
d No – if you copy large sections of the question, the examiner will not count these words in the final word count. This means you may lose marks for length.   e big   f members of

2 to say what the paragraphs are about

3 *I believe, I think, in my view*

Extension idea Ask students to underline any other words and phrases in the sample answer which they think would be useful when they write an essay. When they've finished, ask them to work in small groups and compare what they've underlined. Finally, round up with the whole class and perhaps brainstorm other useful phrases which you can then write on the board.

❼ *Alternative treatment* Elicit these ideas with a general class discussion; decide if they're advantages or disadvantages and write them on the board:

- *People feel they are part of a social group* (A)
- *Less privacy – people know who you are and what you are doing* (D)
- *Less crime – people look after each other and protect them* (A)
- *People more responsible for the area and work together to improve it* (A)
- *Limited social life – just people from the village* (D)
- *Children could play in the street safely* (A)
- *Limited opportunities for work, study and travel.* (D)

Suggested underlining
small villages, knew everyone, large cities, know only a few people, advantages and disadvantages of living in a small community

❽ *Extension idea* When students have finished, they change partners and compare their plans.

❾ This Writing task is perhaps best done for homework.

Sample answer
Until recently, the majority of people lived in the village where they were born. However, now people tend to live in large cities and, as a result, the way people live has changed.

There were a number of benefits to living in a small village. Firstly, everyone knew everyone else and, in the village my grandparents came from, everyone spoke to everyone else, so no one ever felt lonely. Secondly, there was always someone to look after the children and to teach them good behaviour, so children grew up being polite and respectful. Also, they could play safely in the street and there was little crime. It was a quiet life which everyone understood.

However, there were a number of disadvantages. The nearest primary school was in the next village and the nearest secondary school in a town some miles away. This meant that most children did not get a good education and most people had to work in agriculture. If young people were ambitious, they had to move away from the village and few people had the chance to do this. Also, when someone was ill, it was a long way to the nearest hospital.

All in all, I think people from my grandparents' generation were happier. However, in the modern world, with all the possibilities which exist today, I think it is a pity to be limited to a small village. Nowadays, there are more advantages to living in a large city.

Extension idea 1 Before they hand their essay in for correction, it's a good idea for students to work in pairs and:

- read what their partner has written;
- tell each other what is good about their answers;
- make suggestions for improvements;
- suggest corrections to mistakes in the English.

Extension idea 2 Photocopy and hand out the sample answer above. Ask students:

- which ideas they agree and disagree with;
- to underline the irregular verbs in the answer and to say what the base form of each verb is.

Spelling Changes when adding -*ed*

❶ Many of the verbs in this section are included because IELTS candidates often spell them incorrectly – as shown by the CLC.

Answers
2 appeared   3 carried   4 ended   5 opened
6 played   7 saved   8 stopped

Extension idea Ask students to work in pairs and add one more example of their own to each rule. Round up these examples with the whole class and write them on the board. If students still need practice with spelling, ask them to spell the words out as you write or another student writes them.

❷ **Answers**
2 remembered   3 preferred   4 dropped
5 developed   6 happened   7 stayed   8 studied
9 destroyed   10 remained

Vocabulary and grammar review
Unit 1

❶ 2 city centre   3 outskirts   4 country
5 suburbs   6 sea

❷ 2 g   3 b   4 h   5 a   6 f   7 e   8 d

❸ 2 industrial   3 busy   4 pretty   5 quiet   6 tall

❹ 2 enjoys; has   3 lives; works   4 are leaving
5 is studying; wants
6 are changing; read / are reading

Unit 2

❶ 2 able   3 know   4 learn   5 how

❷ 2 d   3 b   4 h   5 e   6 a   7 c   8 f

❸ 2 wrote   3 stopped; went   4 spoke   5 developed
6 happened; arrived   7 occurred; destroyed
8 rose; fell

❹ 2 but   3 also   4 and   5 but   6 However

Unit 2 photocopiable activity:
People in the past   Time: 40-60 minutes

Objectives
- To practise the use of the past simple
- To practise comparing ideas and giving opinions
- To practise writing using *also*, *but* and *however*

Before class

You will need one photocopy of page 28 for each student.

❶ *As a warmer* Write the phrase *the pace of life* on the board, with *pace* circled. Below it, write the following three options: *time*; *speed*; *relaxation*. Ask students to tell you which option best matches the meaning of *pace* (speed). Once you have checked the meaning, go on to ask students whether they think the pace of life in the past was slower or faster than today.

Give one copy of the activity sheet to each student. Ask them to work in pairs to identify the past simple form of each verb. Go through the answers with the class, paying particular attention to errors in the pronunciation of *-ed*. Before writing each answer on the board, ask students to spell it, so that you can monitor their control of spelling changes.

Answers
be – was   enjoy – enjoyed   feel – felt   have – had
mean – meant   spend – spent   suffer – suffered
take – took   travel – travelled   worry – worried

❷ Students read the text and work together to complete the gaps with their answers from exercise 1.

Answers
2 suffered   3 spent   4 worried   5 felt   6 had
7 travelled   8 took   9 enjoyed   10 meant

❸ Remind students of the importance of linking ideas and making opinions clear in academic texts. Get feedback from the whole class and write answers on the board so that students can refer to them when writing their own texts later on.

Answers
Linking ideas: *and, but, however, also* (also accept: *firstly, secondly, because, as a result, all in all*)
Making opinions clear: *I believe, in my view*

❹ Explain to students that they are going to discuss some ideas which will help them to plan and write for another Task 2 question. Ask them first to work alone, looking carefully at each point on the list and deciding if they think it was an advantage or disadvantage for children in the past. They should then work in pairs or small groups and compare ideas. Encourage them to discuss the points in as much detail as they can, and to give examples from their own knowledge or experience. When all the pairs are ready, go through each point with the class.

❺ Students plan their answer to the task, using their ideas from the discussion and referring to the model answer. Remind them to use the words and phrases from this exercise for linking ideas and making opinions clear.

When students have finished writing, encourage them to exchange texts with a partner and to check for errors in the use of the past simple. Alternatively, you may wish to make a list of these errors when marking the texts yourself, and give out the list in a follow-up class for students to correct in pairs.

People in the past

❶ What is the past simple of these verbs?

be   enjoyed   mean   travel   feel   suffer   take   spend   worry   have

❷ Use the verbs above to complete this answer to a Writing Task 2 question. Use each verb once.

> In many parts of the world, the pace of life was slower in the past than it is today.
>
> What do you think were the advantages and disadvantages of having a slower pace of life?

Give reasons for your answer and include any relevant examples from your own knowledge and experience.

Write at least 250 words.

The pace of life in today's society is much faster than in the past, because of changes in people's habits and in the world of work. In the past, there were both advantages and disadvantages to having a slower pace of life.

There ¹ _were_ a number of benefits of people's way of life in the past. Firstly, people probably ² _____ less from stress because they were not often in a hurry. Secondly, they ³ _____ more time with friends and family, especially at mealtimes and on traditional holidays. People ⁴ _____ less about being the best in their job or about earning a lot of money. They probably ⁵ _____ happier. However, in my view, the slower pace of life also ⁶ _____ several important disadvantages. People ⁷ _____ much less, either for work or holidays, so their lives were more limited. Basic tasks such as carrying objects, cleaning and washing ⁸ _____ up a lot of their time. As a result, they ⁹ _____ their free time less than people today. The slower pace of life also ¹⁰ _____ that it was more difficult for people to change or improve their situation by studying or finding a better job.

All in all, I believe that the disadvantages of the slower pace of life in the past were greater than the advantages. People had more free time but they were not always able to benefit from it because they had less control over their own lives, both at home and at work.

❸ Underline words in the answer which help to link ideas or make opinions clear.

❹ Discuss these points about children's lives in the past and decide if they were advantages or disadvantages.

- not having a TV, computer or mobile phone
- spending free time playing outside with other children who lived nearby
- not being under pressure to be successful at school
- enjoying dangerous activities like climbing trees or swimming in rivers
- walking home from school, rather than being taken in their parents' car
- spending more time with family members than with babysitters

❺ Now write your own answer to this question. Give reasons for your answer and include any relevant examples from your own knowledge and experience. Write at least 250 words.

> In many parts of the world, children's lives were very different from today.
>
> What do you think were the advantages and disadvantages of life for children in the past?

Vocabulary extension
Unit 2

Abbreviations: n/sln/pln = noun / single noun / plural noun; v = verb; adj = adjective; adv = adverb; p = phrase; pv = phrasal verb; T/I = transitive/intransitive; C/U = countable/uncountable

academic *adj* related to education, schools, universities, etc.

achievement *n* [C] something good that you have succeeded in doing

ambition *n* [C] something you want to achieve in your life

applicant *n* [C] someone who asks for something officially, often in writing

artistic *adj* showing skill and imagination in creating things, especially in painting, drawing, etc

award *v* [T] to officially give someone something such as a prize or an amount of money

candidate *n* [C] someone who is taking an exam

considerable *adj* large or important enough to have an effect

courage *n* [U] the ability to deal with dangerous or difficult situations without being frightened

deserve *v* [T] If you deserve something good or bad, it should happen to you because of the way you have behaved.

encourage *v* [T] to make someone more likely to do something, or make something more likely to happen

ensure *v* [T] to make certain that something is done or happens

gain (a qualification) *v* [T] to get something useful or positive

impressive *adj* Someone or something that is impressive makes you admire and respect them.

innovation *n* [C/U] a new idea or method that is being tried for the first time, or the use of such ideas or methods

knowledge *n* [U] information and understanding that you have in your mind

objective *n* [C] something that you are trying to achieve

obtain *v* [T] to get something

outstanding *adj* excellent and much better than most

persuade *v* [T] to make someone agree to do something by talking to them a lot about it

postgraduate *adj* describes university studies or students at a more advanced level than a first degree

professional *adj* relating to a job that needs special training or education

pride *n* [U] a feeling of satisfaction at your achievements or the achievements of your family or friends

recognise *v* [T] to officially show respect for someone for an achievement

satisfaction *n* [U] the pleasant feeling you have when you get something that you wanted or do something that you wanted to do

skill *n* [C/U] the ability to do an activity or job well, especially because you have practised it

talent *n* [C/U] a natural ability to do something

training *n* [U] the process of learning the skills you need to do a particular job or activity

vocational *adj* Vocational education and skills prepare you for a particular type of work.

❶ Complete the sentences by writing the word in brackets in the plural form.

0   A lot of ......*people*....... (person) visit Paris every year.

1   São Paulo is one of the largest .... (city) in the world.

2   My .... (foot) were very tired after a day's sightseeing in Sydney.

3   Most .... (child) enjoy having holidays by the sea.

4   More .... (woman) go out to work now than did in the past.

5   Research shows that our .... (life) are happier if we have good relationships with others.

❷ Choose the correct form of the present tense to complete each sentence.

0   *I think* / ~~*I'm thinking*~~ that my city is a pleasant place to live.

1   Many people in Switzerland *speak* / *are speaking* several languages fluently.

2   I don't have much free time nowadays because *I study* / *I'm studying* for an important exam.

3   The population of my city *is growing* / *grows* fast – it will soon have 10 million inhabitants.

4   It *rains* / *is raining* a lot in Seattle, especially in the winter months.

5   *I'm spending* / *I spend* a week working in Hong Kong at the moment.

❸ Complete the sentences by writing the correct form of the word in brackets.

0   The way of life is more ......*relaxed*...... (relax) in the outskirts of the city.

1   People in my city are usually very .... (help) towards strangers.

2   The beach near my home can get very .... (crowd) in summer.

3   My family likes visiting Thailand because people there are so .... (friend).

4   I find it .... (enjoy) to go sailing at the weekends.

5   It is important to have a .... (health) lifestyle, wherever you live.

4 Complete the paragraph with words from the box. You may use any word more than once.

and	but	however	also

A hundred years ago most inhabitants of my region lived on farms in the countryside,
0 ....*but*........ nowadays a lot of people live in the city. Many people now live far away from
their families, **1** .... they don't see their parents, brothers and sisters very often.
People **2** .... have smaller families these days. **3** .... , it is much easier to
keep in contact with people now than it was a hundred years ago. These days people living
in the city are often very busy **4** .... they do stressful jobs. Most people work long
hours nowadays, **5** ....they have more money to enjoy their leisure time.

5 Complete the sentences by writing a preposition (*by, with, to,* etc.) in each gap.

0 My parents live in a small village ....*on*............ the top of a hill.

1 People who work in the city centre are often .... a hurry.

2 I'd like to study engineering .... university.

3 Paris is fairly quiet in August because most of the population is ..... holiday.

4 My husband is Turkish. He comes .... the capital, Ankara.

5 The south of Spain is known .... its lovely sandy beaches.

6 Complete the paragraph by writing the verb in brackets in the past tense.

Wilfred Thesiger **0** ....*was*......... (is) an English explorer, born in Addis Ababa in Ethiopia,
North Africa in 1910. He **1** .... (study) at school and university in England, and
then returned to North Africa in his twenties. During the 1940s Thesiger travelled many
thousands of miles by camel across Ethiopia, Iraq, Iran, Kurdistan and Pakistan. He became
good friends with the many local people he **2** .... (meet) along the way, and even
3 .... (wear) the same clothes as the inhabitants of the countries he visited. Thesiger
4 .... (write) several famous books about his travels, and **5** .... (take) over
23,000 photographs.

Unit 3 Getting from A to B

Unit objectives

- **Reading:** skimming and scanning; introduction to labelling a diagram; introduction to matching headings
- **Listening:** introduction to labelling a diagram; introduction to multiple-choice questions; using verbal signals to alert listeners to the answers
- **Speaking Part 2:** introduction to Part 2; making notes; phrases to introduce a talk; introduce new points and finish a talk
- **Pronunciation:** introduction to word stress
- **Grammar:** adjectives with -ed and -ing; making comparisons
- **Vocabulary:** high-frequency IELTS vocabulary: *existing*, *ensure*, *efficiency*, etc.; words connected with traffic problems: *congestion*, *smog*, etc.; *cause* and *make*
- **Writing Task 1:** introduction to tables; comparing information; writing in paragraphs; analysing tables and charts
- **Spelling:** spelling changes when adding -er and -est to adjectives

Starting off

❶ *As a warmer* With books closed, tell students that the next unit is about transport. Ask them to work in small groups and make a list of as many different forms of transport as possible (e.g. *train*). Give them three minutes for this.

With books open, ask the whole class which form of transport is the cleanest and why. Elicit opinions and reasons. Then ask students to do the exercise in the book.

Note: *the cleanest* here may refer to how clean the people operating the form of transport keep it in terms of litter, etc., or how clean it is in terms of environmental impact and pollution. Both interpretations acceptable here.

Alternative treatment Before students do the exercise in the book, check that they can pronounce the different adjectives correctly, putting the stress on the correct syllable, especially *healthiest* ('hel.θiəst), *comfortable* ('kʌm.fə.tə.bl), *dangerous* ('deɪn.dʒr.əs), *exciting* (ɪk'saɪ.tɪŋ) and *quietest* ('kwaɪətst).

Extension idea Ask students in small groups to think of two more adjectives to add to the list, e.g. *the most relaxing, the most enjoyable*. Write suggestions from the whole class on the board. Ask students to discuss *Which form of transport is…?* for the adjectives they have suggested.

Reading 1 Labelling a diagram

❶ *As a warmer* With books closed, tell students they are going to read a passage about cars. Tell them to work in small groups. Ask: *What are the advantages and disadvantages of travelling by car, not public transport?*

With books open, remind students that they should always read the title, subtitle and look at any illustrations before scanning the passage. Give students two or three minutes for both parts of this exercise and be strict about the timing you decide.

> **Answers**
> 1 the passage is about electric cars and their technologies.
> 2 powered by renewable energy, zero emissions, convert more than 90 percent of power into movement, technology is already available.

❷ Give students three minutes to scan the passage and underline the words. Tell them to use the context, not guess, to help them decide which is the correct definition.

Alternative treatment 1 Before choosing the correct definition, ask students to decide what type of word each item is (noun, verb or adjective). (*answers:* 1 adjective 2 adjective 3 noun 4 adjective+noun 5 adjective+noun 6 noun 7 verb 8 verb)

Alternative treatment 2 If you wish your students to deal with reading tasks without being pre-taught vocabulary, you can leave this exercise till after they have done Exercise 4.

> **Answers**
> 2 a 3 d 4 g 5 h 6 e 7 b 8 c

❸ Ask students to try to use their own words when they discuss what the diagram shows. Tell them to underline the parts of the passage which each picture refers to so that when they answer the questions, they can find the parts easily (pictures 1, 2 and 3: third paragraph; picture 4: fourth paragraph).

Alternative treatment Especially with a weak class, to help students think of the sort of information they need, ask:

Which answer…?

– *needs a number* (2)

– *a place* (3)

– *might be the name of something you find in the car* (5)

– *may be the name of a machine* (6)

> **Suggested answers**
>
> **1** Part 1 shows a car being charged with electricity at home.
>
> Part 2 shows an electric car travelling through city streets.
>
> Part 3 shows a car being charged with electricity in the street.
>
> Part 4 shows a car having its battery changed at a switch station.
>
> **2 1** noun (something a car is connected to)
>
> **2** number (a distance)
>
> **3** noun (a destination)
>
> **4** noun (something a car can receive power from that is low)
>
> **5** noun (something that can locate switch stations)
>
> **6** noun (something that can be used to change batteries)
>
> **3** Part 1: *it starts with the installation of a home charge point, and through this, the vehicle will be plugged into the electricity grid whenever it is in the garage, typically at night.* (paragraph 3)
>
> Part 2: *In the morning, with a fully charged battery, the car is capable of as much as 160 km in urban motoring conditions.* (paragraph 3)
>
> Part 3: *In addition to the home charge point, the battery can be topped up by charge points at work and at supermarkets.* (paragraph 3)
>
> Part 4: *For longer trips, a navigation system directs the driver to the nearest switch station, where the depleted battery can be replaced with a charged one by a robot within a couple of minutes.* (paragraph 4)

❹ Tell students to look at the instructions. Ask:

– *Can you use less than two words?* (yes)

– *Can you use two words and a number as well?* (yes)

When students have finished, ask them to compare their answers in pairs. Tell them to check that their answers are written exactly as they are written in the passage.

> **Answers**
> **1** (electricity) grid   **2** 160 km   **3** work   **4** price
> **5** Navigation system   **6** robot

❺ ***Extension idea*** Ask students to say how popular they think electric cars are / will be in their country and why.

Listening
Labelling a diagram; multiple-choice

❶ *As a warmer* With books closed, tell students they're going to listen to an announcement telling passengers about different facilities on a ferry. Ask them to work in pairs and think of different facilities passengers can use when they're travelling by ship (e.g. a restaurant). Give them two or three minutes for this. When they have finished, they can change partners and put their ideas together.

> The aim of diagram-labelling tasks is to test students' ability to listen for detail, to follow directions and understand expressions of location.

When students look at the diagram, tell them that, before they listen, it's important to see:

• where they are (if they're on the diagram);

• what things are already labelled, as these will almost certainly be mentioned when they listen and will help them hear the things they need to fill the gaps;

• what information they need for each gap.

> **Answers**
> **1** at reception   **2** the restaurant and lounge
> **3** the games area and cinema   **4** the cabins
> **5** 2, 4 and 5   **6** 1   **7** 3

❷ Remind students that they hear each recording only once. Tell them that the recording will often contain words and phrases which signal that a question is about to be answered and these will help them to focus on the right question while they listen. In this exercise, they look at the sort of phrases they will hear that signal the answer.

> **Answers**
> **b** 4   **c** 3   **d** 2   **e** 1

3 🎧 Tell students they should write the word for each answer when they hear it. In the exam they will have some time at the end to check their answers and transfer them to the answer sheet.

- Play the recording once. After students have listened, give them some time to check that their answers make sense and they are correctly spelled. They can do this in pairs.
- Play the recording again for students to check and complete their answers.

> **Answers**
> 1 snack 2 entrance 3 keys 4 shopping 5 viewing

Extension idea Let students read the recording script while they listen a third time to check if their answers are correct.

4
> Multiple-choice questions can test listening for details, main idea and opinions. In Listening Part 1 as demonstrated here, multiple-choice questions will focus on information, facts and details.

Tell students that, in the exam, they have a short time to read the questions before they listen. They should use this time to underline the key ideas in each question, but not in the options as there won't be enough time for that. Underlining the key ideas:

- helps students to focus on the meaning of each question;
- reminds them of what the question is asking when they are actually listening.

> **Suggested underlining**
> 7 children have; restaurant
> 8 available; reduced price
> 9 situated; lounge
> 10 special event

5 As with Exercise 2, the purpose of this matching exercise is to alert students to the sorts of phrases which signal when a question is being dealt with in the recording. Since students only listen once, it is likely, especially in the early parts of the listening exam, that the recording will include verbal clues to help students find their place.

- Use the example: elicit why phrase a matches Question 5 (answer: students should match *unique* and *only* with *special*, and *crossing* with *voyage*).
- When you go through the answers with students, elicit the vocabulary which matches up. This will alert students to the idea that they will usually not hear exactly the same words in the recording as in the Question, but usually a paraphrase. You can point this out to students if necessary.

> **Answers**
> b 9 c 8 d 7 e 6

6 🎧 Play the recording only once. Afterwards, ask students to compare their answers in pairs.

- Play the recording again for students to check.
- Ask them to look at the recording script to finally decide if their answers were correct or not.

> **Answers**
> 6 B (*reaching our destination at about eight tomorrow morning*)
> 7 A (*a special section in the restaurant with kids' food*)
> 8 C (*you can get your train tickets here ... If you buy them first class, you can get them for 20 percent off*)
> 9 C (*You can also watch the latest TV programmes there*)
> 10 C (*has the chance to win a free holiday ... and the best sentence wins the prize*)

Extension idea Ask students to underline the words in the recording script which give the answers. Point out again that they will often hear paraphrases of the correct option in the questions, not exactly the same words.

Speaking Part 2

1 *As a warmer* With books closed, ask students to work in pairs and discuss: *In what situations might you have to speak on your own for two minutes or more?* To get them started, suggest: *when you have to speak at a meeting.*

- When you round up, ask: *What do you find difficult about speaking on your own, even in your own language?*

  Ask students to open their books and read the exam information. Ask: *What problems do you think you might have doing this?*

- If you have students who have done this sort of activity before, ask them about their experiences.

- Tell students it's important to underline the key ideas in this practice task so that they answer the question as completely as possible. In the real test, they will not be able to underline anything, so they need to get used to picking out the key ideas in their heads as quickly as possible. Although the exam information says they must speak for one to two minutes, they should try to speak for the full two minutes or until the examiner says 'thank you'.

② 🎧 Tell students that making good notes will help them to continue speaking for two minutes. If they note down useful vocabulary and follow the order of the points on the card, they will be able to speak with less hesitation.

③ Elicit from students why it's useful to use phrases like these when giving the talk (*answer*: it helps to structure the talk and signal clearly to the examiner which part of the task you're talking about and where you've reached).

Extension idea Ask students to work in small groups, look at the task and think of other phrases they could use to introduce the talk, etc.

• Round up with the whole class and write the phrases you think are useful on the board.

• Ask students to copy them to the table.

Note: Now is a good moment to do the Pronunciation section on word stress, based on Kyung-Soon's answer.

④ Since this is the first time they have done this task, give students three or four minutes to think and make notes. If they wish, they can discuss their ideas for their notes with a partner. Tell them that their notes should be notes – they should not attempt to write out the whole of what they are going to say because they will not have time in the exam and it will sound unnatural.

Alternative treatment If your students are unused to making notes in English, you should ask them to look at Kyung-Soon's notes in Exercise 2. Ask:

– *Has she written complete sentences?* (no)
– *Do her notes contain words which express ideas or meaning, or do they contain small words which are important for grammar?* (words which express ideas or meaning)

If this concept is hard for students, write these words on the board: *I, she, have, was, did, to, the, a, with.* Ask students: *Does she use any of these words in*

her notes? Why not? (because we add these small grammar words when we're speaking and making complete grammatical sentences – notes carry the essential meaning to remind us what we want to say).

⑤ A common problem when students do Speaking Part 2 for the first time in class is that they treat it as another discussion activity. Tell the student who is listening that they should only listen and not speak during their partner's turn.

Alternative treatment Ask the student who is listening to listen carefully and check that their partner has:

• covered all the points on the task card;

• used some introductory phrases.

Extension idea 1 When students have finished, ask them to work in small groups.

• Ask them to discuss what problems and difficulties they had when doing the task.

• Round up with the whole class and ask them to suggest solutions or strategies to deal with the difficulties.

Typical problems at this early stage in preparation are: not understanding the demands of the task; not speaking for long enough or not having enough to say; hesitating or freezing; repeating the same point too many times; straying from the subject; not knowing the word they want to use, etc.

Extension idea 2 Especially if you have done Extension idea 1, ask students to:

• work alone for a few minutes and think how they could improve the talk they gave;

• work with a different partner and take turns to give the same talk again.

Repeating speaking tasks in this way can be very valuable: it gives students extra practice and confidence and a lot of learning takes place between doing the task the first time and doing it again, especially learning from the way their partners have dealt with the task.

⑥ Give students several minutes to think and prepare their notes.

Alternative treatment Before they make notes, tell students to work in pairs and ask: *What sorts of things can you learn on a journey?*

• Ask them to brainstorm a number of ideas.

• Round up and write their ideas on the board.

• Then ask them to write their notes.

Extension idea If you did the alternative treatment in Exercise 4, take the opportunity for more work on making notes. Ask students to work in pairs and compare their notes. Ask them to look and see if their partner has put in their notes the sort of small words you wrote on the board when doing Exercise 4, or have they written complete sentences?

If necessary, choose a student whose notes are too long and write them on the board. Ask the class to suggest what words could be excluded to make the notes more like notes.

❼ **Answers**
2 a, c, d, f   **3** e

Extension idea Ask students to look at the phrases and the ideas in their notes and think which phrases they can use with their ideas.

Ask them to look at the phrases in Exercise 3 and see if any of those are useful for this task as well.

❽ **Alternative treatment** Write on the board:

Did your partner …?
– speak for two minutes
–
–

Elicit other things that students should do when they do Speaking Part 2 and write them as bullets on the board (e.g. use phrases to structure the talk, speak only in English, cover all the points on the task card, etc.).

• Tell students that when they do the exercise, the student who is listening should think about the points on the board and when their partner has finished, they should give feedback and make suggestions.

• Round up useful feedback from the whole class. Make the feedback positive. Ask: *What did your partner do well? What could he/she do better?* Discuss ideas with the whole class.

• Finally, ask students to change partners and do the task again.

Pronunciation Word stress 1

❶ 🎧 Tell students that good pronunciation is important to make sure the examiner can understand them. When the wrong syllable is stressed in a word, it becomes difficult to understand and communication can break down. The Speaking Band descriptors make reference to how well the candidate can be understood at different levels.

Answer
'motorbike

Extension idea Ask students to repeat *motorbike* when they hear it. Write this sentence on the board: *The transport I used was a motorbike.* Ask students to read the sentence with the correct stress on *motorbike*.

❷ **Alternative treatment** Ask students to say how many syllables there are in each word (answers: transport 2, studying 3, public 2, independent 4, holiday 3, university 5, travel 2, language 2, powerful 3, engine 2, exciting 3, expensive 3, memories 3, interesting 3 or 4 depending on how it is pronounced).

If your students have dictionaries, or access to an online dictionary (such as CLD, http://dictionaries. cambridge.org/default.asp?dict=L) in class, ask them to check where the stress is placed in each word. They can then listen, either to CLD or to the recording with this book to check their answers.

Answers
'transport   'studying   inde'pendent   'holiday
uni'versity   'powerful   ex'citing   ex'pensive
'memories   'interesting

❸ 🎧 Play Kyung-Soon's complete answer, so that they hear the words used in context.

❹ **Extension idea** Ask students to write down, on a piece of paper, five words of more than one syllable that they're not sure how to stress.

• Then, students exchange papers with a partner and check in a dictionary for the correct stress of the words given them.

• Finally, they read the words to their partner. Their partner notes the stress by listening, and then reads the words back to check and practise.

Reading 2 Matching headings

❶ **As a warmer** Ask students to look at the photo. Ask: *How do you feel when you're in a traffic jam? Why?*

Alternative treatment Ask students to do the activity in small groups. When they've finished, ask one student from each group to present the group's ideas to the whole class.

❷ Students should skim the passage to answer this question. Give them two minutes to do so.

Answer
four: congestion pricing; flexitime; more roads; increasing public transport

❸ This exercise pre-teaches vocabulary which occurs in the passage.

Alternative treatment If you would prefer your students to deal with the passage without pre-taught vocabulary, you can leave this exercise till after they have done the task in Exercise 4. In this case, ask students to scan the passage and underline the words from this exercise when they find them. Tell them to use the context of the passage to help them match up the words with their definitions.

> **Answers**
> 2 a   3 d   4 c   5 g   6 e   7 h   8 f

❹ Tell students that to do this task efficiently, it's important to be very familiar with the headings before reading the passage.

> **Suggested underlining**
> ii   Changing working practices
> iii Closing city centres to traffic
> iv   cars more environmentally friendly
> v   not doing enough
> vi   Paying to get in
> vii Global problem

Note: Students may be disconcerted that, for many of these headings, the whole phrase is the key idea and needs to be underlined. Remind them that the point of underlining is to help determine what the key idea is and therefore what the question is asking.

For the second instruction, ask the whole class to suggest what heading **i** means (*answer*: someone has suggested a solution to the problem which won't actually solve the problem). They then do the rest of the headings in pairs (*suggested answers*: ii asking people to work in different ways; iii not allowing vehicles into the centre of cities; iv cutting pollution from cars; v should be doing more; vi paying money to enter; vii a problem which affects the whole world).

Extension idea As stated before, being familiar with the headings before reading makes it easier to do the task efficiently.

- Ask students to close their books, work in pairs and try to remember the seven headings.
- When they've finished, they should compare their answers with another pair of students and then check by opening the book.

❺ The purpose of Questions 1 and 2 are to help students into this task type. Tell them that the best way to do it is to read the first paragraph and decide the answer; read the second paragraph and do the same, etc. (i.e. read each paragraph carefully one by one).

Encourage them to underline words in the paragraphs which give them the correct answers.

> **Answers**
> 1 *global problem* links with *affect people throughout the world* and *dozens of cities across both the developed and developing world.*
> 2 vi (*Paying to get in* links with *congestion pricing, charge a toll to enter*)
> 3 C ii (*employers to implement flexitime / employees travel to and from work at off-peak traffic times / employers can also allow more staff to telecommute* (= work from home)
> D i (*Some urban planners still believe the best way to ease traffic congestion is to build more roads … But such techniques do not really keep cars off the road …*)
> E v (*environmentalists complain that such funding is tiny compared to the $50 billion being spent on roads, bridges and highways*)

Extension idea You can give your students some extra practice in Speaking Part 2 as a follow-up to this reading passage. Write the following speaking task on the board:
Describe a journey you made which took longer than normal.
You should say:
– how you were travelling
– where you were going
– why you were going there
– and how you spent the time on the journey.
Give students time to make some notes. Then ask them to take turns to speak for one to two minutes on the subject.

Vocabulary *make* and *cause*

❶
> **Answers**
> 1 cause   2 make

❷ Tell students to use dictionaries when they are not sure about a word, especially when doing written work for homework.

> **Answers**
> 1 cause   2 make

❸
> **Answers**
> 1 caused   2 made   3 caused   4 makes

Extension idea Write these sentence beginnings on the board:

– *The heavy rain made …*

– *The heavy rain caused …*

– *The rise in fuel prices made …*

– *The rise in fuel prices caused …*

Ask students to complete sentences with their own ideas.

❹ Tell students to take care when using *make* and *cause* in their writing, as IELTS students often confuse them.

> **Answers**
> **1** ~~make~~ cause   **2** ~~make~~ cause   **3** correct
> **4** ~~makes~~ causes

Writing Task 1

❶ **As a warmer** With books closed, tell students that they are going to conduct a survey to find out information about how people in their class travel to the school or college.

- Tell them to work in small groups and discuss: *What type of information could we find out in the survey?*

- To get them started, elicit types or means of transport.

- With books open, before they start, elicit the questions students can ask to find out the information needed (*How do you come to class? How long is your journey? How far do you have to travel? How long does it take?*).

Alternative treatment Ask students if there is other information they thought about when they were doing the warmer (e.g. cost, activities during journey, etc.). Elicit suitable questions.

Ask students to change partners to present this information to their partners. If they did the alternative treatment in Exercise 1, they should include this here.

❷ Tell students that tables are a common way of presenting information in Writing Task 1. They should first look at the table in this exercise to find the maximums and minimums in each column (as focused on in the questions in this exercise).

If they can find relationships between maximums and minimums in different columns, this will also help them to summarise the information.

Alternative treatment Before students start, elicit what is meant by *average*. You can do this by asking: *What is the average distance for one person alone in a car?* (17 miles) *Do all people who travel alone*

in a car travel exactly 17 miles, or do some people travel more and others less? (some travel more and others less) *So what do you think 'average' means?* (An average amount is calculated by adding some amounts together and then dividing by the number of amounts. (CLD))

To reinforce the idea of 'average', you can refer students to the table in Exercise 1 and ask them to work out the average distance and average time for people in their group (by adding the total and dividing by the number in the group).

> **Answers**
> **1** car – more than one person   **2** cycle/walk
> **3** most: train/bus   least: cycle/walk
> **4** fastest: car – more than one person   slowest: walk

Extension idea Ask students: *How do the means of transport and the distances and times for this US city compare with those of people in your group travelling to class?*

Note: Now is a good moment to do the Key grammar section on making comparisons, and after that, the Spelling section on adding -er and -est to adjectives.

❸ Tell students when necessary to refer to the Language reference while doing this task.

> **Answers**
> **2** shortest   **3** longest   **4** least   **5** fastest
> **6** slowest   **7** quickest   **8** best

❹ Although at this level candidates are not expected to be able to divide their summaries into paragraphs, they will raise their score if they can organise the information logically and structure their writing. Using paragraphs helps to do this.

> **Suggested answers**
> **1** Paragraphs 1/2: …in the USA.// People who…
>   Paragraphs 2/3: …17 miles.// People travelling…
>   Paragraphs 3/4: …20 minutes.// Cars tend…
>   Paragraphs 4/5: 3 mph.// Overall …
> **2** Paragraph 2: a
>   Paragraph 3: c
>   Paragraph 4: b
>   Paragraph 5: d

Extension idea Ask students to look at the sample answer and the table and discuss:

– *Where is the information in the table given in the sample answer?*

– *Is there any important information missing?* (no)

❺ Tell students that, very often, Writing Task 1 will contain information in two different forms (e.g. here a table and a bar chart) and that students will have to find the relationship between the information from the two sources in order to write their summary.

Tell them they should look at:

- what type of information is being shown;
- maximums and minimums in the table and the chart;
- any relationships between maximums and minimums.

Suggested answers

1 the percentage of people who use each form of transport and their average age

2 car (one person)

3 cycle/walk

4 train / bus travellers

5 cycling / walking travellers

6 CO_2 emissions from different modes of transport per person per kilometre

7 cycling / walking, train / bus

8 car (driver only)

---

❻ Remind students that it's important to include an overview of the information. Ask them to look at the table and chart to see where the information in this overview is shown.

Answers
most; more

---

❼ *Alternative treatment* Ask students to work in pairs and underline words and phrases from the sample answer in Exercise 4 which they think they might be able to use in this answer.

Sample answer

The table and chart show the percentages of commuters using different modes of transport in Houston, Texas, their average age, and how much carbon dioxide each type of traveller produces.

The most popular form of transport is the car, with 48 percent of people travelling to work alone and a further 11 percent sharing cars to work. On the other hand, 37 percent of commuters use trains or buses, while just 4 percent cycle or walk.

Commuters using public transport are, at 47, on average three or four years older than people using private cars and these, at 43 or 44, are four or five years older than those who walk or cycle.

People travelling alone by car produce the most carbon dioxide, slightly more than 0.3 kilos per person per kilometre. By comparison, people who share transport produce 0.08 kilos, whereas those using public transport produce only a tiny amount.

Overall, the most popular form of transport, the car, is also the one which produces the most pollution.

Extension idea 1 Whether you ask students to write their answers in class or at home, when they have finished, ask them to exchange answers with a partner. Ask them to read their partner's answer and check the following things (you can write these on the board):

– *Have they covered all the important information?*

– *Have they made comparisons?*

– *Have they included some figures?*

– *Have they written an overview?*

– *Have they written at least 150 words?*

– *Have they written in paragraphs?*

When they have finished reading their partner's answer, they should give each other advice on how they can improve it. Where necessary, they rewrite it before handing it in.

Extension idea 2 Photocopy the sample answer and give it to students to compare with their answers.

Key grammar
Making comparisons

❶ When students have completed the table, go through the Language reference on page 123 with them.

Answers
3 higher   4 the highest   5 more expensive
6 the most expensive   7 healthier   8 the healthiest
9 more steadily   10 the most steadily

Extension idea Ask students to add one example of their own to each rule. They then compare their examples in small groups.

❷ **Answers**
2 easier   3 lower   4 healthiest
5 most dangerous   6 more quickly

❸ When they have finished, ask students to compare their answers in small groups. When you round up, ask groups to read out sentences they are not sure about and sentences they think are good.

❹ Tell students to refer to the Language reference on page 123 if necessary when doing this exercise.

In class

❶ As a warmer Elicit from the class the names of some well-known cars. Write their names on the board and add the following gapped phrases:

The .... *parking easy.*

The .... *a lot of pollution.*

The .... *driving exciting.*

❺ Tell students they should be especially careful when using adjectives and adverbs for comparison in their writing and speaking, as candidates frequently make mistakes. Point out, however, that they will achieve a higher band score if they demonstrate they can use them correctly.

- For each gap, ask students to say whether *makes* or *causes* can fit in each space, and to decide which car best matches each description.

- Put students in groups of three or four. Tell them that they are going to read about three different cars. Give each group one copy of the information table and a set of cards, which should be shuffled and placed face down in front of each group.

- Explain that they are going to practise comparative and superlative sentences. Write the following adjectives on the board: *easy (to park)*; *noisy*; *expensive*; *enjoyable (to drive)*; *comfortable (for passengers)*; *big*; *friendly*; *economical*; *fast*; *slow*. Tell students that they are going to play a game which involves completing sentences with comparative or superlative forms of the adjectives on the board. Demonstrate a turn by writing these sentences on the board:

Spelling
Changes when adding -er and -est to adjectives

❶ Extension idea Ask students to work in pairs and add two more examples of their own for each rule. When they have finished, they should compare their examples with another pair.

> 1 *The Nifty has* .... *engine of all the cars, with a size of 1100cc.*
>
> 2 *The Tega has a* .... *engine* .... *the Samiro, with a size of 2000cc.*

Elicit from students what could go in the gaps (1 *the smallest*, 2 *smaller, than*).

- When the groups have finished, ask them to decide together which of the three cars is the best overall. Encourage them to use the comparative language and the collocations from the warmer.

Extension idea When students have done the writing task in exercise 8, ask them to check their own writing and a partner's writing for spelling mistakes with -*er* and -*est*.

- Ask one member of each group to report their findings to the class. Write these phrases on the board to help them to structure their talk.

> *I'm going to talk about ...*
>
> *The good things are ...*
>
> *The bad things are ...*
>
> *In all, we think this car is the best, because ...*

Unit 3 photocopiable activity:
Driving decisions   Time: 30 minutes

Objectives
- To practise comparative and superlative adjectives
- To practise phrases for beginning and ending a talk, and introducing new points
- To revise collocations with *make* and *cause*

Extension idea Students write a short paragraph comparing the cars, using key information from the table. When correcting students' work, pay attention to the formation and spelling of comparative and superlative forms.

You will need to make one copy of page 41 and cut it up so that each group of students has one information table and one set of cards.

Driving decisions

	NIFTY	SAMIRO 3S	TEGA 2
Engine type	petrol	petrol	electric hybrid
Engine size	1100cc	3000cc	2000cc
Engine noise	low	high	very low
Top speed	150 km/h	200 km/h	90 km/h
Fuel economy (km travelled for £1 of fuel)	50 km	30 km	5 km
Level of CO_2 emissions	low	high	zero
Easy to park (percentage of drivers who rated it easy)	90%	60%	70%
Enjoyable to drive (percentage who rated it enjoyable)	55%	90%	50%
Price	£7,000	£25,000	£30,000

The Tega is .... to park .... the Samiro.
*The Tega is **easier** to park **than** the Samiro.*

The Nifty has low engine noise, but it is .... the Tega.
*The Nifty has low engine noise, but it is **noisier than** the Tega.*

At £25,000, the Samiro is .... the Nifty.
*At £25,000, the Samiro is **more expensive** than the Nifty.*

The Nifty is .... to drive .... the Tega.
*The Nifty is **more enjoyable** to drive **than** the Tega.*

The Nifty is .... to park of all three cars.
*The Nifty is **the easiest** to park of all three cars.*

With a high level of engine noise, the Samiro is .... of all the cars.
*With a high level of engine noise, the Samiro is **the noisiest** of all the cars.*

At £30,000, the Tega is .... of all the cars.
*At £30,000, the Tega is **the most expensive** of all the cars.*

With a 90% enjoyment rating, the Samiro is .... to drive of all the cars.
*With a 90% enjoyment rating, the Samiro is **the most enjoyable** to drive of all the cars.*

The Tega has a .... engine than the Nifty.
*The Tega has a **bigger** engine than the Nifty.*

The Nifty has a .... level of CO_2 emissions than the Samiro.
*The Nifty has a **lower** level of CO_2 emissions than the Samiro.*

With 30 km per £1 of fuel, the Samiro is .... to drive .... the Tega.
*With 30 km per £1 of fuel, the Samiro is **more economical** to drive **than** the Tega.*

With a top speed of 150 km per hour, the Nifty is .... the Samiro.
*With a top speed of 150 km per hour, the Nifty is **slower than** the Samiro.*

The Samiro has .... engine, with a size of 3000cc.
*The Samiro has **the biggest** engine, with a size of 3000cc.*

The Tega has .... level of CO_2 emissions.
*The Tega has **the lowest** level of CO_2 emissions.*

Vocabulary extension

Unit 3

Abbreviations: n/sln/pln = noun / single noun / plural noun; v = verb; adj = adjective; adv = adverb; p = phrase; pv = phrasal verb; T/I = transitive/intransitive; C/U = countable/uncountable

atmosphere *n* [C] mixture of gases around the Earth

board *v* [T] to get on a bus, boat, aircraft, etc.

communications *pln* ways of moving between one place and another

commute *v* [I] to regularly travel between work and home

delay *n* [C/U] when you have to wait longer than expected for something to happen, or the time that you have to wait

efficient *adj* working well and not wasting time or energy

the environment *n* the air, land, and water where people, animals, and plants live

exhaust *n* [U] the waste gas from a vehicle's engine

fare *n* [C] the price that you pay to travel on an aircraft, train, bus, etc.

infrastructure *n* [C] the basic systems, such as transport and communication, that a country or organisation uses in order to work effectively

journey *n* [C] when you travel from one place to another

limit *v* [T] to control something so that it is less than a particular amount or number

load *n* [C] something that is carried, often by a vehicle

long-distance *adj* travelling or communicating between two places that are a long way apart

luggage *n* [U] bags and cases that you carry with you when you are travelling

motorist *n* [C] someone who drives a car

motorway *n* [C] a long, wide road, usually used by traffic travelling fast over long distances

passenger *n* [C] someone who is travelling in a vehicle, but not controlling the vehicle

pollution *n* [U] damage caused to water, air, etc. by harmful substances or waste

prevent *v* [T] to stop something happening or to stop someone doing something

profitable *adj* making or likely to make a profit

public *adj* Public parks/toilets/transport, etc. are for everyone to use and are not private.

reliable *adj* able to be trusted or believed

ride *v* [I/T] to travel by sitting on a horse, bicycle, or motorcycle and controlling it

route *n* [C] the roads or paths you follow to get from one place to another place

system *n* [C] a way or method of doing things

ticket *n* [C] a small piece of paper that shows you have paid to do something, for example travel on a bus, watch a film, etc.

timetable *n* [C] a list of times when buses, trains, etc. arrive and leave

the underground *n* [U] a railway system in which electric trains travel along passages below ground

urban *adj* belonging or relating to a town or city

Unit 4 It was all new once

Unit objectives

- **Vocabulary:** deciding what type of word it is; *design*, *inventor*, *yield*, etc.; *lead to*, *assemble*, etc.

- **Reading:** scanning for words and names; introduction to multiple-choice questions; introduction to summary-completion task

- **Listening:** introduction to sentence-completion tasks; introduction to pick-from-a-list questions

- **Speaking Part 2:** making notes; giving reasons and examples; explaining consequences; monitoring performance

- **Pronunciation:** chunking and pausing naturally

- **Grammar:** the present perfect

- **Writing Task 2:** critical-thinking skills for analysing the task; distinguishing between relevant and irrelevant points in answers; analysing the structure of a sample essay: essay and paragraph planning

- **Spelling:** using and misusing double letters

Starting off

As a warmer With books closed, ask students to work in small groups for three minutes and make a list of ten important inventions. When they have finished, ask them to change groups, compare their lists and decide which are the most important ten inventions from their combined lists.

- With books open, ask students if any of the things in the pictures were not on their lists. They then do the exercise in the book.

- When students answer the second question, encourage them to talk in general and suggest a variety of changes arising from each invention. You can elicit how air travel has changed people's lives (e.g. allowing people to travel quickly and easily between countries; encouraging tourism; allowing people to see how people in other countries live; encouraging international business and trade, etc.).

Answers
1 the mobile / cell phone   2 the syringe
3 the plane   4 air conditioning
5 the washing machine   6 the camera

Vocabulary What type of word is it? 1

❶ *As a warmer* Ask students to read the introductory sentence. Ask them: *Why does it help to know if a difficult word is a noun, verb, or adjective?* (it will help you understand the sentence; if you use a dictionary, it will help you choose the correct definition where a word has more than one meaning).

- To practise scanning, give students a minute to find and underline the two words.

- Students should decide that *moisture* is a noun because it comes after a verb (as the object). The ending *-ure* may also help them.

- They should decide that *cited* is a verb because of its ending *-ed* and because it comes between two noun phrases, the subject and the object.

- You can elicit that the position of the word in the sentence will help to decide what type of word it is.

- Go through the Language reference on page 123.

Alternative treatment You can incorporate this vocabulary section into the reading section which follows by doing it after Reading Exercise 2 if you wish to pre-teach the vocabulary, or after Exercise 4 if you wish your students to cope with the exam-style task without the help of pre-taught vocabulary.

Answers
1 *moisture* – noun; *cited* – verb
2 *moisture* – a; *cited* – b

Extension idea If you have a class set of dictionaries, ask students to look up *design* and *plant* in the dictionary and say how many meanings each word has (*design* has at least six, *plant* has more than ten).

Ask them to look at the entries and say whether the words are nouns or verbs.

❷ Give students two minutes to scan the passage and underline the words.

Answers
2 noun a   3 noun b   4 verb f   5 noun d   6 noun c

Reading 1 Multiple-choice questions

❶ *As a warmer* Ask students to work in small groups, compare the two photographs and say how working conditions have improved.

It was all new once   (43)

Extension idea If it hasn't arisen already, ask students: *What other inventions have changed working and study conditions? How and why?*

② ***Alternative treatment*** Remind students that it's important to read the title of the passage and the sub-heading before reading. Ask them to read these and say what they think the passage will be about (*answer*: the history of air conditioning and how it has made life more comfortable).

Tell students that there are often questions about people mentioned in reading passages, so scanning to locate the people is a useful reading skill. Give them a minute for this.

> **Answers**
> **1** the inventor of air conditioning
> **2** an environmentalist

③ Tell students that the best approach to multiple-choice questions is to:

- read the question, but not the alternatives
- locate where the question is dealt with in the passage and read that part carefully
- look at the alternatives afterwards and choose the correct one.

Tell students that if they read the alternatives before they have understood what the passage says, they may become confused and choose the wrong one.

Alternative treatment for Exercises 3 and 4 Ask students to deal with each question one by one (i.e. they read the question – but not the alternatives – for Question 1), locate where it is answered in the passage, read carefully, then read the alternatives and choose the correct answer. They then pass to question 2 and do the same, etc.

> **Students should underline**
> **2** not popular at first   **3** Employers refused to put air conditioning in workplaces   **4** purpose of / research / 1940s and 50s   **5** Jed Brown say

④ While students are doing this exercise, ask them to underline the words in the passage which gave them the answers. When they have finished, ask them to work in pairs and compare their answers. Where they disagree, they should go back to the passage to sort out whose answer is correct.

> **Answers**
> **1** D   **2** A   **3** C   **4** C   **5** D

⑤ ***Extension idea*** When they have finished, ask students to change groups and take turns to talk about one invention they mentioned in their previous group. They should say what the invention is and how it has made life more comfortable.

Listening
Sentence completion; pick from a list

① ***As a warmer*** Ask students:

- *Do you have exhibitions in your town or city? What things do they show?*
- *In what ways are exhibitions useful?*

If you prefer, you can write these questions on the board and ask students to discuss them in groups.

② Sentence-completion tasks test students' ability to extract important facts and details from a text. Tell students that thinking about questions 1–3 will help them to know what sort of information they should be listening for.

Alternative treatment Ask students to think about what type of word they need in each gap. You can elicit that in Question 1, it will be a verb.

> **Answers**
> **1** three
> **2** first section: questions 1, 2; second section: questions 3–5; third section: question 6
> **3** **2** device / checking / temperatures   **3** second / children   **4** inventions / avoid / in the home   **5** device / checking / children   **6** third section / devices / dealing with

③ 🎧 Before they listen, ask students:

- *How many words can you write in each space?* (one)
- *If you hear two words which you think are both correct, can you write them both?* (no)

- Play the recording once as in the exam. Ask students to write their answers while they listen.
- Give students time to check their spelling and then to compare their answers with a partner.
- Play the recording a second time for students to check their answers. Tell them to make sure that the completed sentences make sense and are grammatically correct.

> **Answers**
> **1** protect   **2** ocean   **3** safety   **4** accident   **5** school
> **6** money

④ Ask students to look at the four questions. Ask: *How are these questions different from normal multiple-choice questions?* (answer: There are five options; you must choose two.)

- Tell students that this is like an extended multiple-choice question, but as there is more than one answer, it is particularly important to read the question carefully so that they know what to listen for.

- They should also note how many marks they get. When they see a rubric which says Questions 1–2, it means that each correct answer scores one mark, as there is one mark per question in the Listening Test. In this case they must choose the two correct answers to get one mark per question.

> **Suggested underlining**
> 8 TWO devices; bought
> 9 TWO things; like; building
> 10 TWO problems; coming to the exhibition

❺ 🎧 Tell students that when they listen, they are likely to hear each of the alternatives mentioned in some way, but that they should be careful (for example in Question 1) to choose the reasons for visiting the exhibition and not the ideas mentioned in connection with something else. The answers are often close together and may not come in the same order in the script as in the questions.

- Remind students that Irina will express the same meaning, but not necessarily use the same words as in the alternatives.

- Play the recording once as in the exam. Then give students time to compare their answers in pairs.

- Play the recording again for students to check their answers.

Extension idea Ask students to read the recording script when you play the recording a second time, for them to check their answers.

> **Answers**
> 7 B (*I want to keep up with the latest developments in electronics*), E (*I thought there would be things which would interest my son and he'd enjoy it as well*)
> 8 B (*I got a new laptop recently*), C (*I bought him a camera*)
> 9 B (*It feels very large and spacious*), D (*the ceiling near the entrance … that's something I really like*)
> 10 C (*the car park … was full when I arrived*), D (*we had to stand outside for quite a long time queuing to get in*)

❻ *Extension idea* Ask students: *Do you think it's better to buy electronics on the internet or in a shop? Why?*

Speaking Part 2

❶ *As a warmer* With books closed, tell students that they're going to work on Speaking Part 2 again. Ask them to work in small groups and try to remember what Speaking Part 2 involves. When they have finished, they can check by looking at the Exam overview on page 7.

Tell students that, in the exam, they should choose what they find easiest to talk about for two minutes, not what they think will impress the examiner most. Ask them to give reasons for their decisions (i.e. outline to their partners what they can say about the device they chose).

❷ 🎧

> **Answers**
> 2 a 3 d 4 c 5 h 6 b 7 g 8 e

❸ Tell students that they will score higher marks if:

- they keep going for two minutes – the examiner will encourage them to do this;

- they speak coherently with structured thoughts and ideas;

- they use longer, more complex sentences.

> **Answers**
> 1 because 2 for example; for instance 3 so

Extension idea Write on the board:

- *My parents gave me a new laptop because …*

- *My parents gave me a new laptop, so …*

- *I bought a new mobile phone because …*

- *I bought a new mobile phone, so …*

Ask students to work alone and complete the sentences. They then compare their sentences with a partner. Students can use these sentences for the suggested Alternative treatment in Pronunciation Exercise 4.

Note: Now is a good moment to do the Pronunciation section on chunking and the Key grammar section on the present perfect, which are based on Amani's answer.

❹ Give students two or three minutes to make notes.

Alternative treatment Before they do this exercise, remind students about the work they did in Unit 3 on introducing the talk, introducing new points and finishing the talk. Elicit phrases they can use to do these things here.

Extension idea Ask students to work in pairs and compare the notes they've made and the ideas they have had. Give them time in this case to update their notes with any ideas their partners have given them.

❺ Before students start, elicit what they should do while reading the task (*answer*: underline key ideas).

⑥ *Alternative treatment* Write the following checklist on the board:

Did your partner …

1 talk directly about the topic?

2 read from his/her notes without looking at you?

3 deal with all the points?

4 give examples, reasons, express consequences?

5 answer using his/her own words?

6 keep talking for two minutes?

Ask: *Which of these things are good things to do when you are doing Speaking part 2?* Students then discuss in pairs. Where they decide something is not a good thing to do, ask them to rewrite the question so that it reflects good advice (suggested answers: 1 yes 2 no – use the notes as prompts, but look at the examiner when speaking 3 yes 4 yes 5 no – use your own words where possible rather than repeating the words in the prompt – it shows ability to use language creatively 6 yes).

They then take turns to do the speaking task with the student who is listening giving feedback based on the checklist.

- When the first student has given feedback, round up the feedback with the whole class.
- Encourage positive feedback.
- Elicit suggestions from the whole class for dealing with problems / negative feedback.
- Repeat the process after the second student in each pair has given feedback.

Pronunciation Chunking 1

① Chunks are groups of words which, in the speaker's mind, form units of meaning. Speakers are more likely to pause before and after these chunks.

🎧 Be prepared to play the recording several times, so that students can recognise where pauses occur.

Answers
I've had this camera / for two years./ My parents gave it to me / for my birthday / when I was 18./ I didn't ask / for a camera, / so it was a complete surprise, / but it's been / really useful.

② 🎧 To help students predict where the pauses will occur, if you haven't already done so, point out that chunks are groups of words which form units of meaning and that the pauses will come before these.

When students listen to check their answers, tell them that because there are no fixed rules for this, their answers are not necessarily wrong if they are different from the recording. The speaker here pauses in the most likely places.

Answers
Since I got the camera, / I've carried it with me / everywhere I've gone on holiday. / For example, / in July / I went on holiday to Denmark and Sweden. / They're lovely places / and in summer / it's still light at midnight, / so I got some great photos there.

③ Students will need to read the sentences several times to achieve some naturalness. When they have finished, ask for volunteers to read the sentences out to the whole class. Other students should say if they have 'chunked' naturally.

④ Tell students to write fairly long sentences using *because, so, for example* and *for instance.*

⑤ When they have read their sentences to each other once, they should change partners and read again.

Key grammar Present perfect

① If your students are unfamiliar with the term *past participle,* ask them to look at the examples of past participles and then elicit other examples.

Answers
it's been; I've carried; I've gone; I've taken

② Point out that the present perfect always combines ideas of time in the past and time in the present:

- something which started in the past and continues to the present;
- something where we don't state the time, so it may have happened any time from the past up to the present moment.

When students have done the exercise, go through the Language reference on page 124 with them.

Answers
1 I've had; it's been; I've carried
2 I've gone; I've taken

③ Remind students that many common verbs have irregular forms, and that in order to use this grammar correctly and confidently, they will have to know them. Students can find a list in the Language reference on page 124.

❹ **Answers**
2 ~~has brought~~ have brought   3 ~~are~~ have been
4 ~~are~~ have been   5 ~~become~~ has become

❺ Go through the Language reference on page 124 with your students after they have answered the questions.

Answers
1 for   2 since

Extension idea Write on the board:

How long have you…?

– lived in this town/city?

– had a mobile phone?

Ask students to write two sentences, one with *for* and one with *since* to answer each question. When they have finished, ask students to compare answers in pairs.

❻ **Answers**
2 since   3 for   4 since   5 since   6 for

Reading 2 Summary completion

❶ ***As a warmer*** With books closed, write on the board:

– *What indoor games (not sports) do you play?*

– *Which are your favourites?*

– *How long do you spend playing games each week?*

Ask students to work in groups and discuss.

Answers
1 1 b   2 c   3 a

2 Rubik's Cube: you have to turn the pieces of the cube so that each of the faces of the cube is one colour.

Chinese tangram: You have to form shapes using the pieces.

Sudoku: You have to fill the squares with numbers 1 to 9 so that each column, each row, and each box that make up the puzzle contains all of the digits from 1 to 9.

❷ Before students do this task, elicit what type of information they should scan for (times or dates). Give them one minute to find the information.

Answers
1 while he was working as a teacher   2 1979–80

Extension idea For more scanning practice, you can

• write on the board: *Tibor Laczi; Tom Kremer.* Give students one minute to find out their jobs (*answers*: Tibor Laczi – businessman; Tom Kremer – inventor and marketer).

• ask students to find and underline the names of five cities mentioned in the passage (Budapest, Nuremberg, London, Paris and New York).

❸ Before students do this task, they can look at the Language reference on Deciding the type of word again. They worked on this when they did the previous Reading task in this unit.

• When they do the task, they should scan for these words. You can give them 90 seconds. They should then use the context to help them choose the correct definition.

Alternative treatment If you want your students to do the IELTS-type task without being pre-taught vocabulary, omit this exercise unitl Exercise 5.

Answers
2 verb a   3 verb f   4 verb b   5 verb e   6 noun d

❹ Point out to students that, in the exam itself, they will have to complete a summary of part or one aspect of a passage as the exam advice here indicates. They have to scan the passage to locate the part they need to concentrate on. In this instance, since the passage is much shorter than a full IELTS passage, the summary takes information from all parts of it.

• The instructions here suggest the technique they should use with this task type in the exam. By answering these questions, they can then scan in the passage for the specific information and types of words they need.

• When they answer these questions, students may not be able to give very exact or precise answers, but it's still useful to help them focus on what they should look for.

Suggested answers
1 noun – a name
2 noun – the way something is organised, a shape
3 adverb – a direction
4 noun – part of the Cube
5 adjective – description of the colours
6 noun – the name of someone or something related to the Cube   7 noun – something that is sold

❺ Tell students to look at the instructions and ask: *Can you write answers of just one word, or must you write two?* (*answer*: one or two, but not more)

- Before they answer the questions, draw their attention to the Exam advice.

- Point out that IELTS candidates often lose marks by not copying words exactly, or spelling them wrongly.

- Remind students that they should always check their answers to completion exercises when they've finished to make sure that they make sense, reflect the ideas expressed in the passage, and are grammatically correct.

- When students have finished, ask them to work in pairs and compare their answers.

- Point out that for Question 7, there are two possible correct answers. Tell them that in the exam, although the instructions say 'no more than two words', they should only write one of the answers.

> **Answers**
> **1** Magic Cube **2** layers **3** diagonally **4** interior
> **5** identical **6** inventor **7** puzzle

Extension idea 1 To reinforce the idea that students should check they have spelled their answers exactly as in the passage, write these answers on the board.

1 Majic Cube 2 layer 3 diagonaly 4 interior 5 identicall 6 inventer 7 puzlle.

Say: *Some of the answers are spelled correctly and some contain mistakes. Work in pairs and correct the mistakes by checking in the passage.*

Extension idea 2 Ask: *Why do you think Rubik's Cube has been so successful?* (*suggested answers*: the object is simple, but the solution is complex; it's small and easily carried; it's cheap; you can't lose pieces, etc.)

Extension idea 3 Write the following Speaking Part 2 question on the board.

Describe a typical game people in your country enjoy.
You can say:
– what it consists of
– who plays it
– when people play it
– and explain why people enjoy it.

- Give students a minute to prepare and make notes.

- Then ask them to work in pairs and take turns to give their talks.

- If you wish, ask them to give each other feedback after their talks.

Writing Task 2

❶ *As a warmer* Ask students to look at the photos and work in small groups. Write these questions on the board and ask students to discuss them:

- *What do the three photos have in common?* (people using electronic technology/devices, or people looking at screens).

- *How are pictures 1 and 2 different?* (in 1 the person is not taking any physical exercise; in 2 the person is using a device to take exercise, being active both physically and mentally).

- *Is picture 3 more similar to picture 1 or picture 2?* (this should give rise to some discussion: the person is not physically active, but is mentally active).

When students have finished, round up ideas with the whole class.

Once students have familiarised themselves with the writing task by underlining the key ideas, the questions which follow are intended to help:

- analyse the question;

- think through the possible implications of the question; and

- form their opinions on the topic.

When students have finished, point out that they must cover both these ideas in their answer: *people do less physical activity and this is having a negative effect on their health*. If students only discuss one of these points, they will lose marks.

Students often have difficulty with the concept of 'To what extent do you agree or disagree?' Tell students that they are not expected to have a black or white position on a topic, but that there will be a wide range of possible opinions and positions. They can agree with one part of the question, partly disagree with another, etc. They must express their opinions, but they should support them with reasons and examples.

Extension idea Ask students to change groups and report what they have discussed. Encourage each student to speak at length, to accustom them to speaking at length as they have to do in Speaking Part 2.

> **Suggested underlining**
> electronic inventions, less physical activity, negative effect on their health

❷ IELTS candidates often write things in their answers which are not relevant to the task. They will lose marks for this. Tell students it's important to analyse the question and plan before they write: they must answer the question as exactly as possible.

Answers

2 R

3 I (the question is about health, not enjoyment)

4 R

5 I (the question is about electronic inventions, not about general reasons why people's health is better)

6 I (it's not about sports either)

❸ **Answers**

1 5   2 1   3 4   4 2   5 3

Extension idea Draw students' attention to the introductory phrases in each paragraph (*As far as work is concerned; However; In conclusion; On the other hand; and There is no doubt that*) and their function in introducing the topic and linking paragraphs to each other. Ask students to suggest, or write other sentences which start with *As far as x is concerned* and *There is no doubt that ...* as these are phrases they may not have used before.

❹ *As a warmer* Write on the board:

- *How are the people communicating in each photo?*

- *What are the advantages of each method of communication?*

- *Which of them do you use? Why?* Ask students to work in groups, look at the photos and discuss.

• When they have finished, round up students' ideas with the whole class before looking at the writing task in the book.

• When students discuss the questions in the book, focus on *include any relevant examples from your own knowledge and experience*. Tell them that they should answer the question in general, but they can talk about their own experience to support their opinions, hence Question 4.

• Make sure students realise the two points they have to discuss – modern forms of communication have reduced the amount of time people spend seeing their friends and this has had a negative effect on their social lives. Students very often lose marks for not answering both parts of a question.

Alternative treatment You can use the questions for a general class discussion to vary class dynamics.

Suggested underlining
Modern forms of communication, reduced the amount of time people spend seeing their friends, negative effect on their social lives

❺ *Alternative treatment* Ask students to work in pairs, brainstorm ideas for their answer, and write their plan together.

❻ This writing task is probably best done for homework. Tell students that in the exam they will have about 40 minutes for the task. However, at this stage in the course it's better to do the task well than to adhere strictly to a time limit. They should, however, write at least 250 words.

Sample answer
Electronic messaging and email have changed our social lives and the way we communicate with our friends. However, it is not at all certain that our social lives are worse as a result. In many ways, they are better.

In the past, people communicated by letter or by phone. They used to meet and see each other only when they had time. Because people led busy lives, often they did not have any communication with some of their friends for months. As a consequence, their relationships suffered.

Nowadays, we can be in constant contact with all our friends using social websites and instant messaging without even leaving our rooms. As a result, our social relationships are much closer. For example, in my case I spend about an hour chatting to friends from all over the world everyday on my computer. I know how they are, what they are thinking and what they are doing. In the past this was not possible and I might have communicated with some of these friends only once or twice a year.

I think it is also difficult to argue that modern forms of communication have reduced the amount people see each other. In my experience, the amount people go out and meet each other has increased. It has become easier to organise parties, and young people especially are able to introduce their friends to each other and in this way increase their social circle.

In conclusion, I disagree entirely with the statement in the question and firmly believe that modern communications have greatly improved people's social lives.

Extension idea To reinforce the teaching point made in Exercise 2, before students hand in their work, ask them to exchange it with a partner. They should then read each other's work and decide if all of the answer is relevant. If they feel there is any part of the answer which is not answering the question, they should give feedback on that.

Spelling Using and misusing double letters

❶ Tell students that, in most cases, they simply have to learn the spelling of words rather than look for rules. However, they should remember rules for adding *-er*, *-est* to adjectives or *-ing* and *-ed* to verbs.

- Point out that in words beginning with a vowel (e.g. *office*), the vowel is often followed by a double consonant (though this is not a rule – see *employee*).
- Words of more than one syllable ending in *-l*, the *'l'* will usually be single not double.

Answers

1 office 2 sitting 3 affected 4 physical 5 better
6 generally 7 difficult 8 harmful

---

❷ Tell students that native speakers recognise correct spelling by the visual shape of the word rather than knowledge of spelling rules. Correct spelling comes with extensive reading and the resulting familiarity with the shape of words.

Answers

2 installed 3 annoyed 4 attractive 5 attention
6 apart 7 successfully 8 different 9 benefit
10 attempted 11 appearance 12 communicate

Vocabulary and grammar review *Unit 3*

❶

❷ 2 has caused 3 make 4 have made 5 has caused
6 causes

❸ 2 more efficient 3 further/farther 4 greatest
5 hottest 6 worse 7 highest 8 lower
❹ 2 hottest 3 wettest 4 driest 5 sunniest 6 cloudiest

Unit 4

❶ 2 Output 3 designed 4 experimenting
5 assembled 6 object
❷ 2 successfully 3 office 4 attention 5 Apart
6 benefit 7 different 8 physical
❸ 2 for example / for instance 3 because 4 so
5 because 6 For example / For instance
❹ 2 has just written 3 has risen 4 have bought
5 have done; have found 6 have finished; have not paid
❺ 2 for 3 since 4 for 5 since

Unit 4 photocopiable activity: The technology trail Time: 40 minutes

---

Objectives

- To practise the present perfect simple, *for* and *since*
- To practise extending responses
- To recycle technology and inventions vocabulary

Before class

You will need a photocopy of page 51, a set of counters and one dice for each group.

❶ Put students into groups of three or four and give the game to each group.

- Explain that for white squares, students must speak for at least one minute. Demonstrate by writing *Could you live without electronic devices?* on the board and talking on this subject. Ask students to time you.
- Explain that for grey squares, students must answer a 'grammar check' question. Write *She's been interested in photography for/since more than 10 years.* on the board. Elicit the correct word (*for*).

❷ Students play the game by taking turns to roll the dice and moving their counter to a square. If they land on a square which is already occupied, or has already been answered, they move forward one square. The winner is the first person to reach 'FINISH'.

As students play, monitor for errors. Be ready to sort out any disagreements about answers.

❸ When students have finished, you could write a selection of errors on the board and ask the class to correct them.

Answers for 'grammar check' squares

2 for 4 become 7 since 11 understood 15 since
18 increased 20 for 23 ridden 26 since
29 changed 32 for 35 been 38 Since 40 lost

The technology trail

START	**1** How often do you use a computer?	**2** I've had my computer *since/for* over five years.	**3** Move back one square.	**4** My life *has become/became* more stressful because of technology.	**5** Miss a turn.
11 I've never *understood/understand* the internet.	**10** Do you think it's important to take photos?	**9** Move forward two squares.	**8** Talk about a website you often visit.	**7** He hasn't used his camera *since/for* last summer.	**6** Is your mobile phone important to you?
12 Move back two squares.	**13** Talk about a useful invention.	**14** Miss a turn.	**15** He hasn't been online *for/since* yesterday.	**16** Do you often send emails?	**17** Move forward one square.
23 I *haven't rode/ridden* a bicycle since I was a child.	**22** Do you think it's important to have a mobile phone?	**21** Move back two squares.	**20** I haven't heard from my sister *for/since* almost a month.	**19** Do you use social-networking sites?	**18** The number of internet users in my country *has increased/increase* in recent years.
24 Miss a turn.	**25** Does technology help you with your work/studies?	**26** I've had a mobile phone *since/for* 1997.	**27** Move forward one square.	**28** Have you ever bought anything online?	**29** Technology *has changed/changes* the lives of many people.
35 She *has being/been* interested in science all her life.	**34** Move back two squares.	**33** Talk about something you have bought recently.	**32** Touch-screen phones have been available *for/since* a few years.	**31** Do you read newspapers online?	**30** Move back two squares.
36 Could you live without the internet?	**37** Miss a turn.	**38** *For/Since* buying my phone, I have been able to check my emails easily.	**39** Talk about an invention which helps to save time.	**40** We *have loss/lost* touch with all our friends.	**FINISH**

Vocabulary extension

Unit 4

Abbreviations: n/sln/pln = noun / single noun / plural noun; v = verb; adj = adjective; adv = adverb; p = phrase; pv = phrasal verb; T/I = transitive/intransitive; C/U = countable/uncountable

assist *v* [I/T] to help

attach *v* [T] to fasten, join or connect

attempt *n* [C] when you try to do something

automatic *adj* An automatic machine works by itself or with little human control.

break down *pv* [I] If a machine or vehicle breaks down, it stops working.

combine *v* [I/T] to become mixed or joined, or to mix or join things together

connect *v* [I/T] to join two things or places together

consist of *pv* [T] to be made of or formed from something

demonstrate *v* [T] to show someone how to do something, or how something works

design *v* [T] to draw or plan something before making it

device *n* [C] a piece of equipment that is used for a particular purpose

display *v* [I/T] to show something electronically, such as on a computer screen

electronic *adj* Electronic equipment consists of things such as computers, televisions and radios.

gadget *n* [C] a small piece of equipment that does a particular job, especially a new type

hand-held *adj* describes something that is designed to be held and used easily with one or two hands

industrial *adj* connected with industry

install *v* [I/T] to put software onto a computer

labour-saving *adj* describes a device or method which saves a lot of effort and time

manufacture *v* [T] to produce something, usually in large numbers in a factory

measure *v* [T] to find the size, weight, amount, or speed of something

operate (a machine) *v* [T] If you operate a machine you make it do what it is designed to do.

portable *adj* able to be carried

powerful (machine) *adj* having a lot of strength or force

purchase *v* [T] to buy something

purpose *n* [C] why you do something or why something exists

replace *v* [T] to start using another thing or person instead of the one that you are using now

simple *adj* not difficult to do or to understand

sophisticated *adj* A sophisticated machine or system is very advanced and works in a clever way.

switch on/off *pv* [T] to turn on or off a light, television, etc. by using a switch

tool *n* [C] something that helps you to do a particular activity

weigh *v* [T] to measure how heavy someone or something is

❶ **Choose the best alternative (A, B or C) for each sentence.**

0   My ....C............ to work takes me over an hour every day.

   A travel   **B** transport   **C** journey

1   Some employers try to .... their staff to leave their cars at home.

   A engage   **B** ensure   **C** encourage

2   Commuters in the United States .... a large part of their working week waiting in traffic jams.

   A pass   **B** spend   **C** give

3   If you go to work very early or late, you can .... the rush hour.

   A avoid   **B** prevent   **C** excuse

4   Some cities .... drivers money to enter the city centre.

   A charge   **B** ask   **C** demand

5   You can help .... pollution by sharing your car with other people.

   A drop   **B** fall   **C** reduce

❷ **Complete the paragraph by writing the correct comparative or superlative form of the adjective in brackets.**

I love cycling. If there are traffic jams, cycling can be **0** ......*quicker*...... (quick) than going by car or bus. Cycling is **1** .... (convenient) than travelling by car, because you don't need to worry about finding a parking space. It also costs **2** .... (little) than driving or taking public transport. What's more, driving has a much **3** .... (bad) effect on the environment than cycling does. You get lots of exercise on a bike, so it's **4** .... (healthy) than driving too. I think it's the **5** .... (good) way to travel!

❸ **Match the beginnings of the sentences on the left with the endings of sentences on the right. There are three extra endings which you do not need to use.**

0   The bus arrived   **A** because I'd always wanted to go there.

1   I travelled by train   **B** so I enjoy driving.

2   My bike is broken   **C** because there weren't any traffic jams.

3   I got a plane to New York   **D** so I got on it.

4   The station's near my house   **E** because I don't like flying.

5   I got to work on time   **F** because I arrived on time.

                                   G because I prefer cycling.

                                   H so I walked to the office today.

                                   I so I don't use my car much.

4 **Choose the correct option (*since* or *for*) in each sentence.**

0   I've had my computer *for* / *since* six months.
1   Jane and Bob have been married *for* / *since* 1998.
2   I've played the piano *for* / *since* I was a child.
3   Takeshi has worked for this company *for* / *since* a few years.
4   I've lived here *for* / *since* I finished university.
5   We've known each other *for* / *since* a long time.

5 **Complete the sentences by putting the verb in brackets into the correct form of the present perfect tense.**

0   How long ....*have*.... you ...*been*... a student at this college? (be)
1   I .... never .... such an interesting exhibition. (see)
2   Dad .... to town to buy a new mobile phone. (go)
3   .... you .... in a helicopter before? (fly)
4   I'm annoyed that Emily .... already .... her new video game. (break)
5   This is the fastest car I .... ever .... (drive)

6 **Find a word in italics in the text with the same meaning as each word in the list. There are two words in italics which you do not need to use.**

0   method   ...*technique*...
1   information   ....
2   aim   ....
3   effect   ....
4   connection   ....
5   advantage   ....

Tetris is an electronic game invented by a Russian computer programmer in the 1980s. The *object* of the game is to move various falling shapes into position to make horizontal lines. The ~~technique~~ for achieving this is relatively simple, but there are many different levels of *difficulty* within the game. Some parents and teachers believe that computer games like Tetris have a negative *influence* on young people. However, according to *data* published in a US scientific journal, playing Tetris may actually have an unexpected *benefit*. Research suggests that there is a *link* between Tetris and improved brain *efficiency*, says Dr Richard Haier of the Mind Research Network in Albuquerque, New Mexico.

Unit 5 Animal world

Unit objectives

- **Reading:** scanning; skimming; introduction to sentence completion and pick from a list
- **Listening Part 2:** introduction to table completion and labelling a map
- **Speaking Parts 1 and 2:** expressing feelings and opinions; dealing with not knowing a word or not knowing how to answer
- **Pronunciation:** sentence stress in introductory phrases and phrases which express feelings
- **Vocabulary:** some names of animals *cow, crocodile,* etc.; animal habitats *grassland, farmland,* etc.; words connected with animal behaviour *diet, prey,* etc.; suffixes for nouns, verbs, adverbs and adjectives, synonyms for *rise* and *fall*
- **Writing Task 1:** describing changes over time from bar charts; using sequencers and time markers; planning and comparing
- **Grammar:** prepositions in time phrases; countable and uncountable nouns, *few, little, much, many, number and amount*
- **Spelling:** small words which are often misspelled: *the, they, there,* etc.

Starting off

❶ *As a warmer* With books closed, ask students to think of five animals they can see in their country. (If they don't know the English name for them, they can describe what they look like.) Write on the board:

– *Where is the best place to see these animals?*

– *Have you ever seen them?*

Students should work in pairs and answer the questions (partners needn't be from the same country or talk about the same animals).

> **Answers**
> 1 zebra   2 whale   3 cow   4 tree frog   5 scorpion
> 6 penguin   7 crocodile

Extension idea Write *reptile, mammal, bird, amphibian, arachnid* on the board and ask students to classify the seven animals (*answers*: reptile – crocodile; mammal – cow, whale and zebra; bird – penguin; amphibian – tree frog; arachnid – scorpion).

❷ *Alternative treatment* Ask students to look at the exercise and say what *habitat* means (*answer*: where an animal or plant normally lives or is found).

> **Suggested answers**
> 1 zebra   2 cow   3 crocodile   4 penguin
> 5 whale   6 scorpion   7 tree frog

Extension idea Ask: *Which of these habitats exist in or around your country? What animals are typical there?*

❸ Students may legitimately answer that they've seen these animals in the zoo or on TV.

Reading 1 Sentence completion

❶ *As a warmer* Tell students that they're going to read a passage about a bird. Ask: *What things should you look at or read before you read the whole passage? Why?* (*answers*: students should read the title and subheading and look at any illustrations before they start, as these will orientate them and help them through the passage).

Elicit the meaning of *species* from students (*answer*: a group of plants or animals which share similar characteristics (CLD)). Ask: *Is 'species' singular or plural?* (*answer*: here singular) Tell students that the singular and plural forms are the same.

Give students a minute to answer the questions.

> **Suggested answer**
> a description of the European bee-eater's life and how it migrates

❷ Ask students: *How should you read the passage to find out this information: slowly and carefully, or should you skim and scan?* (*answer*: skim and scan).

Give them two minutes to read and answer the questions. They then compare answers in pairs.

> **Answers**
> 1 farmland and river valleys from Spain to Kazakhstan and Africa
> 2 five to six years

❸ Ask students how they should read the passage to find these words (*answer*: they should scan).

- Tell them that when they have found the words, they should read around them to decide which is the correct definition from the list.

- Tell students that these words are used here as nouns or verbs, but they will find many of them in the dictionary as both nouns and verbs.

Alternative treatment If you wish your students to deal with the exam-style task without being pre-taught vocabulary, you can do this exercise after Exercise 5.

Answers		
2 (noun) g	3 (verb) d	4 (noun) a
5 (noun) e	6 (noun) c	7 (noun) b

Extension idea If you have a class set of dictionaries, ask students to look these words up in the dictionary to see how many can be both nouns and verbs (all except 5 and 6). This should help them to realise the usefulness of identifying what type of word they are looking at.

4 Remind students that the reasons for underlining key ideas are:

- to be clear what the question is asking
- to make it easier to find the part of the passage which gives the answer.

Alternative treatment Especially with weaker classes, work through the first two or three questions with students.

- For Question 1, check they know the meaning of *prey* from Exercise 3 and ask students what they should look for (*answer*: another type of prey apart from bees).
- For Question 2, elicit the meaning of *remove* (to take something away).
- For Question 3, ask them what information they need to fill the gap (somewhere apart from agricultural land where bee-eaters can find food).

Suggested answers
1 1 prey   2 remove the
  3 food; on agricultural land and in
  4 spend the winter in different parts of
  5 because of; one-third; do not survive migration
  6 make nests in
  7 nesting; receive food from
  8 problem; reduced the amount of food

2 1 what bee-eaters eat
  2 something bee-eaters can't eat
  3 somewhere bee-eaters can find food
  4 a part of the world
  5 a reason why bee-eaters do not survive migration
  6 a place where bee-eaters make nests
  7 who or what receive food
  8 something which has reduced bee-eaters' prey

Extension idea Ask students what type of word (noun, verb, adjective, etc.) they need for each answer (*answer*: nouns for all).

5 Elicit the number of words that can be used for each answer (*answer*: one or two). When students answer the questions, tell them they should concentrate on the parts of the passage which provide the answer.

- There may be sentences or vocabulary which they find hard to understand, but which don't provide an answer, e.g. in the penultimate paragraph: *The helpers benefit too: parents with helpers can provide more food for chicks to continue the family line.* Students should not worry about these too much.
- Similarly, students may want to answer a question with a word, the meaning of which they are not sure of, e.g. *pesticides* in Question 8. They should be prepared to take a risk and do this; if they read around the word, they will find that *bee-eaters find it harder to find food as there are fewer insects around as a result of pesticides,* which will tell them that pesticides have reduced the amount of food available to them.
- Remind students that because the IELTS test is designed to assess all levels of English, they will find words and sentences which are hard to understand, so they need strategies like the ones above to help them maximise their marks.
- When students have finished, tell them to read through their answers to make sure they reflect the meaning of the passage, are grammatically correct and that they have copied the word(s) exactly.

Answers
1 (flying) insects   2 poison   3 river valleys   4 Africa
5 predators   6 tunnels   7 chicks   8 pesticides

Extension idea So that students understand how the question will paraphrase the passage rather than repeat it word for word, ask them to underline the phrases and sentences in the passage which gave them the answers. They should then compare the wording of the passage with the wording of the questions. If they have used more than one word for Questions 2, 4, 5, 6, 7 or 8, tell them to check why their answer is wrong.

6 *Alternative treatment* Write *endangered species* on the board. Ask: *Which question asks about endangered species?* (*answer*: the first)

For the second question, ask students to think of other possible causes of species becoming endangered (*possible answers*: hunting, disease, climate change).

Extension idea With stronger classes, you can extend the discussion by asking these questions:

- *What can countries do to protect wild animals and birds?*
- *Why is it important to protect wildlife?*

You will probably have to make this a class discussion and help students by supplying useful vocabulary (e.g. *nature reserves, laws, protecting habitats*).

Listening

Table completion, labelling a map or plan

1 *As a warmer* Ask students to work in pairs, look at the photos and compare the two zoos.

Ask: *Is there a zoo near your home? If so, what is it like? What are the areas called where animals live?* (*answer*: enclosures or cages).

(*Suggested ideas which might arise from the discussion*: as long as they have enough space, animals in zoos are protected, can breed, people can see them safely, they can educate. People can learn about animals, their behaviour and their habitats.)

2 Although students can see the type of information easily by looking at the top line of the table, it's still important to do this before listening and to see which parts of the table contain gaps. Students should also look at the information already given in the table as this will guide them through the listening.

> **Answers**
> **1, 4** location   **2, 6** type of event
> **3, 5** name of event   **7** time

Point out that the answers come in question order, so they will read across the table as they answer.

3 Play the recording once and then give students a couple of minutes to complete the table alone.

- Ask students to compare their answers in pairs.
- Play the recording again for students to check their answers.
- Finally, refer them to the recording script to check spelling and any missing answers.
- When you round up with the whole class, write the correct answers on the board and tell students that if they have anything different, it is wrong.

> **Answers**
> (Note: lower-case letters are also acceptable)
> **1** Insect House   **2** (a) lecture   **3** *Great Migration*
> **4** Theatre C   **5** *Garden Wildlife*   **6** (a) (bird) display
> **7** 3.45

4 Tell students that before they listen in order to label a map, the first thing they should do is find where they / the speaker are located on the map.

- They should then look at the information already given on the map (names of places), paths or streets, etc., to see the various possible routes and know the type of words they can expect to hear on the recording. They will have to answer the questions by following directions, and/or placing things in relation to other features which are already on the map.

- This exercise gives students some of the language they may hear and helps them orientate themselves.

Alternative treatment If your students need it, go through the Language reference on page 124 on prepositions of place with them beforehand.

> **Answers**
> **1** in the main building   **2** G   **3** F   **4** penguins
> **5** E   **6** B and C   **7** C   **8** A

5 Play the recording once. Tell students to answer the questions while they listen.

- Ask students to compare their answers in pairs. Then play the recording again for them to check their answers.
- Refer them to the recording script.

> **Answers**
> **1** F   **2** E   **3** A

Extension idea Ask students to read the recording script and underline words and phrases which say where things are, e.g. *on your right*. They can then copy them into their notebooks.

Speaking Parts 1 and 2

1 *As a warmer* Ask students: *Do people in your culture keep animals at home as pets? What sort of animals do people keep at pets? Do you have pets?*

Tell students that the questions in Speaking Part 1 will always be about themselves, their country and their culture, etc. Some questions will ask for information but others for their opinions or feelings about things. Some may ask for both (as in d).

Tell students that there are often questions asking what they don't like and they should be prepared to talk about those things too.

> **Answers**
> **1** a, b   **2** c, d

2 Give students two or three minutes for this, but don't allow dictionaries and don't help them with vocabulary, otherwise they won't have an opportunity to apply the strategies taught later in this section.

3 Students can make notes and give approximate answers.

> **Answers**
> **a** her cat, birds
> **b** insects, flies (because insects bite)
> **c** many places, not easy – forest
> **d** hunting popular, watching wildlife – doesn't know, going to zoos – yes, but not the same

Extension idea Ask students: *How well do you think she answers the questions?*

- This should prompt comments that she doesn't know some words or answers to some questions.
- You can then take the opportunity to point out that when she doesn't know a word or doesn't know the answer, she has a strategy for dealing with it.
- Tell students that they will get higher scores if they can deal with situations where they don't know the word or the answer.

4

> **Answers**
> **1** love **2** how **3** keen **4** hate **5** what **6** too
> **7** That's **8** difficult **9** called

5
> **Answers**
> **a** 2, 5, 9 **b** 7, 8 **c** 1, 4 **d** 3, 6

Extension idea Ask students to copy these phrases into their notebooks but organised in the categories a–d. Elicit other phrases for each category, write them on the board and ask students to also copy them.

Note: Now is a good moment to do the Pronunciation work on sentence stress.

6 If students have just worked on some of these questions in the pronunciation section, ask them to change partners to do this exercise.

7 Tell students they can use phrases from Exercise 4 when they do this task as well. Again, do not help students with vocabulary. If they have never visited such a place, tell them to think about somewhere similar that they have seen in a film or documentary. Point out that in the IELTS test they may have to use their imagination to do Speaking Part 2 as they cannot change the task.

8 *Alternative treatment* Tell the student who is listening to give feedback on how well their partner:

- managed when they didn't know a word, or wasn't sure how to express an idea;
- used stress when expressing their feelings.

When both students have done the task, they should change partners and do it again.

Pronunciation Sentence stress 2

1 Tell students that we stress the words which carry the meanings we want to communicate. If these words are not clearly stressed, people may not understand exactly what we want to say.

- Native speakers do not normally stress 'grammar words' because both the speaker and listener know the grammar and do not need to hear it clearly.
- When we stress words in sentences, we tend to spend longer saying them, but we don't usually say them louder.
- Tell students that we say the words between the stressed words quite quickly, but it is not necessary to speak more quickly than you find it comfortable to speak fluently. They should concentrate on being clearly understood and communicating what they want to say.

> **Answers**
> **2** know; name; English **3** difficult; question; sure
> **4** hard; say **5** what; activity; called

2 Ask students to listen and repeat.

3
> **Answers**
> **1** had; year; love; beautiful
> **2** hate; insects; horrible

4 Suchin stresses these words in quite an exaggerated way. Encourage students to also exaggerate the stress – as native speakers often do.

Extension idea Ask students to say the sentences to the whole class. Tell them the student who sounds most like a native speaker will be the winner.

5 Give students five or six minutes to write down their answers. Remind them that they should answer each question with two or three sentences.

6 *Alternative treatment* Tell the student who is listening to listen for the stressed words. When their partner has finished, they should say which words their partner stressed. Their partner should then say whether those were the words which he/she underlined when writing the answers in Exercise 5.

Vocabulary What type of word is it? 2

1 *As a warmer* Write on the board:

Nouns: *Verbs:*

Adjectives: *Adverbs:*

Ask students to work in small groups. They should:

- copy the words on the board into their notebooks;
- read the introductory sentence to this section and think of word endings for each type of word;
- as they work through the exercises in this section, they should add to their lists.

When they have done Exercise 1, go through the Language reference on types of word and word endings with them.

Answers
2 noun   3 adjective   4 adjective   5 adjective
6 adverb   7 noun or verb   8 noun   9 noun
10 verb   11 verb   12 noun

② Give students two minutes to scan the passage and underline the words.

Alternative treatment 1 If you wish to incorporate this vocabulary section into the Reading section which follows, you can do the following exercises after Reading Exercise 3 to pre-teach vocabulary from the passage.

Alternative treatment 2 If you prefer not to pre-teach the vocabulary, you can do the following exercises after the exam-style task in Reading Exercise 4.

③ Tell students they should use the context, the shape of the word and the word endings to help them decide what each of the words means. In many cases they may only arrive at an approximate meaning of the word. If students speak the same first language, it's fine for them to use this to express the meanings.

④ When students match the words with the definitions on page 176, they should check with its context in the passage to see how the meaning fits.

Answers
1 k   2 f   3 i   4 g   5 l   6 h   7 b   8 c
9 e   10 d   11 j   12 a

Reading 2 Pick from a list

① *Alternative treatment* Ask students to work in small groups. One student has their book open, the others have their books closed. The student with the book open reads the seven sentences aloud one by one. The other students listen and together discuss whether the sentences are true or false.

When they have finished, one of the other students opens their book, checks the group's answers on page 176 and gives them the correct information.

② Elicit from students that they should also look at the pictures accompanying the passage.

Suggested answer
a whale which travelled further than researchers expected

③ To answer this question, students will have to skim the passage. Tell them to read it passing their eyes over the words to get a general impression of what it's about. Give them two minutes to do this.

After two minutes, ask students to compare their answers with a partner. Then allow them to look back at the passage for a few moments to check.

Answer
Sentence B

④ The aim of the 'pick from a list' task is to scan the passage to find the relevant section(s) and then read in detail to answer the question.

Tell students that in the live exam, the questions may be presented in the following way, which you can write on the board:

Questions 1 and 2

What two aspects of the whale's journey surprised researchers?

A

B

If questions are presented in this way, students will get one mark for each correct choice. If questions are presented as in the Student's Book, students will get one mark for making both correct choices.

- Tell them that they should follow a similar approach to these as to multiple-choice questions: they should read the questions (but not the options) underlining the key ideas. They then scan the passage to find the relevant section and read that carefully to understand it. Finally, they choose the correct options.

- Tell students that if they read the options before understanding the passage, it will only confuse them.

- Point out that the final question in a set of Pick from a list or Multiple-choice questions may refer to the whole passage, not just one part of it, so they may – as in this case – have to quickly read the passage again to answer it.

- When students have finished, ask them to work in pairs to compare their answers and, where necessary, quote from the text to justify their choices. Tell them there must be words in the text which mean the same as the options they choose, otherwise their answers are wrong.

Suggested underlining
2 why whales; migrate; TWO reasons
3 TWO methods; identity of the whale
4 TWO places; passed close
5 more research; in the Northern Hemisphere; TWO methods
6 why; whale made a different journey; TWO reasons
7 TWO methods; finding out where whales migrate

⑤ Answers

1 B, C (The whale's journey was unusual not only for its length, but also because it travelled across almost 90 degrees of longitude from west to east. Typically, humpbacks move in a north-south direction)

2 C, E (*humpbacks move ... between cold feeding areas and warm breeding grounds*)

3 A, E (*researchers photographed its tail fluke and took skin samples for chromosome testing*)

4 A, E (*the animal's shortest possible route: an arc skirting the southern tip of South Africa ... the whale probably took a detour to feed on krill in the Southern Ocean near Antarctica*)

5 B, D (Most humpback-whale researchers focus their efforts on the Northern Hemisphere because the Southern Ocean near the Antarctic is a hostile environment and it is hard to get to.)

6 A, D (She could have been exploring new habitats, or simply have lost her way.)

7 B, E (*Researchers routinely compare the markings in each new photograph to those in the archive ... Scientists will probably observe more long-distance migrations in the Southern Hemisphere as satellite tracking becomes increasingly common*)

Writing Task 1

❶ *As a warmer* Ask students to look at the bar charts and compare them to the bar charts in Unit 1. Ask: *How is the type of information different?* If necessary ask: *Which charts show changes over time?* (*answer:* the charts in Unit 5) *How many years do they show?* (*answer:* four years between 2005 and 2011).

- Ask students to look at the two charts in Unit 5 only. Ask: *What do the two charts have in common?* (*answer:* the place and the years).

- Use the examples: Ask students to look at the charts and say why 1 is true and 2 is false. They then work through the other questions together.

Alternative treatment If you think your class can manage it, ask them to work in pairs or small groups and cover the true/false sentences. They then discuss what the charts show and make comparisons. When they have finished, they should look at the sentences to see if there's anything they have missed.

Answers
3 T   4 F – the number of zebras rose to 75 in 2009 and then fell to 70 in 2009   5 T
6 F – there were 650mm of rain in 2005   7 T   8 T
9 F – numbers of animals have increased   10 T

Extension idea Ask: *When you write your summary, do you think you should explain why there are more zebras when there is more rain?* (no, you should only summarise the information given).

❷ *Alternative treatment* With some classes, before they group the sentences to form paragraphs, it may be beneficial to ask them to copy the correct sentences and write out the corrected sentences accurately in their notebooks; it gives them elementary practice with the task, forces them to focus on how sentences are constructed and statistics expressed, and boosts their confidence with a task they may find intimidating. When they have done this, ask them to exchange what they have copied with a partner and just check that the task has been done accurately.

Answers
a 1   b 2, 3, 4, 5   c 6, 7, 8   d 9, 10

Note: Now is a good moment to do the Key grammar section on page 56 on Countable and uncountable nouns.

- Remind students that they will get higher marks by using more extended vocabulary. Ask them to copy the words into their notebooks.

❸ Elicit the base forms of *rose* and *fell* and the past participles (*rise, fall, risen, fallen*).

Answers
rose: went up, increased   **fell:** dropped, decreased

Extension idea Elicit other synonyms of *rise* and *fall* that students may know.

❹ After students have done the exercise ask:

– *Which word means the same as 'during'?* (over)
– *Which phrase means the same as 'between ... and'?* (*from ... to*)

Note: while there may be differences between *during* and *over*, etc., they are not significant at this level.

Answers
1 in   2 between   3 from   4 during   5 over

Extension idea Ask students to work in pairs and answer these questions (write them on the board).

1 What did you do in 2010?
2 When did you go to primary school?
3 How long have you lived in your present home?
4 Which season do you prefer to go on holiday? Why?

❺ Tell students to be careful with prepositions when using time phrases in their writing.

Answers
2 ~~during~~ from   3 ~~on~~ in   4 ~~on~~ in   5 ~~since~~ from

Extension idea Follow these steps:

1 Tell students they're going to compare activities they do. They can choose the activity from the following: doing homework, taking exercise or watching television. Students work alone and draw a bar chart which shows how much time they have spent doing the activity each week during this course. If they can't remember exactly, they can invent the figures.

2 When they have finished, ask them to work in pairs and look at the two charts together. They should then discuss and compare the information.

3 If you wish, they can then write the summary.

Go through the Language reference section on page 126 on Prepositions in time phrases with students.

6 Tell students this is the writing task they will have to do. The questions are there to help them analyse and understand the information in the charts. They should make notes while answering the questions.

Alternative treatment Especially with stronger classes, ask students to work in pairs, cover over the sentences, study the charts and discuss what they show. When they have finished, they answer the questions in the exercise.

Suggested answers

1 The first chart shows the number of honey bee colonies in the US between 1970 and 2010; the second chart shows the amount of honey produced in the US between 1970 and 2010.

2 **a** countable   **b** uncountable

3 4 million colonies, 130,000 tons of honey

4 The colonies rose but the honey production fell. More colonies produced less honey.

5 The number of colonies fell, but the amount of honey produced rose. Fewer colonies produced more honey.

6 They both fell.

7 Over the whole period the number of colonies and the amount of honey produced have decreased.

---

7 Students compare their finished ideas with another pair.

8 This writing task is probably best done for homework. Tell students they should spend about 20 minutes on this task, but that at this stage in the course, strict timing is not essential.

Sample answer

The charts give information about the number of bee colonies in the United States and how much honey they produced between 1970 and 2010.

In 1970, there were 4,000,000 bee colonies in the country and this rose to approximately 4,200,000

---

in 1980. However, over the next 30 years this number decreased by more than a million every ten years with the result that in 2010, there were about 1,800,000 colonies left.

During the same period, the amount of honey which the colonies produced also dropped. In 1970, American bees produced 130,000 tons of honey. This fell by 20,000 tons to 110,000 tons in 1980. However, in the next ten years, honey production rose to 120,000 tons in 1980. It then dropped to just 70,000 tons in 2010.

Overall, the charts show that both the number of colonies and the amount of honey which bees make have fallen during the 40-year period. However, the relationship is not an exact one because when colonies increased in 1980, honey production fell, while when colonies decreased in 1990, honey production rose.

Extension idea Give students a date for handing in their answers. When they bring them to class, give them a photocopy of the sample answer. Ask them to compare their answers and to make any changes or improvements that they wish before they hand them in.

Key grammar
Countable and uncountable nouns

1 Elicit that they need to see if the words are used in the plural or not. Tell them that students often make mistakes by making uncountable nouns plural and the verb plural also.

Answers
1 [C]   **2** [C]   **3** [U]

Extension idea Tell students that a good learner's dictionary will tell them if a noun is countable or uncountable. Ask them to look up *milk* and *apple* in their dictionaries and to say if they are countable or uncountable (*milk* [U]; *apple* [C]).

2 Point out that we use different vocabulary with countable and with uncountable nouns. Tell them that *amount* and *number* have similar meanings but *amount* is used with uncountable nouns and *number* with countable nouns. Similarly *few* (C), *little* (U), *much* (U), *many* (C).

Go through the Language reference on page 126.

Answers
1 [U]   **2** [C]   **3** [U]   **4** [C]

---

3 **Alternative treatment** Ask students to check the answers they're not sure about in their dictionaries.

Extension idea Ask students to copy the words into their notebooks in two columns: countable and uncountable.

➍ *Alternative treatment* If you did the extension idea in Exercise 3, ask students to add these words to the lists in their notebooks. Tell them these are words they should pay special attention to when they do the IELTS test, to avoid making mistakes.

➎

Extension idea Ask students to work in pairs and write their own sentences using *much, many, few* and *little* with some of the nouns in the box in Exercise 4.

➏ Mistakes with countable and uncountable nouns are very frequent in both parts of the Writing paper. Tell students to pay special attention, to avoid mistakes.

Spelling Small words often misspelled

Many of these words are misspelled due to carelessness, speed of writing, or because they may sound the same or very similar to students. This exercise is to raise students' awareness of these words as a problem area.

Use the example and elicit why the mistake has occurred (probably because they are homophones).

Extension idea When students do the task in the Writing section, ask them to exchange their answers and look for the spelling mistakes which are highlighted in this section.

Unit 5 photocopiable activity: Animal challenge   Time: 30 minutes

Objectives

- To revise vocabulary related to animals and wildlife
- To practise countable and uncountable nouns
- To practise prepositions
- To revise phrases when unsure of a word or answer

Before class

You will need to photocopy page 63 and cut it into two parts, so that half of the students have 'Student A' cards, and the other half have 'Student B' cards.

➊ *As a warmer* Ask students what they can say in English when they don't know a word, or when they aren't sure of the answer. Elicit useful expressions and write them on the board:
  – *I'm not sure how you say this, but …*
  – *I don't know what their/its name is in English, but …*
  – *It's a difficult question. I'm not sure.*
  – *It's hard to say.*

Tell students that they will have a chance to practise the phrases in the second part of the activity.

Divide the class into two groups, A and B. Give a 'Student A' card to all the students in group A. All the students in group B receive a 'Student B' card.

➋ Ask students to work in pairs with other members in their group to read the 'True or False' statements and circle the correct option in each sentence. Go through the answers with the whole class. You should not discuss whether each statement is true or false at this stage.

➌ Students then find a partner from the other group. They read out statements 1–6 and their partner has to guess whether they are true or false.

➍ Then, in 'Question time', students ask each other the three questions and give their partner 30 seconds to answer each one. Remind students that they can use useful phrases from the warmer.

➎ Once all the pairs have finished interviewing each other, ask them to share their views on which part was more difficult to answer and whether they learned anything new.

Animal challenge

Student A

True or False?

1 The *number/amount* of crocodile species in the world is 13.
(True)

2 A tiger in the wild normally lives between 25 *and/to* 30 years.
(False: between 15 and 20 years)

3 A tiger weighs about nine times as *much/many* as a penguin.
(True: a large penguin weighs about 35 kg; a large tiger weighs about 300 kg)

4 There are *fewer/less* elephants in Africa than in Asia
(True: about 10,000 in Africa; about 50,000 in Asia)

5 All dolphins live *in/at* the sea.
(False: there are river dolphins in Asia)

6 Polar bears live *on/in* the Arctic.
(True)

Question time

A Which animals are dangerous to humans?

B Is it right to keep animals in zoos?

C Is it important to protect animals? Why?

Student B

True or False?

1 The *number/amount* of polar bears in the world is about 50,000.
(False: it is about 22,000)

2 A grey whale normally lives between 50 *and/to* 70 years.
(True)

3 A large male African elephant weighs about 30 times as *much/many* as a large male gorilla.
(True: a large male African elephant weighs about 6,000 kg; a large male gorilla weighs about 200 kg)

4 There are *fewer/less* species of spider than scorpion.
(False: there are about 40,000 species of spider and 1,500 species of scorpion)

5 Elephants, pandas and whales can all be kept *in/at* zoos.
(True)

6 Penguins live *on/in* the Arctic.
(False: there are no penguins in the Arctic, only in the southern hemisphere)

Question time

1 Which animals are popular pets where you live?

2 What are the advantages of having a pet?

3 What can children learn from animals?

Vocabulary extension

Unit 5

Abbreviations: n/sln/pln = noun / single noun / plural noun; v = verb; adj = adjective; adv = adverb; p = phrase; pv = phrasal verb; T/I = transitive/intransitive; C/U = countable/uncountable

annual *adj* happening or produced once a year

behaviour *n* [U] the way that you act or perform

cage *n* [C] a container made of wire or metal bars used for keeping birds or animals in

circus *n* [C] a show in which a group of people and animals perform in a large tent

conservation *n* [U] the protection of nature

creature *n* [C] anything that lives but is not a plant

decline *v* [I] to become less in amount, importance, quality or strength

disappear *v* [I] to stop existing

domestic *adj* A domestic animal is kept as a pet.

ecosystem *n* [C] all the living things in an area and the way they affect each other and the environment

endangered *adj* Endangered birds/plants/species are animals or plants which may soon not exist because there are very few now alive.

exotic *adj* unusual, interesting, and often foreign

extinct *adj* If a type of animal is extinct, it does not now exist.

farm *n* [C] an area of land with fields and buildings that is used for growing crops and keeping animals as a business

feed *v* [I] If an animal or a baby feeds, it eats.

herd *n* [C] a large group of animals such as cows that live and eat together

jungle *n* [C/U] an area of land, usually in tropical countries, where trees and plants grow close together

live *adj* having life

mammal *n* [C] an animal that feeds its babies on milk from its body

marine *adj* found in the sea, or relating to the sea

native *adj* Your native town or country is the place where you were born.

natural habitat *p* [C] the natural environment in which an animal or plant usually lives

non-native *adj* Non-native animals or plants do not live or grow naturally in a place, but have been brought from somewhere else.

pet *n* [C] an animal that someone keeps in their home

rare *adj* very unusual

survive *v* [I/T] to continue to live or exist, especially after coming close to dying or being destroyed or after being in a difficult or threatening situation

threaten (of species) *v* [T] to be likely to cause harm or damage to something or someone

welfare *n* [U] Someone's welfare is their health and happiness.

wild *adj* A wild animal or plant lives or grows in its natural environment and not where people live.

wildlife *n* [U] animals, birds and plants living in their natural environment

Unit 6 Being human

Unit objectives

- **Reading:** using the title and subheading; skimming; introduction to Yes / No / Not Given tasks; summary task
- **Speaking Part 3:** introduction to Part 3; generalising
- **Pronunciation:** intonation to show you haven't finished
- **Listening:** labelling a plan; introduction to matching
- **Vocabulary:** groups of people: *graduate, grandparents*, etc.; academic research: *findings, experiments*, etc.; word formation for nouns, verbs and adjectives
- **Writing Task 2:** dealing with two questions; analysing the question, the structure and ideas; expressing reasons; using a range of relevant vocabulary
- **Grammar:** zero and first conditionals
- **Spelling:** words with suffixes: *successful*, etc.

Starting off

❶ *As a warmer* Ask students to work in small groups and look at the title of the unit (*Being human*). Ask them to discuss what differences there are between humans and animals (the subject of the previous unit). When they've finished, ask them to change groups and report and compare their ideas.

Alternative treatment Tell students to look at the words in the box. Ask: *Which two words are not adjectives?* (*answers*: chance, image)

> **Answers**
> 2 image   3 generous   4 familiar

Extension idea Ask students to suggest opposites for each of the adjectives (*answers:* unfamiliar, usual, uninterested, unreal, uncomfortable, mean, interesting).

❷ Elicit possible answers to picture 1 from the whole class (e.g. they think they need to take more exercise, cut down on car pollution, reduce their travelling costs).

Ask students to talk about the other pictures in pairs. Then they compare their ideas with those of another pair of students.

> **Suggested answers**
> 1 They think they need to take more exercise / cut down on car pollution / reduce their travelling costs.
> 2 He'd like to feel younger / be more adventurous.
> 3 He ought to give more money to charity / be less selfish.
> 4 She ought to visit a new place for her holiday / be more adventurous.

❸ Elicit the fact that all the statements are reasons not to change. This leads into the extension below and/or the Reading passage.

Extension idea Tell students to work in small groups. Ask:

- *Which of the changes mentioned in this exercise would you like to make? Why?*
- *What other changes would you like to make in your lives? Why?*
- *Why do some people find it difficult to change?*

Reading 1 Yes / No / Not Given

❶ Remind students that the title and subheading are intended to help them understand the topic of the passage and what the writer is going to say about it.

> **Suggested answer**
> People want to change but find it difficult.

❷ This is a skimming exercise.

- Tell students to read the passage before they look at the options. If they look at the options first, it will only confuse them when they read the passage.
- Remind them that to skim, they should not read everything carefully, but pass their eyes quickly over the sentences, picking out familiar vocabulary which gives them a general impression of what the passage is about and how it is structured.
- Give students three minutes and be strict about the time limit.

> **Answer**
> C

Extension idea 1 The passage contains words for different types and groups of people (e.g. *graduate*, *grandparent*).

- Ask students if they remember any words like these from the skimming they did in Exercise 2.
- Ask them to find as many words like this as possible and copy them into their notebooks.
- When they have finished, ask them to work in pairs and check their lists and their spelling. This is good practice in copying words correctly from the passage.

(*answers*: family; friends; writer; college graduate; teenagers; (young) person; adventurer; grandparent; psychologist; (young) men and women; partner; children; grandchildren; individual; toddlers; children; adults)

Extension idea 2 Ask students: *Have you seen the film mentioned in the first paragraph? If so, what happened to McCandless?* (he eventually died)

❸ *Alternative treatment* This exercise pre-teaches vocabulary which occurs in the passage. If you would prefer your students to deal with the IELTS-style task in Exercises 4–7 without having the vocabulary pre-taught, you can skip this exercise and use it as a vocabulary follow-up after students have done Exercise 7.

> **Answers**
> **2** f   **3** a   **4** e   **5** b   **6** c

> Yes / No / Not Given (YNNG) questions test students' ability to scan for the writer's ideas and opinions and then to read the relevant part of the passage in detail to fully understand them.

Tell students that:

- these questions are similar to True / False / Not Given, but whereas TFNG questions deal with facts and information, YNNG deal with writers' opinions and claims. Explain what a claim is (something that the writer believes to be true, but that cannot be proved and that other people might not believe). Students do not need to worry too much about this distinction, but should expect to see the words *claims* or *opinions* in the rubric.
- as in TFNG questions, unless the question specifically contradicts an idea or opinion in the passage (NO), the answer is NOT GIVEN.
- some of the words or phrases in the question will be the same as or similar to words in the passage. Students should scan the passage to find similar words and then read carefully around to decide their answer.

In this exercise, the key words that help students find the right place in the passage have been underlined for them.

> **Suggested answers**
> **a** Christopher McCandless / Oxfam International
> **b** young people / decisions / Christopher McCandless
> **c** *Into the wild* / John Krakauer's
> **1 a** YES (*In an act of kindness, …*)
> **2 b** NO (*His decisions were so unusual for his age …*)
> **c** NOT GIVEN (The writer refers to the title, but does not say whether it is a good or bad one.)

❻ Ask students to skim the questions. Then, elicit the type of words they should underline to look for in the passage (particularly nouns, often nouns denoting groups of people).

> **Suggested underlining**
> **1** teenagers / young adults   **2** Grandparents / job
> **3** Life demands / different   **4** toddlers / repetitive activities   **5** Children / adventurous / adults
> **6** you / change

❼ When students have answered the questions, ask them to compare their answers with a partner. Where they disagree, tell them to look back at the passage to reach agreement. Follow up by going through the Exam advice with them.

> **Answers**
> **1** YES (*However, studies do show that in teenage years …*)
> **2** NOT GIVEN (grandparents and work are mentioned but there is nothing about getting a well-paid job)
> **3** NO (*all over the world … people's lives generally follow similar patterns*)
> **4** YES (*One toddler may want to play a different game every day*)
> **5** NO (*Young children who avoid new experiences*)
> **6** YES (*you are better off making a new start today*)

Extension idea There are several difficult phrases in the passage that students should be able to understand from the context. Write these phrases on the board:

- *follow in the footsteps of*   – *life demands*
- *age-related pattern*   – *creatures of habit*

Ask students to scan for the phrases, look at how they are formed, read around them carefully, and then discuss what they mean with a partner. Tell them to quote from the passage if it helps them explain.

(*answers*: *follow in the footsteps of* = do the same thing as (often a career path); *age-related pattern* = a trend that is linked to people's age; *life demands* = activities that are expected of people in society; *creatures of habit* = a comparison to animals – doing the same things as part of a life or daily routine)

Ask students which of these phrases was most/least important to them in the exercises based on this passage. Remind them that some difficult vocabulary can be 'skimmed over'.

8 *Alternative treatment* Give students a minute or two to work alone and think about what they're going to say. When they are ready, tell them to take turns to talk for a minute or two about the subject. Their partners should listen and ask follow-up questions.

Reading 2 Summary completion with a box

1 *As a warmer* With books closed, tell students: *The next reading passage in the book is about memory. In this book you've already read 11 reading passages. Work in small groups and try to remember the subjects of the reading passages you have read, for example, what was the first one about? Something to do with cities ...* And elicit from the whole class that the first one was about the world's friendliest city. Students then have to remember the subjects of the other ten.

Give students two minutes to do the activity.

Extension idea Write the following words on the board and ask students: *Which makes reading passages easier to remember?*

– *interesting*   – *unusual*   – *recent*

2
Suggested answers
1 study / piece of research   **2** sleep **3** mistakes/errors

3 Before they start, elicit from students what they should look for when they read. Ask: *What are the key ideas in the question?* (*answer*: group of people / benefit most). Tell students to pass their eyes over the passage looking for groups of people and then check what Fenn says about them. Give them three minutes.

Alternative treatment As with the previous reading passage, ask students to scan the passage and list all the groups of people mentioned (elderly people, colleagues, college students, study participants).

Answers
older people / the elderly

4
Answers
2 conducted   **3** research **4** experiments   **5** participants **6** colleagues

5 This task may test students' understanding of ideas as well as facts. Remind students that when Reading tasks have a title, it is there to help them and it will usually help them to find the part of the passage that they need to concentrate on.

- Give students 30 seconds to find the right paragraph.
- Tell them they will not need to read the rest of the passage carefully to complete the summary. Skimming before they approach the questions will save them a lot of time locating the part of the passage they need for the reading task.
- Elicit what information they need for Question 2 (a number). Students then do the rest of the exercise in pairs.

Suggested answers

1 paragraph 3
2 **1** an adjective describing the times of the day
  2 a number   **3** an amount   **4** an adjective
  describing the results   **5** how many words

6 Before students complete the summary, elicit why G is the correct answer to Question 1 (answer: the passage says one group of students was trained at 10 a.m. and tested at 10 p.m. Another group was trained at night and tested in the morning).

When they've completed the summary, ask them to

- read their completed summary to make sure it makes sense;
- compare their answers with a partner.

Answers
2 C   **3** E   **4** J   **5** A

7 *Alternative treatment* If you think your class is suitable for this, write on the board:

Describe some research or an experiment which you have carried out.

You should say what its purpose was, when you did it, who you did it with and what the results were.

Give students a minute or two to prepare. You can go round helping them with vocabulary and ideas. When they are ready, ask them to work in pairs and take turns to speak for one or two minutes on the subject.

Speaking Part 3

1
Answers
2, 3 and 4

Extension idea Elicit why each of the defects 1–5 would lose marks.

Point out to students that for questions in Part 3, there are no right and wrong answers, so they should always have something to say. Ask:

- *Is the candidate giving reasons and examples or talking about a number of different possible methods?* (*answer:* talking about a number of different possible methods)

- *What word does he use to begin the answer?* (*answer: well*) You can point out that *well* is often used at the beginning of answers just to introduce what we're going to say, and to give a little extra time to think.

❷ ❸ Students work in pairs to complete the answer.

> **Answers**
> 1 calendar   2 diary   3 list   4 hand

❹ *Alternative treatment* Ask:

- *Does the candidate say that everyone uses these methods?* (*answer:* no)

- *What words and phrases does he use to say that not everyone does each of these things?* (*some people, others, if you're really busy, sometimes*)

> **Answers**
> others, you're, you'll, your, you, someone's

❺ Elicit one or two possibilities from the whole class.

> *Extension idea* Ask students to work in pairs with someone from another group and take turns to ask and answer the questions. Encourage them to use words and phrases they looked at in exercise 4.

❻ 🎧 *Alternative treatment* Ask students to read Anna Maria's answer before they listen and predict the answers to questions 1 and 2.

> **Answers**
> 1 question 1
> 2 1 birthdays   2 keys   3 phone   4 lunch date
>   5 meeting
> 3 You / some older people / they / their / you

Note: Now is a good moment to do the Pronunciation section on intonation.

❼ *Alternative treatment* Ask students to work in pairs and prepare possible answers. When they're ready, ask them to change partners to do the exercise.

Pronunciation Intonation 1

❶ 🎧 There is a rising intonation when people are giving lists of things, and on the final thing, the voice falls to indicate that the speaker has finished.

> **Answers**
> It rises on *diary* and *lunch date* and falls on *remember* and *meeting*.

Extension idea Ask students to work in pairs and practise reading the two extracts with the correct intonation.

❷ 🎧

> **Suggested underlining**
> 1 dentist, appointment   2 sorry   3 work
> 4 meeting, car journey

❸ *Extension idea* Write the following 'shopping list' on the board: *apples, bread, coffee and toothpaste*.

- Ask students where their voices should rise and fall in the list (*answer:* rise on *apples, bread* and *coffee*; fall on *toothpaste*). Read the list and ask them to repeat.

- Ask students to write their own shopping list on a scrap of paper. They then work in pairs and take turns to read their shopping lists to each other.

- They change partners and, from memory, take turns to repeat the list they had with their first partner.

- If their memories allow, they then change partners again and repeat the combined shopping lists from their work with both their previous partners.

Listening Matching; pick from a list

❶ *As a warmer* Ask students to close their books.

- If you and your students all come from the same country, write the names of three or four well-known people in your country from cinema, TV, business, politics, sports or culture on the board.

- If you and your students come from a number of different countries, write the names of internationally known personalities on the board.

- Ask students:

– *Why do you think these people are successful?*

– *Which do you think is the most successful?*

With books open, tell students to try to suggest a number of ideas for each picture. When they have finished question 1, round up ideas from the whole class and write vocabulary from the ideas they suggest on the board (e.g. *talent, skill, luck, money, hard work, studying,* etc.).

When students do question 2, they needn't agree on the answer, or their answer may be a combination of several ideas they thought of when discussing question 1.

Alternative treatment Write these words on the board and check students understand them: *talent, skill, luck, family influence, wealth*. They can use these words and other ideas to answer questions 1 and 2.

❷ Make sure students know what they have to do.

- Ask students to work in pairs and discuss what they think each of the options A–F means. To get them started, ask: *Which of the options means wealthy or rich?* (B)
- Tell them that they will not hear exactly the same words when they listen to the recording.
- Tell them to suggest paraphrases for each of the options using other words as a way of trying to predict how the ideas might be expressed.

Answers

A individual, not like others

B wealthy, rich

C a family member; e.g. father, mother, etc. / family connections

D create, design

F sensible, clever

G new work, job, position

There are two extra options.

❸

Answers

1 C   2 A   3 E   4 D

❹

Answers

2 yes, she was / didn't follow the rules / individual …

3 sensibly published her ideas straight away / clever

4 without him, we wouldn't have / a new snack was created

Extension idea Ask students to check the words they should note down and their answers to Exercise 3 by looking at the recording script.

❺ Remind students that they will not have time to underline all the alternatives if they have a task like this in the exam.

Suggested underlining

5–6 TWO criteria / choose a successful person

7–8 TWO things / students agree to do before they meet

9–10 TWO things / agree / linked to success

Extension idea Ask students to work in pairs, look at the alternatives and say what each of them means, or how each idea might be expressed in the recording using other words. (*Suggested answers*: age – how old;

gender – man or woman; fame – well-known; individual talent – ability; global importance – important all over the world; conduct more research – look for more information; write a biography – write about the person's life; find photos – look for pictures; write a talk – prepare a presentation; plan a seminar – prepare the seminar; wealth – how much money / a lot of money; experience – what they've done in their lives; talent – ability; effort – how hard they worked; location – where they live/are)

❻ Play the recording once. After students have listened, give them a few moments to complete their answers, then ask them to compare them with a partner. Play the recording again for students to check their answers.

Answers

5–6 B (*Yeah, OK, let's pick a woman*) and E (*we should pick someone who's done something great; Yeah – that changed the world.*)

7–8 B (*let's both find out as much as we can. It's always better to have too much information! Yeah, you're right.*) and C (*What about pictures? OK – well, we might get some from the library – but I can look on the internet as well.*)

9–10 C (*in most cases you need to have some natural ability; Yeah – I agree*) and D (*you do have to work hard and be determined. Yeah – and really want to succeed.*)

Extension idea 1 Ask students to look at the recording script. Tell them to underline the words used to express the answers.

Extension idea 2 If your students did the extension idea in Exercise 5, ask them to compare the words used to express the ideas in the recording script with their suggestions from the extension idea.

❼ Students discuss their ideas in pairs. Get feedback from the class.

Vocabulary Word building

❶ ***As a warmer*** Remind students of the work they did on word endings and types of word in Unit 5. As revision, ask them to work in small groups and brainstorm word endings for nouns, verbs and adjectives, giving an example of each. When they have finished, ask them to look back to Unit 5 and at the language reference on page 126.

Refer students to the Exam overview and rating criteria on page 7. Tell them that the Examiner will look at the accuracy, range and relevance of the vocabulary that they use both in the Speaking and Writing papers. They can aim to raise their band score by including topic-related vocabulary.

- Ask students to work in pairs to complete the table.

Answers
2 succeed   3 hard work   4 talented
5 practise/practice   6 regularly   7 naturally
8 skill   9 achieve   10 famous

2 When they have checked their answers, go through the Language reference on page 126 with them.

3 In the Vocabulary sections in Units 4 and 5, students worked on deciding what type of word it was by looking at: its position in the sentence and in relation to other words; its ending.

Tell students in this exercise, they need to look at the position of the word to decide what type of word it is and then which ending is correct.

Answers
2 natural   3 fame   4 talented
5 achievement   6 succeed   7 regularly   8 skilful

Writing Task 2

1 *As a warmer* Tell students to work in pairs and ask: *In what ways are you successful? How did you become successful in these things?*

Alternative treatment Before doing the exercise, remind students to underline the key ideas in the writing task while they read it. Ask them to compare what they have underlined with a partner (*students should underline: Is hard work the key to success or is talent also important?*).

Answers
1 a lot of / much   2 hard work; talent

2 When students finish, round up with the whole class.

Alternative treatment Before doing the questions in the book, write these words on the board: *businessman, lawyer, doctor, singer, footballer.*

- Ask: *What talents do these people need to be successful?* Students should suggest a variety of different abilities, such as: good with money, good at speaking, persuasive, etc.

- Ask: *Do you think any of these people can do these jobs successfully without talent?* Ask students to suggest examples from their experience.

3 *Alternative treatment* Before they choose the correct options, ask students to read the essay. When they've finished ask them to work in pairs. Ask: *What points did you agree with and why? What points did you disagree with and why?*

Answers
1 Paragraph 2: *If you want to be good at something, you must practise hard and regularly.*
Paragraph 3: *However, talent is important too.*
2 No, it contains ideas added by the writer: money and luck
3 Other factors also contribute to success. *So there can be many factors that contribute to success. It is stated at the end of the paragraph*
4 *A range of factors contribute to success and it depends on the person.* It is mainly in the introduction and conclusion, but is stated throughout the sample answer. He does stick to his opinion throughout.
5 footballers / himself as a singer / business people

Note: Now would be a good time to do the Key grammar section on zero and first conditionals on page 65, which is based on the sample answer.

4 Remind students to underline the key ideas while they read the task.

5 This Writing task is probably best done for homework. Although in the exam students will have 40 minutes, at this stage in the course it's reasonable to take longer, say one hour, so that they complete the task in a satisfactory manner.

Extension idea 1 Give students a deadline for handing in the essay. When they bring it back, ask them to work in pairs and exchange essays.

- Their partner should read through their essay and, with a pencil, underline any mistakes she/he spots.

- They then work in pairs, correcting the essays where possible. You should act as monitor and consultant for any queries they may have.

- When they have finished, they should hand in the corrected essays for you to do further correction.

Extension idea 2 Photocopy the sample answer below. When students have finished writing their essays, ask them to compare them with the sample answer. Ask:

– *Are there any ideas in the sample which you think would be good in your answers?*

– *Are there any words or phrases you would like to use?*

Give them time to change and, if necessary, rewrite their answers before handing them in.

Sample answers
In many countries today, you find talent shows on television. They are certainly entertaining because many people watch them and talk about them. However, I also think they are a good way to make people famous.

Talent shows are popular because viewers enjoy seeing people like themselves on television. They

Talent shows are popular because viewers enjoy seeing people like themselves on television. They can also vote for their favourite performers and help someone succeed, which makes the shows very exciting. Though many competitors lose, this is normal in a competition and they still have their memories of taking part.

Some people say that the people who run talent shows make too much money. For example, we have a show on television in my country and the judges earn thousands of dollars. However, this is not unusual for an entertainment programme and these people are very powerful. If someone wins a show like *The X-Factor* they will earn a lot of money too.

This is very different from the past. Twenty years ago, you could only become famous through meeting someone who had an entertainment business. This meant that it was difficult to show your talent unless you were quite wealthy. Nowadays, anyone who is talented and wants to perform can enter a competition and win. What is more, they will get a lot of support with their future career. I think this is much fairer.

In conclusion, I agree that talent shows are entertaining but I also think they help many people who want a career in the music industry. Although people lose, everyone likes to see an ordinary person get lucky and become famous.

Spelling Suffixes

Alternative treatment Ask students to check the correct spellings in a dictionary or an online dictionary, either in class or for homework.

> **Answers**
> 1 attendance   2 beginning   3 development
> 4 unnecessary   5 laziness   6 achievement
> 7 successful   8 developing   9 happened   10 really
> 11 careful   12 argument

Extension idea Write the following suffixes on the board: *-ance, -ment, -ily, -ful.*

Ask students to think of two more words which end in each of these endings. They can then check their spelling in a dictionary or an online dictionary.

Key grammar
Zero and first conditionals (*if / unless*)

❶ *Alternative treatment* Write on the board:

1 *People are usually successful if ...*

2 *I'll be happy if ...*

- Ask students to copy the sentences into their notebooks and complete them in any way they like.

- When they're ready, ask them to compare their answers with their partners. (*suggested answers*: 1 People are usually successful if they work hard.; 2 I'll be happy if I get a good grade in my exam).

- Point out that both sentences can be completed with the present simple. Elicit what the difference in grammar is between them (*answer*: 1 both verbs are in the present simple 2 the *if*-clause is present simple and the main clause is future (*will*)).

- Underline the conditional clause (starting with *if*), tell students it's the conditional clause and then ask students to do the exercise in the book.

> **Answers**
> 1 If you want to be good at something
> 2 If a professional footballer does not train
> 3 unless I have a good singing voice
> 4 if you meet the right people

Extension idea Elicit the meaning of *unless* in 3 (answer: if not). Ask: *How would you say this sentence with 'if'?* (answer: *I won't make money if I don't have a good singing voice*).

❷ When students have answered these questions, go through the Language reference.

> **Answers**
> 1 1 and 4   2 2 and 3
> 3 1 Present simple + modal *must* and infinitive
> 2 Present simple + future simple
> 3 future simple + present simple
> 4 Modal *can* and infinitive + present simple

❸ Elicit when you should use the comma (*answer*: when the conditional clause comes before the main clause – i.e. if the sentence starts with *if* or *unless*).

> **Answers**
> 2 If children get a good education, they **can/will** deal better with problems.
> 3 If parents **don't** help children to learn how to be on their own, they will never feel comfortable taking a role as a leader.
> 4 People can solve all kinds of problems if they ~~will~~ begin to understand that everyone's view is important.
> 5 I would say that if you are always depressed, you **won't / will not be able to/can** do things well.
> 6 A child cannot communicate well if he **isn't / is not** given enough attention.

❹ Elicit suggestions for the answer to question 1 from the whole class. Ask students to do 2–5 in pairs.

> **Suggested answers**
> 1 … I have some money to spend.   2 … I'll go out and celebrate.   3 … they should practise it a lot.
> 4 … don't go in the water.   5 … I can afford it.

Vocabulary and grammar review
Unit 5

❶ **Down**   2 migration   4 diet   5 prey
Across   3 breed   5 predators / predatory   6 habitat

❷ 2 adjective   3 noun   4 adjective   5 verb   6 adverb
7 noun   8 verb

❸ 2 little   3 amount   4 few   5 much   6 little
7 much; many   8 little

❹ 2 On   3 between   4 during   5 from   6 Over

Unit 6

❶ 2 colleagues   3 donate   4 participants
5 experiences   6 conventional   7 findings
8 backgrounds

❷ 2 happiness   3 Safety   4 disappointment
5 criticised/criticized   6 achievement   7 absence
8 success(es)

❸ 2 g   3 a   4 f   5 h   6 b   7 c   8 e

❹ 2 work   3 won't open   4 want   5 publish   6 can't
7 will achieve   8 are

Unit 6 photocopiable activity:
What's the best age? Time: 40-50 minutes

> **Objectives**
> * To revise zero and first conditionals
> * To revise *because* and *because of*
> * To revise vocabulary related to human life and development
> * To practise brainstorming arguments for and against a topic
> * To build spoken fluency in a debate format

Before class

You will need one photocopy of page 73 for each student.

❶ Ask students to look at the conditional sentences in exercise 1. Tell them to work in pairs and complete the gaps using *if* or *unless*. Then ask them to decide whether each sentence is an example of a zero or first conditional. Go through the answers with the whole

class. Explain that sentences like these can be useful both for the Speaking test as well as for Writing Task 2.

> **Answers**
> a if (zero)   b unless (first)   c If (first)
> d unless (first)   e Unless (first)   f If (zero)

❷ Students now work in pairs to complete the sentences with the correct adjective. When they have finished, write the answers up on the board. When taking answers from the class, ask the students to spell the words before you write them up.

> **Answers**
> a comfortable   b energetic   c adventurous
> d successful   e experienced   f wealthy
> g insecure   h patient

❸ Put students into groups of four and tell them that they are going to discuss the topic on the activity sheet. Within each group, one pair will argue 'for' and the others 'against' (in the case of a group of three, ask one stronger student to work alone). Each side should think of two or three reasons why their argument is correct, brainstorm ideas and write them in the appropriate box on the activity page. Weaker students may prefer to rely on the ideas from question 2. Before the students start to prepare, elicit linking words such as *because, because of, as, for example* and *so* and write them on the board. Students can also use some of the conditional sentences from exercise 1, or make their own.

* To help students understand the brainstorming process, give a brief demonstration, by eliciting/ revising the arguments 'for' and 'against' the question from the Writing Task on page 64 of the Student's Book: 'Is hard work the key to success, or is talent also important?'

* Each pair then has a chance to speak for one or two minutes to the other pair in the group, expressing their ideas. It is up to each pair to decide who will speak on which point, but every student should have an equal chance to speak. After each turn, the other pair has a chance to ask questions or say if they agree or disagree.

* After the discussion, conduct a feedback session based on any errors you may have noticed, especially in the use of zero and first conditionals, *because* or other linking words. Write these on the board for students to correct in pairs.

What's the best age?

❶ Complete these sentences with *if* or *unless*. Then decide if they are examples of zero or first conditionals.

a People are likely to be unhappy .... they are worried about their future.

b Children will find life difficult .... they get a good education.

c .... people feel satisfied with their achievements, then they will be happy.

d You can't be happy .... you are able to deal with change.

e .... you have a positive attitude, you will never be happy.

f .... you are physically and mentally healthy, you have a better chance of happiness.

❷ Complete these sentences with the adjective form of the nouns in brackets.

Young people

a They feel .... (comfort) with change and unfamiliar situations.

b They are more .... (energy) and are less likely to feel tired.

c They are .... (adventure) and ready to discover new things.

d They think they will be .... (success) in later life.

Older people

e They are more .... (experience) in dealing with difficult situations.

f If they earn money during their life, they are more likely to be .... (wealth).

g They may be less .... (insecurity) and worry less about the future.

h They are often more .... (patience) and able to wait before making decisions.

❸ Brainstorm ideas for this topic.

People are always happier when they are young.

Ideas FOR

People are always happier when they are young because ...

Ideas AGAINST

People are sometimes happier when they are older because ...

Vocabulary extension
Unit 6

Abbreviations: n/sln/pln = noun / single noun / plural noun; v = verb; adj = adjective; adv = adverb; p = phrase; pv = phrasal verb; T/I = transitive/intransitive; C/U = countable/uncountable

background *n* [C] a person's education, family and experience of life

cast *v* [T] to choose an actor for a particular part in a film or play

charitable *adj* A charitable event, activity or organisation gives money, food or help to people who need it.

composer *n* [C] someone who writes music

creativity *n* [U] the ability to produce new ideas or things using skill and imagination

demonstrate *v* [T] to express or show that you have a feeling, quality or ability

entertain *v* [T] to keep someone interested and help them to have an enjoyable time

event *n* [C] something that happens, especially something important or unusual

expertise *n* [U] a high level of knowledge or skill

familiarity *n* [U] a good knowledge of something, or experience of doing or using it

get to the top *p* achieve the most important position in a group or organisation

have charisma *p* to have a natural power to influence or attract people

have a change *p* to do something different that you enjoy because it is a new experience

(be) inspired *adj* showing a lot of skill and good ideas

impress someone *v* [T] to make someone admire or respect you

have a good/bad relationship *p* the way in which two or more people feel and behave towards each other

lie awake *p* to be in bed but unable to sleep

make a change *p* to make something become different or new

mood *n* [C] the way someone feels at a particular time

musician *n* [C] someone who plays a musical instrument, often as a job

on screen *p* appearing on a computer or television screen

originality *n* [U] the quality of being interesting and different from everyone or everything else

overshadow *v* [T] to cause someone or something to seem less important or successful

play in a band *p* to be one of a group of musicians who play modern music together

paparazzi *pln* photographers whose job is to follow famous people and take photographs of them for newspapers and magazines

rare *adj* (of a skill or talent) very unusual

show business *n* [U] the entertainment industry, including films, television, theatre, etc.

star quality *n* [U] a special ability that makes someone seem very successful or better than other people

singer-songwriter *n* [C] a person who sings and writes the music and words of songs

❶ Complete the dialogue using the words in the box. There are three words which you do not need to use.

turn	ahead	continue	straight	take
follow	past	cross	reach	

A: Excuse me, can you tell me how to get to the zoo?

B: Sure. Go **0** ......*past*........ the supermarket, then go **1** .... on down

the road, as far as the square. You need to **2** .... the square, and

then **3** .... left at the theatre. Then **4** .... that road until you

5 .... a big car park. The zoo's a bit further along on your right.

A: That's great, thank you.

❷ Choose the correct option in each of the sentences.

0 We saw a *few* / ~~*little*~~ interesting animals in the woods today.

1 *Many* / *Much* people think it is wrong to keep wild animals in zoos.

2 Older animals generally need *fewer* / *less* food than younger animals.

3 There is only a small *number* / *amount* of mountain gorillas left in Africa.

4 Very *few* / *little* information is known about how tigers live in the wild.

5 How *many* / *much* research have you done into animal behaviour?

❸ Read the paragraph and then complete the sentences below, writing one word from the paragraph in each gap.

The giant panda, with its distinctive black and white markings, is one of the world's most famous and easily recognised animals. Unfortunately, it is also one of the most endangered. The giant panda is native to the bamboo forests of central and south-western China, and its diet is composed nearly exclusively of bamboo. It is a large, gentle animal, and even in the wild it has almost no predators. However, it is facing near-extinction because the size of its natural habitat has decreased greatly. This is because huge sections of China's bamboo forest have been cut down and converted to farmland. Although many giant pandas now live in captivity – in zoos and wildlife research centres – scientists have had problems encouraging them to breed in these places. As a result, population figures for giant pandas are still very low.

0 The giant panda is among the most ...*endangered*... animals in the world.

1 The giant panda's .... consists almost entirely of bamboo.

2 The giant panda has hardly any .... in the wild.

3 The giant panda's .... has become much smaller.

4 Large areas of bamboo forests have been turned into ....

5 It has been difficult to get giant pandas to .... in captivity.

❹ Choose the correct option in each of the sentences.

0 You can only enter the wildlife park if you *take* / ~~*will take*~~ a guide with you.

1 Lions don't attack people unless they *think* / *will think* that their young are in danger.

2 If you *look after* / *will look after* a pet rabbit well, it can live for up to 12 years.

3 Unless we stop cutting down rainforests, many rare animals *disappear* / *will disappear*.

4 Wildlife in the countryside will increase if farmers *reduce* / *will reduce* their use of pesticides.

5 If you look carefully, *you see* / *you'll see* the birds in their nest.

❺ Choose the best alternative (A, B or C) for each of these sentences.

0 Health experts .....*estimate*..... that about 60 million US adults don't get enough sleep.

    (A) estimate   **B** require   **C** postpone

1 Our research department has recently .... a study about sleeping habits.

    A achieved   **B** performed   **C** conducted

2 The study .... on the amount of sleep that we need.

    A focused   **B** aimed   **C** directed

3 Our researchers .... the sleeping habits of a hundred people.

    A received   **B** suggested   **C** observed

4 They tried to .... the reasons why people have problems with sleeping.

    A improve   **B** identify   **C** introduce

5 The findings .... that 6–8 hours is an ideal night's sleep for all adults.

    A relate   **B** indicate   **C** donate

❻ Complete the paragraph by using the correct forms of the words in brackets.

Malcolm Gladwell is a Canadian journalist who thinks he understands the key to success. He has studied the lives of hundreds of **0** .....*famous*..... (fame) people, from 1960s pop superstars The Beatles to software billionaire Bill Gates, and found some interesting links. Gladwell says that simply being **1** .... (talent) doesn't necessarily mean you will become **2** .... (success). Whatever you do, you have to practise **3** .... (regular) – he believes you need around 10,000 hours of practice to get to the top in your career. What's more, you shouldn't underestimate the **4** .... (important) of timing and luck – as well as having a lot of natural **5** .... (able), people who succeed are often also lucky enough to be born in the right place at the right time.

Unit 7 Literacy skills

Unit objectives

- **Listening:** form completion and multiple choice
- **Vocabulary:** study-related phrases (*attending a lecture, writing an assignment*, etc.); *raise* and *rise*; words describing trends (*dramatic fall, peak*, etc.)
- **Reading:** skimming and scanning; introduction to matching information; table completion
- **Speaking Parts 2 and 3:** introducing opinions and giving reasons
- **Pronunciation:** word stress
- **Writing Task 1:** analysing and describing trends; overviews; trends in the past versus trends from the past to the present.
- **Spelling:** spelling changes when forming adverbs from adjectives
- **Grammar:** prepositions in describing trends

Starting off

❶ As a warmer With books closed, ask students to work in small groups and give them three minutes to brainstorm study/learning activities at university. Don't help them with vocabulary.

When they open their books, ask them how many of the ideas in Starting off they thought of.

> **Answers**
> 1 d 2 a 3 c 4 b 5 f 6 e

Extension idea 1 Ask students: *Do you think that socialising with other students is a way of learning or studying? Why (not)?*

Extension idea 2 Write these groups of words on the board and ask students: *How are they different?*

- *lecture, lesson and seminar*
- *lecture and presentation*
- *assignment and homework*
- *teacher and tutor*

(*answers:* a lecture is a formal talk by an expert or a university teacher, usually without participation from students; a lesson is a more general term for the period of time when a person is taught about something; a seminar is a discussion between the teacher and students; a presentation is a talk giving information about something, but may not be as formal as a lecture

– it can be given by a student; an assignment is a piece of work students have to do as part of their studies, typically in a university context; homework is work given to do at home, more in a school context; a tutor is a teacher who works with one student or a small group.)

❷ Alternative treatment Before students do this:

- write these words on the board and ask them to put them in order from most to least frequent: *every day from time to time never quite often seldom sometimes*

  (*answer:* every day, quite often, sometimes, from time to time, seldom, never)

- ask students to suggest other frequency adverbs to add to the list (e.g. *usually, nearly always*)

- remind students of phrases to express likes and dislikes – you can elicit these – from Unit 5

Extension idea Ask students to close their books. Then write on the board: *attending, socialising, giving, writing, using, talking, surfing* and *participating*. Ask students to work in pairs and remember the rest of the phrase which goes with these words.

Make sure they use the correct preposition and point out that these verbs and nouns are collocations.

Listening Form completion; multiple choice

❶ As a warmer Tell students they're going to listen to someone talking about an online course. Ask students to work in small groups and brainstorm: *What things can you study online?*

- As a follow-up, ask: *What sort of things are difficult or impossible to study online? Have you ever studied English online? Why (not)?*

Extension idea Ask students to work in small groups and make a list of the advantages and disadvantages of studying online.

❷ Before they answer the questions, ask them to look at the instructions for the task. Ask:

- *How many words can you write in each gap?* (up to two)

- *Can you write two words and a number, or should you write two words or a number?* (two words and a number)

- *Can you write just one word, or one word and a number?* (yes)

❸ 🎧 Remind students that in the exam they will hear the recording once only. However, in Listening Part 1, they hear an example, and the extract containing the example is played twice.

- When they have listened, ask them to work in pairs and compare their answers. If necessary, play the recording again.

Answers
1 Sachdeva   2 New Valley   3 PN6 3BZ
4 0787 345 077   5 next week

Extension idea Ask students to look at the recording script to check their answers. Remind them that any words or numbers spelled incorrectly are wrong.

❹ Tell students that in the exam, there will be a short pause for them to read the questions in the second half of the listening. Point out that multiple-choice questions are written as either an incomplete sentence with three possible endings (e.g. Question 6) or a question with three possible answers (e.g. Question 7). Their approach to both types of question should be the same. To read the questions actively, thinking about what each of them is asking, students should underline the key ideas in the question itself – the stem – but not in the options. This will also help remind them of the question.

Suggested underlining
7 course pack include   8 course cost
9 first assignment   10 feedback include

❺ 🎧 Tell students that as they hear the piece only once, they should answer while they listen. When they have finished, ask them to compare their answers with a partner.

Answers
6 B   7 A   8 B   9 C   10 C

❻ 🎧

Suggested underlining
6 advertising agency / like to write better   7 CDs / instructional DVDs / lesson texts   8 was £340 / £375 now   9 what I want / how it will help
10 students get together / share ideas

❼ ***Extension idea*** You can ask these extra questions:
- *How difficult is it to write well in your own language?*
- *Would you be interested in doing a course to improve your writing in your own language?*
- *Do you think it would be better to do a course like this online or face to face?*

Vocabulary *Raise* or *rise*?

❶ The main difference between these two verbs is that one is transitive (it takes an object) and the other is intransitive (it doesn't take an object). Make sure students realise that an object is a noun which follows a verb. To illustrate the difference further, you can write these two sentences on the board and elicit which word is correct in each sentence and why:
- *The sun rises / raises.*
- *She rose / raised her hand.*

When students have done the exercise in the book, elicit why each answer is correct.

Answers
1 raise   2 rise   3 raised   4 rose

❷ Remind students that candidates often make mistakes with these words, so they should take special care when using them in their own writing.

Answers
2 ~~rised~~ risen   3 ~~raises~~ rises   4 ~~rise~~ raise
5 ~~rised~~ rose

Extension idea Ask students to write four sentences of their own, two with *raise* and two with *rise*. When they have finished, they should show their sentences to a partner. Round up by asking students to read out any sentences they're not sure about.

Reading
Matching information; table completion

❶ ***As a warmer*** Ask students in small groups to brainstorm different types of reading matter, e.g. newspaper articles (you can write this on the board). Give them three minutes.

- When they have finished, round up with the whole class and write a list of their ideas on the board.
- Then ask them in groups to discuss: *How much of these things do you read each week/month?*

When they have discussed the questions in the book, round up with the whole class. Elicit ideas from them about how to improve their reading (e.g. read extensively, practise skimming and scanning with articles from the newspaper, practise reading without using a dictionary, guessing the meanings of words from the context, etc.).

❷ Before students do this exercise, elicit why it's important to read the title and subheading. (*Answer*: It will help to guide you through the passage. It gets you off to a comfortable start because you know what you're going to read about.)

> **Answers**
> a definition of speed reading / reasons for needing to read quickly

Extension idea Before they read, ask students to work in groups and predict what the passage is going to say to answer the two questions in the subheading. Again, round up students' ideas with the whole class.

❸ This exercise practises skimming and scanning skills. Give students three minutes to read the passage.

> **Answers**
> (any three from the following) decide what information you want first / skim quickly and extract key facts / ignore irrelevant detail / read silently / chunking / practice / be engaged in the material / want to know more

Alternative treatment If you did the extension idea in Exercise 2, ask your students to read the passage quickly and find out:

- which of their answers to the questions in the subheading are mentioned in the passage;
- what other ideas are mentioned.

Give students three minutes to read the passage. They then work in small groups to discuss their answers.

Extension idea Ask your students what problems they have had so far with the passage. Did they have enough time? This is an opportunity to talk about skimming and scanning with them again and to encourage them to do it in the exam. Elicit why it is useful (it gives an idea of the contents and structure of the passage, which makes it easier to locate answers to questions and deal with tasks later on).

❹
> While Matching Headings will focus on the global idea, theme or purpose of each paragraph, Matching Information asks students to locate specific information which may be embedded somewhere in any of the paragraphs. In Matching Headings tasks there is one answer for each heading (and some distractors); in Matching Information tasks there may be more than one piece of information in a single paragraph (so the paragraph letter will occur more than once in the key), while other paragraphs may not match any of the information (so the letter will not occur in the key).

Students should look carefully at the instructions and at the wording of each question, which tell them what to look for in the passage; for example in Question 1 they need to look for words and phrases that describe groups of people; in Question 4 they are looking for a reason and in Question 5 they are looking for a definition.

If the rubric 'You may use any letter more than once' is present, it means that sometimes a paragraph may contain more than one piece of information. Other paragraphs may not contain any of the information.

- This task type tests students' abilities to skim, scan and read in detail.
- The words in the questions will not repeat words from the passage but will contain a rephrasing or summary of an idea.

Students often have problems doing this task because they haven't read the instructions carefully.

> **Answers**
> **1** one letter **2** no – because there are more paragraphs than questions **3** yes (see the NB in the instructions)

❺
> **Suggested underlining**
> **2** fastest / speeds **3** how/ reader / confused
> **4** why / reading / interesting **5** definition / speed reading **6** consider before / reading

❻ *Alternative treatment* With weaker classes, you can tell them that Paragraph A is either 1 or 2. Ask them to choose, then elicit the reasons why it is 2 (see answer key below). If necessary, tell them that Paragraph B is 1, 4 or 5 and elicit the reasons why it is 1. They then do the rest of the exercise alone. When they have finished, ask students to work in pairs, comparing their answers using words from the passage to justify their choices.

> **Answers**
> **1** B (*Professional workers … students…*)
> **2** A (*top competitors average around 1,000 to 2,000 words a minute*)
> **3** G (*He or she will skip back often, losing the flow … and muddling their overall understanding*)
> **4** H (*In order to do this effectively a person must be engaged in the material …*)
> **5** A (*Speed reading is not just about … It is also about … finished reading*)
> **6** C (*the trick is deciding what information you want first*)

Extension idea Ask students: *Did you need all the paragraphs to answer the questions? Which paragraphs did you not need? (D, E and F)*

Ask students to work in pairs and suggest one piece of information which is found in each paragraph. Doing this is a challenging exercise, but it should help students understand how the task works and how paragraphs are organised (*suggested answers*: D – why you can't speed read when you read aloud, E – how to organise words into groups; F – how organising words into groups helps).

❼ Answers
E, F, G

❽ Elicit how many words students can write in each gap.

Tell students to look at the title of the table. Ask: *What is 'chunking'?* (reading blocks of words at a time)

Ask them to look at the gaps (Questions 7–13) and decide:
  – what type of word they need for each gap;
  – what information they think they need.

Tell them to answer the questions in order. When they have finished, ask them to check their answers with a partner and check for spelling mistakes.

Answers
7 words **8** eyes **9** information **10** slow reader
11 often **12** tired **13** concentrate

❾ Take this opportunity to get feedback from students about parts of the exam that are worrying them, and to discuss strategies for improvement.

• Recap on reading strategies (looking at titles and subheadings; skimming the passage for main ideas) and strategies for dealing with questions (underlining key ideas; using titles of summaries and tables to find the right place; scanning for proper nouns, numbers, etc.).

• Elicit the range of question types covered so far and discuss any concerns.

Speaking Parts 2 and 3

❶ *Alternative treatment* Ask students to gather this information for the whole class.

• They then use the figures to draw a chart showing the information. You can discuss with them what type of chart will show the information most clearly (probably a bar chart).

• They then write a short summary of the information. It needn't be the length of a Writing Part 1 as this depends on how much information they have gathered.

• When they have finished, post their summaries on the wall for the whole class to see, or ask students to pass them round and compare them.

❷ Point out that in the exam itself, candidates will have one minute to make some notes.

❸ *Alternative treatment* Before students do the task, ask them if these are good things to do in Speaking Part 2. List the good things on the board.

– *Introduce your talk with a short phrase* (yes – you can elicit possible phrases, e.g. *I'm going to talk about.../ The subject of my talk is...*)

– *Stop talking after a minute* (no – keep going for two minutes or till the examiner says *thank you.*)

– *Talk about several books or articles* (no – the subject is a book or article; be relevant)

– *Look at the examiner while you're speaking* (yes)

– *Give reasons and examples* (yes)

– *Ignore your mistakes* (no – correct yourself if possible)

– *Finish with a concluding sentence* (yes – again elicit possible conclusions e.g. *So, to finish off ... / Finally, I'd like to say*).

Students should take turns to give their talks. The student who is listening should complete the checklist on the board for their partner and give feedback when he/she has finished.

• Round up the feedback from the whole class when everyone has finished, and give advice where necessary for dealing with difficulties which arose.

• If suitable, ask students to change partners and give their talks again, this time putting into practice feedback they have received.

❹ *As a warmer* With books closed, elicit from students what Speaking Part 3 involves. They looked at this in Unit 6, so this is a reminder. Ask them how the questions are different from Speaking Part 1. (Part 1 questions are about the candidate's life and experience; Part 3 questions are more general and require a more general, less personal answer though they may require candidates to express their opinions on general topics.)

Alternative treatment With books closed, write the two questions on the board. Ask students to think for a few moments, then ask and answer the questions.

When students have finished, tell them to discuss how they could answer the questions better. They then change partners and repeat the questions.

Answers
1 B **2** A

Extension idea Ask students to work in pairs and say why the answers are good answers to the questions. (*Suggested answer*: they don't repeat the words of the question, but use their own words, they give several reasons). If students did the alternative treatment above, ask them to compare what they said with the answers in the book.

❺ ❻ Ask students to listen to the speakers while they underline phrases introducing opinions and reasons in the speech bubbles in Exercise 4. They should then copy them to the table (or to their notebooks) for reference.

Extension idea Ask students to think of other phrases they can add to the table.

Answers	
introducing an opinion	**giving a reason**
I think	*because*
In my view	*one reason is*
Well, I'm not sure	*another reason is*
I think it depends	*perhaps because*
I would say that	*as*
maybe	

Extension idea Ask students to look at the recording script to check their answers (*answers*: Introducing an opinion: *I think, In my view, Well I'm not sure, I think it depends, I would say that, maybe*; Giving a reason: *because, one reason is, another reason is, perhaps, because, as*).

Note: This would be a good moment to do the Pronunciation section on word stress, which is based on the candidates' answers.

❼ Tell students they should think of several ideas to answer each question. Tell them to think about how they can use phrases from the table to answer the questions. Remind them that they should give general, not personal answers.

Extension idea For the second question, ask students: *What word does B use in Exercise 4 which means they can't read or write?* (*illiterate*)

- Remind them they will gain extra marks if they can answer using this vocabulary rather than repeating the words of the question.

- Elicit synonyms for: *dislike* (*hate, not enjoy, not find enjoyable*), *problems* (*difficulties*), *encouraged* (*persuaded*). Ask students to think about how they can use these synonyms in their answers.

❽ When students have finished, round up by asking: *Who had a particularly good answer to the first question? What was it?*, etc. Students can then say what was good and what could be improved.

Pronunciation Word stress 2

❶ 🎧 Remind students that they can check word stress in any good learner's dictionary. You can also refer them to the word lists in the Language reference.

Alternative treatment Before doing the exercise:

- ask students to look at the words in the box and decide how many syllables each of them has (*particularly* 5; *relax* 2; *activities* 4; *imagination* 5; *education* 4; *illiterate* 4).

- ask them to predict where the main stress will come in each word before they listen.

Answers
re'lax ac'tivities imagin'ation edu'cation i'lliterate

Extension idea 1 When students have finished, ask them to work in pairs and take turns to read out the words.

Extension idea 2 Ask them to read words aloud from the word list for this unit in the Language reference.

❷ 🎧 Ask students to exaggerate the stress on the words in italics to make it very clear. Ask the students who listen to check that their partner places the stress on the correct syllable.

❸ 🎧 Ask students to say the words as if they are emphasising them, so that they will exaggerate the stressed syllable. Tell them they are only doing this for the purposes of the exercise and that obviously they shouldn't always exaggerate the stress.

❹ *Extension idea* Ask students to make their own sentences using other words from Exercise 3.

❺ Round up with the whole class by asking students to volunteer sentences which are true for them. Where suitable, you can use what students say to start short class discussions (on, for example, how much students enjoyed their secondary education).

Writing Task 1

❶ *As a warmer* Write on the board:

- *numbers of students*
- *literacy rates*
- *spending on education*
- *unemployment*

Ask students to work in small groups and say if they think each of these is rising or falling.

Alternative treatment Before students complete the phrases on the graph, ask them to say the names of the months on the horizontal axis.

- Ask them to look at the words in the box and say which words are synonyms (*increase* and *rise*; *decrease*, *fall* and *decline*). When they do the exercise, they should then, by elimination and from the context, work out the meaning of *peak*.

- Remind students that good English style avoids repeating the same vocabulary too often, hence the large number of synonyms.

- Elicit what these words mean, based on context:
  - *slight* (small and not important)
  - *dramatic* (very sudden or noticeable)
  - *sharp* (sudden and very large)
  - *gradual* (happening slowly over a period of time).

Point out that *sharp* and *dramatic* are interchangeable, whereas *gradual* includes a time element and does not mean the same as *slight*.

> **Answers**
> 2 rise/increase   3 peak   4 fall/decrease
> 5 fall/decrease

②
> **Answers**
> 2 dramatic rise/increase   3 peak   4 sharp fall/decrease   5 gradual fall/decrease

Extension idea Draw students' attention to the verbs used with these noun phrases: *there was, this was followed by* and *reached*. Ask students to write similar sentences about, for example, numbers in their class or in their school. The sentences needn't be true.

③ Especially if you did the extension idea in Exercise 2, point out that the examiners will be looking for a variety of style and an ability to use different vocabulary and grammatical forms. The sentences in Exercise 2 might read quite monotonously to an examiner if this was the answer to a Writing Task 1.

> **Answers**
> 2 rose/increased dramatically   3 peaked   4 fell/decreased sharply   5 decreased/fell gradually
> 6 fluctuated

④ Do sentences 1–3 together as a whole-class activity. Then ask students: *Which preposition...?*
  - *is used to show the first amount in a trend (from)*
  - *is used to show the final amount in a trend (to)*
  - *is used to show the total amount of the change (of)*
  - *is used with peaked or peak? (at)*

> **Answers**
> 2 of   3 at   4 to   5 from/to

Note: Now is a good moment to do the Key grammar section on prepositions to describe graphs.

⑤
> **Answers**
> 1 dropped/fallen/decreased + significantly/considerably/steadily
> 2 steeper/more significant/greater

⑥
> **Answers**
> a downward

⑦
> **Answers**
> 1 rose
> 2 increased more sharply   3 upward

⑧ Ask: *Which tense do you usually use to talk about the past?* (past simple) *Which do you use to talk about the present?* (present simple) *Which do you use to talk about the past and the present together?* (present perfect). If necessary, refer students to the Language reference sections on pages 121 and 124.

> **Answers**
> 1 Graph A   2 Chart B   3 In Graph A the present simple and present perfect; in graph B, the past simple.   4 The present simple is used to talk about what the graph shows now. The present perfect is used to describe a trend which started in the past and continues to the present. The past simple is used to describe a trend which ended in the past.

⑨ **Alternative treatment** Before they do the exercise, ask students to cover the summary below the graph and work in pairs. Ask them to discuss:
  - *What does the chart show?*
  - *What are the trends?*
  - *Can you give an overview?*

> **Answers**
> 2 shows   3 have followed   4 have always been   5 didn't have   6 rose   7 remained   8 has risen
> 9 has also increased   10 has been   11 has become

⑩ Tell students to take notes while they discuss.

Extension idea Ask students to write a brief plan outlining the main idea of each paragraph.

⑪ Tell students to:
  - look back through the writing section and try to use language taught in the section;
  - write using their plans;
  - check their finished summaries carefully.

> **Sample answer**
> The graph gives information about Starmouth School library between 2009 and 2012. It shows how many library books pupils read over this four-year period.
>
> According to the graph, there were different trends for boys and girls. The number of books read by girls increased steadily between 2009 and 2010, from about 25 to 40. After that, the numbers rose dramatically to 140 books in 2012. This was the highest figure in the period.

Boys started off reading more books than girls, but their numbers followed a different pattern. Between 2009 and 2010, there was an increase of 30 from 50 books to 80 books, and then a gradual rise to 100 books in 2011. However, in 2012, their numbers fell back to 80 again.

Overall, there was a strong upward trend in the number of books read by girls. Although boys read more books than girls in 2009, their reading fell to below the level of girls in 2012.

Spelling Forming adverbs from adjectives

❶ To remind students about adverbs, write on the board: *There was a quick rise in the number of students. The number of students rose …* and elicit what word is needed (*quickly*).

> **Answers**
> 2 e 3 a 4 b 5 d

Extension idea Ask students to write one more example for each rule.

❷
> **Answers**
> 2 clearly 3 factually 4 extremely 5 easily
> 6 logically 7 repetitively 8 thoroughly

❸ Warn students to pay special attention when writing adverbs in the exam as candidates often make mistakes. Remind them that they will lose marks for misspelling in the Listening and Reading papers.

> **Answers**
> 2 ~~steadly~~ steadily 3 ~~dramaticlly~~ dramatically
> 4 ~~slighty~~ slightly 5 ~~gentley~~ gentle 6 ~~rapid~~ rapidly

Key grammar
Prepositions to describe graphs

❶ When students have answered the questions, go through the Language reference section on page 128.

> **Answers**
> 1 in (d, h) 2 over/during (a, b) 3 from/to;
> between/and (e, f) 4 in (g) 5 by (f)
> 6 from/to (c)

❷ *Alternative treatment* Photocopy the graph or ask students to cover it. Elicit sentences from students to describe the data in the chart.

> **Answers**
> 1 from; to 2 at 3 by 4 to; over 5 by
> 6 between

❸
> **Answers**
> 2 ~~on~~ in 3 fall ~~down~~ to 4 ~~During~~ From
> 5 70% **in** 2010 6 ~~of~~ in

Unit 7 photocopiable activity:
University trends Time: 30-40 minutes

Objectives
- To practise the use of the present perfect and past simple when describing graphs
- To practise describing trends and changes
- To practise writing introductory sentences and overviews for Writing Task 1

Before class

Photocopy page 84 and cut it into two parts, 'Student A' cards, and 'Student B' cards.

❶ Divide the class into two groups, A and B. Give a 'Student A' card to all the students in group A. All the students in group B receive a 'Student B' card. Ask students to work in pairs with other members of their group to read through the description of the graph and circle the correct verb form or preposition.

> **Answers**
> **A** 1 has fluctuated 2 From 3 rose 4 to 5 in
> 6 fell 7 by 8 peaked 9 at 10 decreased
> 11 between 12 have remained
>
> **B** 1 has risen 2 From 3 to 4 In 5 was 6 fell
> 7 to 8 rose 9 by 10 to 11 decreased
> 12 have increased

❷ Explain to students that they are going to read their text aloud to a member of the other group to see if they are able to guess what their graph looks like.

Each student finds a partner from the other group and sits so that they can listen but not see each other's graphs. They take turns to read their completed description and see if their partner can guess which of the five graphs on their sheet corresponds to it.

> **Answers**
> **Student A:** graph 4 **Student B:** graph 1

❸ Students write an introductory sentence and final overview for their own graph in the spaces. To help them get started, elicit which tenses will be used (present simple for the introduction and present perfect for the overview). They then look at each sentence and check for errors and accuracy.

Student A

University students attending lectures over the past 12 months

Since the beginning of the year, student attendance at lectures [1] *has fluctuated/fluctuated.* [2] *From/during* January to April, numbers [3] *rised/rose* steadily from 50 students per lecture in January [4] *by/to* around 170 [5] *in/on* April. This figure [6] *fell/has fallen* [7] *by/of* 20 students to a total of around 150 students in May. Attendance [8] *peaked/peak* in June [9] *at/in* approximately 230 students per lecture, but then [10] *decreased/has decreased* dramatically [11] *between/since* July and September. Since September, numbers [12] *remained/have remained* stable until now.

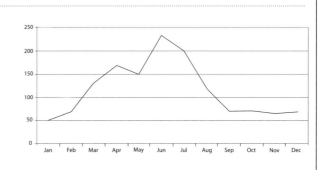

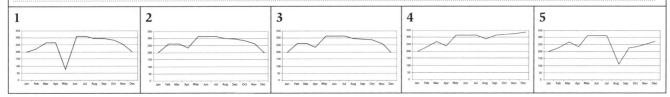

Student B

University students using the library over the past 12 months

Since the beginning of last year, the number of students using the library [1] *rose/has risen* steadily. [2] *From/Over* January to March, there was a gradual increase from 200 library users [3] *to/by* 265 per day. [4] *In/At* April there [5] *was/has* been a slight drop, when numbers [6] *have fallen/fell* [7] *to/over* 235, but in May users [8] *rose/has risen* [9] *by/of* 75 [10] *to/at* a total of 310. Numbers [11] *have decreased/decreased* slightly again in August, but since then, they [12] *have increased/increased* steadily until now.

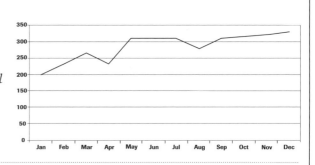

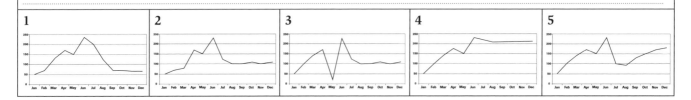

Vocabulary extension

Unit 7

Abbreviations: n/sln/pln = noun / single noun / plural noun; v = verb; adj = adjective; adv = adverb; p = phrase; pv = phrasal verb; T/I = transitive/intransitive; C/U = countable/uncountable

additional qualifications *pln* official records showing that you have extra skills, qualities or experience

(get into) bad habits *p* something that you start to do that is bad for your health or is annoying

campus *n* [C/U] the land and buildings belonging to a college or university

colleague *n* [C] someone that you work with

concept *n* [C] an idea or principle

do homework *p* to do the work which teachers give their students to do at home

enable (somebody to do something) *v* [T] to make someone able to do something, or to make something possible

further education *n* [U] education at a college for people who have left school but are not at a university

get a place *p* to be given a position in an organisation such as a university

get a qualification *p* to be given an official record showing that you have finished a training course or have the necessary skills, etc.

give priority *p* to consider that something or someone is more important than other things or people

have a chance *p* to be given the opportunity to do something

institution *n* [C] a large and important organisation, such as a university or bank

keen to do something *p* wanting to do something very much

level *n* [C] someone's ability compared to other people

make progress *p* to improve skills, knowledge, etc.

measure performance *p* to judge how successful someone or something is

non-academic *adj* related to technical subjects or practical skills rather than studying

one-to-one *adj* describes an activity in which one person is teaching or giving information to another person

participate in *p* [T] to be involved with other people in an activity

pressure *n* [C/U] difficult situations that make you feel worried or unhappy

program(me) *n* [C] a plan of activities to be done or things to be achieved

schedule *n* [C/U] a plan that gives events or activities and the times that they will happen or be done

self-discipline *n* [U] the ability to make yourself do things that you do not want to do

semester *n* [C] one of the two time periods that a school or college year is divided into

spare time *p* time when you are not working

take (a course or subject) *v* [T] to do a series of lessons about a particular subject

textbook *n* [C] a book about a particular subject, written for students

undergraduate *n* [C] a student who is studying for their first university degree qualification

Unit 8 Tourist attractions

Unit objectives

- **Reading:** scanning; summary completion; matching features; recognising the rephrasing of words in a passage
- **Vocabulary:** *tourist* and *tourism*; adjectives describing opinions and facts
- **Listening:** sentence completion; table completion; listening for a rephrasing of words in the question
- **Speaking Parts 1 and 2:** describing places; subjective and objective descriptions; avoiding hesitation
- **Pronunciation:** chunking; pausing naturally
- **Writing Task 2:** tasks with two questions; analysing the task; structuring the answer; writing a conclusion
- **Grammar:** relative pronouns
- **Spelling:** introductory and linking phrases

Starting off

❶ *As a warmer* With books closed, ask students to work in pairs and think of six different holiday activities, for example *sightseeing*.

With books open, ask students to match the holidays with the photos and ask: *Did you think of any other activities which are not on this list?*

> **Answers**
> 1 d   2 b   3 e   4 c   5 a   6 f

❷
> **Answers**
> 1 1 Chamonix, France   2 Inca Trail, Peru
> 3 Hong Kong   4 Zambia   5 Prague, Czech Republic
> 6 the Arctic Ocean
>
> 2 1 the exercise, fresh air and mountains   2 the exercise, fresh air and mountains; the sense of achievement   3 the wide variety of products, the cheap prices   4 the range of wildlife, the scenery, the relaxing environment   5 the amazing buildings and architecture, the sense of history   6 the snow and ice and very different environment, the wildlife
>
> 3 students' own answers

Extension idea Ask students: *Which of these holidays do you think you would not enjoy? Why not?*

Reading
Summary completion; matching features

❶ *As a warmer* With books closed, tell students they are going to read about two unusual places to go on holiday. Tell them to work in small groups and ask: *What unusual holiday destinations have you heard about? Why do people go there?*

Tell students that when a passage in IELTS is accompanied by pictures or photos, they should always look at these, as they are included to help candidates understand or orientate themselves with the passage.

> **Answers**
> The Arctic is a region at the North Pole and Antarctica is a continent covering the South Pole.
>
> things such as tourism, scientific research, exploration, etc. happen there

Extension idea Ask: *Would you like to go to the Arctic or Antarctica? Why (not)? What do you think tourists can do there?*

❷ To help students with the first question, you can ask some supporting questions. For example: *What is happening to the ice in the North and South Poles?* (*answer*: much of it is melting) *Why?* (*answer*: higher global temperatures/global warming/climate change).

With the second question, to help students understand *icy wildernesses*, ask what *these* refers to earlier in the sentence (*answer*: the Arctic and Antarctica). Ask: *What base word can you see in 'wildernesses'?* (*answer*: wild) *How do this and 'icy' relate to the Arctic and Antarctica?*

> **Answers**
> 1 Both suggest that tourists may not be able to go there in the future.   2 The environments / the landscapes   3 something about the increase or changes in numbers of tourists to these regions

❸ Students needn't discuss these questions for more than a minute or two – their answers can be yes or no and a brief reason.

Elicit that they should skim the passage by running their eyes over the words to get a general impression and find the answers. Give them three minutes to do this, and be strict about the time.

Extension idea If you wish to give your students practice scanning, write the following words on the board and ask students to scan the passage in two minutes and find what they refer to.

– 370,000   – 17 percent   – 100

(*answers*: 370,000 – the number of cruise ship visitors to Norway in 2007; 17 percent – the fall in the percentage of visitors to Antarctica last season; 100 – the limit to the number of passengers who can go ashore to Antarctica at one time following the meeting of the Antarctic Treaty)

④ Students worked on summary completion in Unit 4.

- Ask students to look at the instructions. Ask: *What should you write in the gaps?* (*answer*: up to two words and/or a number)

- Ask: *Which IELTS reading tasks often have titles?* (*answer*: flow charts, summaries, tables, notes, labelling diagrams and plans, etc.)

- *How does the title help you?* (*answer*: it tells you what the flow chart, summary, etc. is about; if you use it well, it helps you to quickly find the part of the passage you need to read carefully.)

- Ask students to look at the title and say what aspect of polar tourism the summary will focus on (the figures). Ask them to scan the passage to find which paragraph starts giving them figures. (*answer*: paragraph 2)

- Ask students to quickly read through the summary to see what type of information they need and to look at the passage to see where they will find it. (*answer*: in paragraphs 2–5)

Alternative treatment Focus on Question 1. Students may see *in* and say a place or a time. Ask them how they know it's a time (*answer*: by reading the rest of the sentence). Ask them to work in pairs to decide the type of information for the other gaps and then compare their ideas with another pair.

Extension idea 1 Focus on some of the words and phrases in the summary which relate to figures. Ask students:

– which preposition means 'more than'? (*over*)

– which preposition is used to say how much something has changed, risen or fallen? (*by*)

– which preposition means 'during'? (*over*)

– which phrase means 'up to' or 'this is the maximum number'? (*as many as*)

Extension idea 2 Ask students to read the passage again and underline phrases which express a rise or fall in numbers (e.g. *have increased from about a million in the early 1990s to more than 1.5 million today*) (suggested answers: *In 2007, 370,000 cruise passengers visited Norway, twice the number that arrived in 2000; has enjoyed an annual growth rate of 9 percent since 1990; a rise of 7.3 per cent from 2006; with a sharp increase in cruise ship arrivals of 250 percent since 2004; last season saw a drop of 17 percent to 38,200; there has been a 760 percent rise in land-based tourism*).

⑤ Tell students that, like in the live test, they won't always find the information in the passage in the same order as it occurs in the summary, so they may need to scan backwards and forwards for it. Point out that is very important to do this. Candidates often lose marks because they only read ahead.

- When they have finished ask them to read their summary again to make sure it makes sense and is grammatical.

- Ask students to work in pairs and compare their answers. Tell them to make sure they have copied words and numbers exactly as they are written in the passage.

Alternative treatment With weaker classes, you can do this task step-by-step. Ask: *What information are you looking for in Question 1?* (*answer*: when tourism began). Tell them to start scanning the paragraphs with figures in them – they will find the answer immediately.

Ask: *What information is needed for Question 2?* (*answer*: the number of people who travel there now) Tell students to read a little further, etc.

⑥ Matching Features tests students' ability to scan the passage for options (in this case, names of people) and then read that part/those parts of the passage carefully to find the information which goes with each name. The names are listed in the same order as in the passage.

Students should read the instructions carefully. Sometimes (as here) the box contains fewer options than the number of questions. In this case they will need to use some letters more than once. Other times, the box contains more options than the number of questions and they will not need to use all the letters.

Ask students first to read the instructions for the task and the questions. Ask: *Can you use the letters A–D once only?* (answer: no, more than once)

Give students a time limit of one minute to scan for the four names in the passage. Tell them to check the entire passage as sometimes the names can occur more than once.

Alternative treatment To help weaker classes, once students have underlined the key ideas in each statement, tell them that the answer to Question 11 is A and ask them to say why (*answer*: she says *25 percent go* for a second time).

> **Answers**
> **2** **8** tourists believe / should not delay   **9** dangers / travelling Antarctica   **10** famous people / look at the impacts / global warming   **11** some tourists / more than one trip **12** no evidence / visitors / hurrying
>
> **3** **8** D (*There's an element of 'do it now'.*)
> **9** B (*Tourism in Antarctica is not without its risks*)
> **10** C (*Hillary Clinton and many other big names have been to Svalbard in the northernmost part of Norway to see the effects of climate change.*)
> **11** A (*Looking at six years' worth of data, of the people who have been to the polar regions, roughly 25 percent go for a second time.*)
> **12** C (*So far, no surveys confirm that people are quickly going to see polar regions before they change*)

7 Tell students that the wording of the questions will be different from the wording of the passage, so they can only answer the questions by understanding what the passage is saying. This exercise reinforces the need (throughout the IELTS test) to look for synonymous meaning rather than identical words.

> **Answers**
> **2** risks   **3** effects   **4** climate change
> **5** go for a second time   **6** quickly going

8 Before students do the discussion task, ask: *How can large numbers of tourists affect the environment?* To prompt students you can write these words on the board: *air travel, traffic, hotels and other buildings,*

You may also elicit good aspects of tourism such as employment, money, development, etc.

Vocabulary *Tourism or tourist?*

1 To focus student's reading of the information, ask:

– *Which word ('tourism' or 'tourist') refers to people?* (*tourist*)

– *Which word refers to the general activity?* (*tourism*)

– *Which would you be if you went on a holiday?* (*tourist*)

– *What activity would you be doing?* (*tourism*)

– *Which word is countable and which is uncountable?* (*tourist* [C], *tourism* [U])

Remind students that they studied countable and uncountable nouns in Unit 5. If necessary, refer them to the Language reference section on page 126.

> **Answers**
> **1** tourists   **2** tourism   **3** tourism   **4** tourist

2 Use the example. Ask students: *What is the difference between the two corrections? Why was the original sentence wrong?* Remind them of the need for the '*s*' in the third person singular and the present simple, and that *tourism* is uncountable and therefore always singular.

Tell students to refer back to the information in Exercise 1 when doing this exercise.

> **Answers**
> **2** ✓   **3** ~~tourism spend~~ tourists spend
> **4** ~~to the tourism~~ to tourism   **5** ~~number of tourism~~ number of tourists / amount of tourism   **6** ✓
> **7** ~~tourism~~ tourist   **8** ~~mass tourists~~ mass tourism / tourists

Extension idea Ask students to write four sentences of their own about tourists and tourism in their country or region. Encourage them to use some of the compound nouns from Exercise 1. When they have finished, ask students to compare their sentences with a partner's.

Listening
Sentence completion; table completion

1 *As a warmer* Write on the board:

Describe the last time you visited a museum. Say why you went, who you went with, what you saw and what you liked and disliked about it.

- Tell students they are going to work in pairs and take turns to talk about the task.

- Give them time to work alone and make notes. They then take turns to give their talks.

Alternative treatment Before they do the exercise, elicit approximate meanings of these words from the museum programme (some of which they have seen previously in this course) from the whole class: *demonstrations, experiments, witness, global warming* and *3-D*.

Extension idea When they have finished, ask one student from each group to report to the whole class what they have decided and why.

2 Students did sentence completion in Unit 4. Before they look at the questions, tell them to read the instructions so that they are clear about what they can write in the gaps.

Alternative treatment Ask students to underline the key ideas before they decide what information they need (*suggested underlining*: 1 Keep your / in a safe place 2 pass through the / to enter and leave 3 buy a / use a camera 4 costs 5 Look after your / mobile phone 6 all the sentence).

Answers
1 noun / something you own   **2** noun / type of entrance   **3** noun / something you buy   **4** noun / something you own   **5** number of minutes

❸ 🎧 As in the live exam, play the recording once only. Give students time at the end to check their answers, particularly their spelling.

- Ask them to work in pairs and compare answers.
- They then listen again to check.

Answers
1 ticket   **2** grey gates   **3** permit
4 wallet   **5** 5 / five minutes

Extension idea 1 Ask students to call out answers to the questions and spell them. You write their answers on the board and ask the class in each case if the answer is correct and correctly spelled.

Extension idea 2 Play the recording a third time, while students read the recording script. They can then check their answers for themselves.

❹ 🎧 Remind students that they will not usually hear exactly the same words as they read in the questions, but they will hear words which mean the same.

Alternative treatment Ask students to look at the recording script to do this exercise. If you didn't do Extension idea 2 in Exercise 3, you can play the recording as they read.

Answers
1 put   **2** secure   **3** come back   **4** go   **5** purchase
6 take photographs   **7** don't lose   **8** get to   **9** early

❺ Students did table completion previously in Unit 5. Remind them that they should look at:

- the instruction to check what they can write in the gaps:
- the title, as well as other parts of the table.

Alternative treatment Ask students to look at Question 5. Ask what *re-creation* means. Give clues such as *re-write, re-enter, re-read*. Ask: *Will the word you need begin with a vowel or a consonant?* (a consonant) *How do you know?* (it has *a*, not *an*, before it).

Answers
6 noun that goes with 'along'   **7** adjective that describes 'ocean'   **8** a time   **9** adjective that describes a type of dinosaur   **10** noun – a place

❻ 🎧 As in the live exam, play the recording once only, but give students time to check their answers, especially their spelling, afterwards.

Ask students to compare their answers with a partner before playing the recording again for them to check.

Answers
6 journey   **7** Wild   **8** 1.45 p.m.   **9** new   **10** desert

Extension idea You can do either of the extension ideas from Exercise 3 again with this exercise.

❼ *Extension idea* Say to students: *Imagine you have been given a large amount of money to set up a museum in your town. What museum would you set up?* Ask them to think for a while and then explain to their partners.

Speaking Parts 1 and 2

❶ *As a warmer* Ask students to work in pairs. Ask: *Do you ever have foreign visitors to your town? Why do they visit?*

Alternative treatment With books open, before students do the exercise, ask them if they remember phrases from Unit 1 to describe where places are. Elicit as many phrases as possible (e.g. *in the country*) and then refer them back to Unit 1 to remind them.

- Elicit things they can say to describe the place (e.g. *industrial, rural, residential, modern, old*, etc.).
- Tell students to take turns and speak for about two minutes about the place they come from.

❷ 🎧

Answers
1 modern, industrial   **2** What else; Let me think

Extension idea 1 Recap the two phrases Ulia has used to avoid hesitation (*let me think; what else?*) Ask students if they can think of other phrases to avoid hesitation (*Suggested answers: I mean…, you know, anyway*, etc.).

Extension idea 2 Ask students to change partners and say how Ulia's description of Balakovo is similar to or different from the place they come from.

❸ Give students a couple of minutes to prepare their answers. Encourage them to think of reasons why they would recommend places (in question 3) and to give some details of the festivals in their local area.

Write these openings on the board to help them start:

1 I live in a town/village that/which

2 It's very important because

3 I'd recommend X – it's a place that/where

4 We have a festival called X that/which

Extension idea 1 When they have finished, ask students to discuss together how they could have answered each question better.

- When they are ready, round up their ideas with the whole class.

- Then ask students to change partners and do the exercise again.

Extension idea 2 Ask students if they remember answering a similar question to question 1 when they did the Speaking section in Unit 1. How is their answer different this time?

This should give rise to useful consideration of what goes into a good Part 1 answer, while also highlighting the progress they've made over the course so far.

❹ **Alternative treatment** If your students bring dictionaries to class, or you have a class set, you can take this opportunity for some dictionary work.

- Ask students if there are any words they are not sure of the meaning of.

- Ask them to use their dictionaries to look up meanings and then match adjectives with their opposites.

Answers
2 noisy F   3 dirty F   4 quiet F   5 urban F
6 unpopular F/O   7 stressful F/O
8 unimpressive O   9 poor F   10 dull F/O
11 outdated F/O   12 awful O

Extension idea Ask students to think of two more adjectives to describe the place where they come from. Round up their suggestions with the whole class and write their ideas on the board so students can copy them into their notebooks.

❺ **Suggested answers**
2 a busy, urban   3 a fashionable, wealthy
4 beautiful, ancient   5 a peaceful, rural
6 an exciting, colourful

Extension idea Tell students to change partners and take turns to read out their answers without the nouns (i.e. the adjectives only). Their partners should say which picture they are describing in each case.

❻ 🎧 You may need to play the recording twice to give students time to write everything down. When they've finished, ask them to compare their answers in pairs and to check spelling.

Answers
1 clear / impressive / not dirty
2 amazing / colourful / wonderful / breathtaking
3 ancient / beautiful / impressive
4 fantastic / memorable

Extension idea Ask students to guess the meanings of any adjectives they don't know. If they have access to dictionaries, they can check meanings there.

Note: Now is a good moment to do the Pronunciation section on page 83 on chunking.

❼ Tell students, while they are preparing their talks, to think of adjectives from Exercises 5 and 6 which they can use. When they give their talks, tell them to use phrases to avoid hesitation.

The students who are listening should note down adjectives their partners use when they speak.

❽ As always, give students a minute to prepare their talk and make some notes.

Alternative treatment If you need a variety of pace, you can leave this last exercise for another moment and use it as revision later in the unit.

Pronunciation Chunking 2

❶ **As a warmer** Students did work on chunking in Unit 4. Ask them what they remember about it.

🎧 **Alternative treatment** As students already know a little about chunking, ask them to predict which versions of the sentences in this exercise will be easier to understand before they listen. Ask also: *Which sounds more natural? Do people use chunking when they speak in your language as well?*

Answer
with a pause

❷

Answer
b

Extension idea Ask students to work in pairs and take turns to read the sentences aloud.

❸ 🎧 **Alternative treatment** Ask students to work in pairs and predict where Ulia will pause before they listen. They then listen to check their answers and make any changes.

Answers
I'd like to talk about a holiday / which I took in 2005 / It's a holiday that I remember very well / because we had such a fantastic time / I went with three other girls / who are all friends of mine / and we still talk about this holiday today

❹ Tell students that to do this naturally, they needn't read quickly but can take their time.

❺ 🎧

> **Answers**
> It was funny / because usually I'm a person / who's quite scared of things, / and I didn't think I / would put a mask on my face / or go under the water - / but I wanted to see the coral / so much

Extension idea Ask students to work alone and write two sentences about the place they come from. They should then take turns to read their sentences aloud to their partners with suitable pauses.

Writing Task 2

❶ ***As a warmer*** Tell students to work in pairs and discuss: *What holiday resorts are there in your country/countries? Do they attract local people more or foreign tourists more?*

With books open, ask students: *Why should you underline the key ideas in the writing task?* (to be sure you have understood what is being asked and that you cover all the points).

Alternative treatment
- Say: *The introduction at the start of this section says the task may contain two questions to write about. What are the two questions here?* (Why do you think this happens? How was tourism different in the past?).
- Ask: *In the question 'Why do you think this happens', what does 'this' refer to?* (the whole of the introductory statement).

> **Suggested underlining**
> tourists / straight to their holiday resort / almost never leave it / no experience of the local culture / why / this happens / How / tourism different in the past

❷
> **Suggested answers**
> The photo shows a resort, which tourists almost never leave, where everything is provided for them and they will only meet other tourists, not local people. It is an example of mass tourism.

❸
> **Answers**
> 2 F 3 F 4 T 5 F 6 T 7 T

❹ Before students work in pairs, ask: *What is meant by 'transfers'?* (buses or taxis which take them from the airport to their hotel).

- Elicit one or two other ideas from the whole class about why tourists have no experience of local

culture (*suggested answers*: their hotels discourage local people from entering or are too expensive for locals; hotels serve international food, not local food; holidaymakers are taken in closed buses from place to place, etc.).

- Elicit one or two ideas about how things were different in the past (e.g. tourists had to find their own transport to the hotel, the hotel was also used by local people, served local food – not international food, etc.).

Extension idea When students have finished, ask them to change partners and compare their ideas with their new partner.

❺ ***Alternative treatment 1*** Ask students to read the sample answer. Ask: *Which ideas expressed in the sample answer are also in the notes you made for Exercise 2?*

Alternative treatment 2 Ask students to write out a rough plan of the sample answer in note form, paragraph by paragraph. If they're not sure how to do this, ask them to look at the notes on the sample answer in Unit 2. (*Suggested answers*: Paragraph 1: with air travel possible to reach distant places, new holiday experience; Paragraph 2: in past, travellers organised own travel – many stories; Paragraph 3: cheap package hols mean tourist go straight to hotels, don't meet local people; Paragraph 4: stay in hotels, don't go out of resort; Paragraph 5: in past, backbackers met local people – this lost.)

> **Answers**
> 1 paragraphs 3 and 4 2 paragraphs 2 and 5
> 3 writer's views: from *I think ... holiday experience* in the introduction; the last sentence of paragraph 3; the next to last sentence of paragraph 5 writer's experience: the second and third sentences of paragraph 5

❻ Apart from work done previously in this book, some of your students may be unfamiliar with the conventions of academic essays if they don't have them as part of their educational culture. At this point it would be a good idea to check that they all understand the basic structure of an IELTS-style essay that has: a) an introduction; b) 2–4 paragraphs that form the body of the essay; and c) a conclusion.

- Discuss the correct answers with the whole class when you round up, but reassure students that the conclusion doesn't need to be lengthy – two sentences are enough.
- Point out that the purpose identified in question 1 is an essential characteristic of a concluding paragraph. The conclusion can contain some or all of the four features listed as correct in question 2.

Alternative treatment Ask students to look at the concluding paragraphs in the sample answers from Units 2, 4, and 6 and to identify the characteristics listed in the questions in this exercise.

> **Answers**
> 1 C **2** A, C, D, F

❼ Tell students to read the three concluding paragraphs as continuations of the sample answer in Exercise 3. Ask any or all of these questions:

– *Which seems to continue and conclude the essay in the most natural manner?*

– *Which ties in most logically?*

– *Which is most relevant?*

– *Remember from Unit 4 that you'll lose marks for irrelevance; do any of the paragraphs here contain things which seem irrelevant, or are introducing new points not clearly connected with the rest of the essay?*

> **Answers**
> Conclusion C is the best because it sums up the writer's view and makes a recommendation. Conclusion A contains the writer's view and has a concluding phrase, but does not link the points in the essay. Conclusion B begins with a concluding word but introduces a new idea and doesn't link the ideas in the essay.

Extension idea 1 Work on discourse markers from the sample essay in Exercise 3 and the concluding paragraphs in this exercise. Ask students to work in pairs, look at the sample essay and the conclusions and note down words or phrases which (you can write these on the board):

1 introduce an idea about the past (for this one you can elicit the opening phrase 'In the last century' from the whole class as an example);

2 introduce a contrasting idea about the present;

3 introduce an opinion;

4 introduce a new idea linked to one already mentioned;

5 show that the writer is finishing.

(Answers: 1 In the last century, In the past, This is very different from the past when ...; When I was a child; 2 Now, Nowadays, these days; 3 I think, In my opinion, In my view; 4 Another problem is, Therefore; 5 In conclusion, finally)

Extension idea 2 If your students have done Extension idea 1, ask them to think of one or two more phrases to add to each of the categories on the list they made.

Note: Now is a good moment to do the Key grammar section and the Spelling section, especially if you have done Extension idea 1.

❽ Remind students to underline the key ideas as they read. When they have finished, they should compare what they have underlined.

Alternative treatment Especially with weaker classes, help them to think through this exercise.

- Ask them to list negative effects and positive effects of tourism. Before you start, elicit why it's a good idea to think of positive effects as well (because the question asks 'How true is this statement?').

- Elicit from the whole class some negative effects (e.g. tourism changes local culture, it can conflict with local culture, it raises prices, it can be harmful to the environment, can cause litter, etc.).

- Elicit some positive effects (e.g. tourism provides employment, opens up the country to new ideas and cultures, brings in money, etc.).

- Ask what tourists can do to reduce the harmful effects, (e.g. reading about the place before they visit, respecting local culture, being tidy, etc.).

- Get ideas from the whole class and write them up on the board. Encourage students to note them down for use when they do the writing task themselves.

- Finally, if it hasn't come up previously in the discussion, ask students to suggest things from their own experience connected with the points you've covered in class.

❾ This task is probably best done for homework. Remind students that in the exam they will have about 40 minutes for this, and as it's near the end of the course, they should try to complete their writing in this time.

Alternative treatment Especially with weaker classes, ask students to plan the essay in pairs in class. When they have finished, they should compare their plans with another pair and make any improvements they think suitable.

> **Sample answer**
> Some countries rely on tourism, as it is their main industry. These countries receive large numbers of tourists and have to provide many facilities for them. This brings money into the economy and creates jobs, but it can also cause problems.
>
> In my opinion, one of the worst effects of tourism is the presence of large crowds of people in streets and areas of beauty. When this happens, local people can find it difficult to do things they want to do. Also, the appearance of their home city or village can change so much that they feel they have lost their identity.
>
> Another disadvantage of tourism is that tourists do not usually worry about environmental issues. If

trees have been cut down to build hotels, this does not matter to them. If their children drop litter, they may not do anything about it. However, these problems can be very worrying for people who live in the area all the time.

Generally, I think there are positive things that tourists can do. Firstly, they can think about where they go on holiday and avoid places that are already overcrowded. Secondly, they should read something about their holiday destination before they leave. This will help them understand the people and culture better. Lastly, they should try to look after the area they stay in and observe the rules there.

Overall, I believe tourism has many benefits for everyone. However, it is important that people still think about protecting tourist locations and reducing the undesirable impacts of tourist behaviour.

Key grammar
Relative pronouns: *who, which, what, where*

❶ Remind students that one of the assessment criteria for the Writing paper is the ability to write suitably complex sentences, and that by doing this they will achieve a higher band score.

When students have done the exercise, go through the Language reference section on page 128 with them. For each point in the Language reference section, elicit extra examples from students and write good examples on the board for students to copy to their notebooks.

> **Answers**
> 2 that they could tell   3 who never go outside the resort   4 which is a popular destination   5 where tourists and local people can meet

❷ **Answers**
1 which/that   2 who/that   3 where
4 which/that   5 who/that   6 that/which
7 where

❸ Omission of relative pronouns is a common error in IELTS and may be caused by either first-language interference or carelessness. Tell students that they should set aside some time to read through what they have written and that this is one of the common mistakes that they should look for.

> **Answers**
> 2 ~~destinations are~~ destinations that/which are
> 3 ~~problem causes~~ problem that/which causes
> 4 ~~visitors travel~~ visitors who/that travel
> 5 ~~Children work~~ Children who/that work
> 6 ~~accommodation is~~ accommodation that/which is
> 7 ~~people don't~~ people who/that don't

Spelling Introductory and linking phrases

The mistakes in questions 9 and 10 reflect an inability to spell adverbs correctly. Remind students by eliciting the rules which they covered in the spelling section of Unit 7.

> **Answers**
> 1 century   2 nowadays   3 sometimes   4 problem
> 5 although   6 opinion   7 therefore   8 conclusion
> 9 finally   10 unfortunately

Extension idea The mistake in question 5 is perhaps a confusion with *thought*. Students, not surprisingly, often have problems with words ending in *gh* and *ght*.

- Dictate these words and ask students to write them down: *high, height, thought, right, though, through, weight*. You will have to give an example of each word in context as there are possible homonyms for some of them.

- When you have finished dictating, ask students to compare their answers in pairs and then dictate the spelling of each answer to you. Write the words on the board and ask the class if they are spelled correctly.

Vocabulary and grammar review Unit 7

❶ 2 raising   3 rises   4 raised   5 Raise   6 has risen
7 rose

❷ 2 There was a fall of 20% / a 20% fall in the amount of study time.

3 There was a considerable improvement in reading speeds.

4 There has been a slight drop in (the) sales of electronic books this month.

5 There will be an increase of 10% / a 10% increase in the number of lecture hours.

6 There was a peak in the cost of fees in 2011.

7 There is a rise in the number of words people know as they get older.

8 There was a fluctuation in literacy levels in rural areas during the 1990s.

❸ 2 of   3 to   4 Between   5 at   6 by   7 from   8 to
9 over

Unit 8

❶ 2 impressive   3 outdated   4 fashionable   5 dull
6 stressful

❷ 2 ✓   3 lively, historical   4 fascinating, colourful
5 ✓   6 exciting, healthy   7 ✓

❸ 2   Riyadh is the city in Saudi Arabia where I grew up
/ that I grew up in.

3   The horses that/which we rode in the country park
were very beautiful.

4   People who/that travel by train can enjoy the
passing scenery.

5   Greece is the country where the first Olympic
Games took place.

6   Tourists who/that are more adventurous try new
activities.

❹ 2 who/that   3 which/that   4 where   5 which/that
6 who/which/that   7 which/that   8 where

Unit 8 photocopiable activity:
Tourist talk   Time: 30 minutes

> **Objectives**
> *   To practise forming sentences with relative clauses
> *   To build confidence in giving extended answers
>   using a range of adjectives
> *   To recycle vocabulary related to travel and tourism

Before class

You will need to photocopy page 95 and cut it up so that
each group of students has one set of grey cards and one
set of white cards. You can also make a photocopy of the
'Rules' for each group.

As a warmer Write the following adjectives on the board:
beautiful, fashionable, urban, sandy, enjoyable, local.

Ask students to discuss in pairs which ones are
adjectives of opinion, and which of fact. Point out
that there are three of each type. Once this has been
established, write up the nouns *beach, area, festival* and
ask students to put one of each type of adjective with
each noun to make a likely combination (with a stronger
group, it may not be necessary to supply the nouns).
When going through their answers, elicit the rule that
opinion adjectives come before adjectives of fact.

> **Suggested answers**
> fashionable urban area
> enjoyable local festival
> beautiful sandy beach

❶ Tell students that they are going to play a speaking
game. Ask them to work in groups of three or four
and place the two sets of cards (grey and white)

in two separate piles, face down, in the middle of
the group. Show the class how to play the game by
demonstrating a typical turn of each type. First,
pick up a 'Speaking challenge' card from one of the
groups, read out the question, and give your own
answer to it in around one minute. Then demonstrate
the 'Grammar check' by asking a student to pick up
a card and read the sentences aloud to you. Give the
answer in a full sentence using the correct relative
pronoun. Deal with any questions from students
about how to play, before starting the game.

❷ During the game, monitor students' use of adjectives
from Unit 8, as well as relative clauses.

❸ When all the groups have finished playing, conduct
a brief language feedback session. Write a selection
of the errors on the board and ask the students to
correct them in their groups, before going through
each one as a class. If you wish to work on chunking,
write some sample sentences on the board and ask the
students to identify where the pauses should come.
Mark these on the board before drilling each chunk
with the whole class.

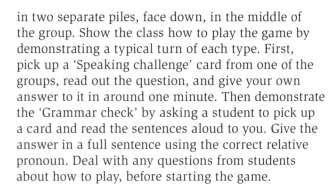

> **Rules**
> *   Take turns to play the game. When it is your turn,
>   choose a 'Speaking challenge' or 'Grammar check'.
> *   The next player to the left then picks up a card
>   from the appropriate pile and reads it out, without
>   showing it.
> *   For 'Speaking challenge', talk for one minute in
>   answer to the prompt. If you succeed, you may
>   keep the card. If not, you must put the card to one
>   side on the waste pile. During the talk, the other
>   students should make a note of any adjectives you
>   use. At the end of the talk, they should let you
>   know how many adjectives you managed to use:
>   if you have used more than four, your card will
>   score double points.
> *   For 'Grammar check', read out the two separate
>   sentences in **bold**. You must join them together
>   into a single sentence using a relative pronoun,
>   without looking at the card. If you got the answer
>   right (as indicated on the card), you may keep the
>   card. If not, you must put the card to one side on
>   the waste pile.
> *   Play then passes to the left until all the cards
>   have been used up, or until a time limit has been
>   reached. The winner of the game is the player who
>   finishes with the highest number of cards kept,
>   plus any bonus points given for the use of more
>   than four adjectives in one turn.

Tourist talk

Speaking challenge

Describe a hotel where you have stayed.	Tal about a place you know which is near the sea.
Describe a meal which you had on holiday.	Describe a historic city which you have visited.
Talk about a monument which tourists visit in your country.	Describe a festival that takes place near your home.
Describe a landscape that you know well.	What tourist facilities are available in your home town?
Talk about a time when you went sightseeing.	Describe something which you learned about another culture on holiday.
What is the impact of tourism on your country?	Which food from your country would you recommend to tourists?
Talk about a time when you went shopping on holiday.	Talk about the weather in your country.
Talk about a relaxing holiday that you have had.	Talk about the different kinds of tourists who visit your country.

Grammar check

There was a guide on the tour. The guide was very helpful. (Answer: There was a guide on the tour who/that was very helpful.)
There are some beautiful mountains. The mountains look wonderful on a sunny day. (Answer: There are some beautiful mountains which/that look wonderful on a sunny day.)
The city has a famous market. You can buy local products in the market. (Answer: The city has a famous market where you can buy local products.)
We need to protect areas of natural beauty. Tourism is having a negative effect on these areas. (Answer: We need to protect areas of natural beauty where tourism is having a negative effect.)
The area is popular with people. These people enjoy shopping. (Answer: The area is popular with people who/that enjoy shopping.)
There's a sandy beach. You can go swimming on that beach in summer. (Answer: There's a sandy beach where you can go swimming in summer.)
In front of the building there is a park. The park is full of flowers. (Answer: In front of the building there is a park which/that is full of flowers.)
We met some local people. They told us a lot about the area. (Answer: We met some local people who/that told us a lot about the area.)
I met some other backpackers. The other backpackers later became my friends. (Answer: I met some other backpackers who/that later became my friends.)
I read a guide book. The guide book helped me to understand the city's history. (Answer: I read a guide book which/that helped me to understand the city's history.)
There is a museum in the city. You can find beautiful paintings in the museum. (Answer: There is a museum in the city where you can find beautiful paintings.)
They gave us a room. The room had a view of the main square. (Answer: They gave us a room which/that had a view of the main square.)

Vocabulary extension

Unit 8

Abbreviations: n/sln/pln = noun / single noun / plural noun; v = verb; adj = adjective; adv = adverb; p = phrase; pv = phrasal verb; T/I = transitive/intransitive; C/U = countable/uncountable

admission *n* [U] the money that you pay to enter a place

atlas *n* [C] a book of maps

bank holiday *p* an official holiday when all banks and most shops and offices are closed

border *n* [C] the line that separates two countries or states

breathtaking scenery *p* very beautiful natural things that you see in the countryside

chalet *n* [C] a small wooden house, often in a mountain area, or for people who are on holiday

collection *n* [C] a group of objects of the same type that have been collected by one person or in one place

exotic *adj* unusual, interesting, and often foreign

exhibit *v* [T] to show objects such as paintings to the public

gallery *n* [C] a room or building that is used for showing paintings and other art to the public

go for a ride *p* to have a journey on a horse or bicycle, or in a vehicle

holiday rep *p* a person who takes care of people on holiday and organises activities for them

honeymoon *n* [C] a holiday taken by two people who have just got married

jungle *n* [C/U] an area of land, usually in tropical countries, where trees and plants grow close together

lake *n* [C] a large area of water which has land all around it

leisure time *p* the time when you are not working or doing other duties

long-haul flight *n* [C] an aeroplane journey that travels a long distance

nearby *adv* not far away

on display *p* If something is on display, it is there for people to look at.

overlook *v* [T] to have a view of something from above

pursuit *n* [C/U] when you try to achieve a plan, activity, or situation, usually over a long period of time

remote *adj* far away

self-catering holiday *n* [C] a holiday in which you cook meals for yourself rather than having them provided for you

take a break *p* to go away for a short holiday or have a period of time away from work, school, etc.

unspoilt area *n* [C] An unspoilt area is beautiful because it has not been changed or damaged by people.

valley *n* [C] an area of low land between hills or mountains

Complete IELTS Bands 4–5 by Guy Brook-Hart and Vanessa Jakeman with David Jay © Cambridge University Press 2012

❶ Complete the paragraph by writing a word from the box in each gap. There are three words which you do not need to use.

receive	speak	come	learn	participate
give	write	attend	use	

I've just started a course at university, and I'm finding it very different from studying at school. I **0** ......*use*........ the university library a lot, and I **1** .... lectures every day. I also **2** .... in seminars a few times a week. As part of my course I have to **3** .... regular assignments, and then I **4** .... feedback on them from my tutor. Next term, I'll have to **5** .... a presentation to my tutor and some other students.

❷ Complete the sentences with the correct form of the verb *rise* or *raise*.

0 College fees are going to ....*rise*......... next year.

1 Literacy levels in this country have .... a lot recently.

2 The government has plans to .... the school leaving age.

3 The number of students graduating from university .... last year.

4 The new principal has .... the standard of education in the college.

5 Sales of e-books are .... in all European countries.

❸ Complete the paragraph by writing a preposition (*by, with, to*, etc.) in each gap.

Tourism in Britain 2000–2010

Foreign tourism in Britain grew steadily during the first seven years of the decade. The greatest rise was in 2004, when the number of tourists visiting Britain increased **0** ......*from*...... 24.7m in 2003 **1** .... 27.8m in 2004. The number of foreign tourists coming to Britain peaked **2** .... 32.8m in 2007. This was followed by a fall **3** .... approximately 10% between 2007 and 2010. While there was a large drop **4** .... the number of American visitors between 2000 and 2010, the value of the Indian tourist trade in Britain grew **5** .... 168% over the same period.

❹ Choose the best alternative (A, B or C) for each of these sentences.

0   I like taking holidays in countries ....*where*........ there are not so many tourists.

    A that   **B** where   **C** which

1   Have you ever met anyone .... has been to Antarctica?

    A where   **B** which   **C** who

2   Bali is an island .... I would love to see.

    A where   **B** who   **C** that

3   The 'Lonely Planet' guides are books .... many travellers find very useful.

    A which   **B** who   **C** where

4   The Arctic is a place .... you can really see the effects of global warming.

    A where   **B** which   **C** that

5   Most visitors prefer to stay somewhere .... is in easy reach of an airport.

    A who   **B** that   **C** where

❺ Read the paragraph and then complete the sentences below, writing one word from the paragraph in each gap.

Taking holidays abroad has become increasingly common in recent years, with southern Spain becoming a top destination for foreign tourists. There are a large number of well-known resorts situated all along its coastline. These offer visitors a wide choice of accommodation – from secluded luxury villas to bustling bargain hotels. Many hotels have swimming pools, bars and restaurants, and even shops, gyms and beauty salons. In fact, there are so many facilities on offer that some tourists spend all their time there. However, those visitors who choose not to leave their hotel miss the chance to discover the fascinating local culture of the area, which includes traditional villages, beautiful ancient cities and historic castles.

0   More and more people have been taking holidays ......*abroad*...... in recent years.

1   The south of Spain has become a very popular tourist ....

2   The coast has a large number of well-known .... for holiday-makers.

3   There are many different types of .... available for visitors to the area.

4   Many hotels in southern Spain provide a range of ....

5   Some tourists miss the opportunity to learn about the .... of the region.

❻ Complete the sentences by putting the adjectives in brackets into the gaps in the correct order.

0   You can get ....*beautiful gold*.... jewellery in Venice.   (gold/beautiful)

1   Dubai has many .... buildings.   (impressive/modern)

2   We went to a .... tea house in Japan.   (traditional/lovely)

3   Most cities have a few .... areas.   (industrial/dull)

4   Harry bought some .... luggage for the trip.   (expensive/new)

5   A .... taxi-driver gave us a sightseeing tour.   (local/friendly)

Unit 9 Every drop counts

Unit objectives

- **Listening:** matching features; diagram labelling; flow-chart completion
- **Reading:** matching paragraph headings; sentence completion; pick from a list
- **Spelling:** words with a final *-e*
- **Vocabulary:** words connected with water filtration – *pump, pressure, drought, well*, etc.; guessing meaning from context; outdoor activities connected with water – *swimming, fishing*, etc.
- **Speaking Parts 2 and 3:** beginning and ending talks; dealing with questions; asking students to compare, name and explain
- **Pronunciation:** intonation to express interest or to show the speaker is finishing
- **Writing Task 1:** describing a diagram; using sequencers and time markers; planning and comparing
- **Grammar:** the passive

Starting off

❶ *As a warmer* With books closed, tell students that the unit they're going to start now is about water. Ask them: *How much water do you think you use every day, for washing, drinking, cooking, cleaning, etc.?* Get the whole class to discuss this together.

- Read the following to students and ask them to write down the figures as listening practice: *the average person in the US uses 466 litres a day just for personal and household use (shower – 60–115 litres; brushing teeth – 3.75–7.5 litres; washing dishes – 35–75 litres; flushing the toilet – 20–36 litres; drinking – 3–4 litres).*

Answers
1 c 2 d 3 b 4 e 5 f 6 a

❷ *Extension idea* Tell students that other interesting statistics are: a flight from Los Angeles to San Francisco (700 miles round trip) consumes 40,000 litres of water; nearly 900 million people have no access to clean water. For further practice in writing numbers, you can ask them to write these figures down.

❸ *Extension idea 2* If it's appropriate for your class, tell students to ask each other about their habits in connection with the statistics (e.g. *How many cups of coffee do you drink a day? Do you have leaky taps?*, etc.).

Listening Matching; flow-chart completion

❶ *As a warmer* Tell students: *You're going to listen to a student preparing to give a talk to other students.* Write these questions on the board and ask students to discuss them in pairs:

- *Why is it important to prepare before you give a talk?*
- *What things can you do to prepare a talk?*
- *How do you think students benefit from giving talks to other students?*
- *Why do people get nervous before giving talks? Do you think being nervous is a positive or a negative thing?*

❷ Students did a matching task in Unit 6. When students look at the instructions, ask them:

- *How many questions are there: three or five?* (five)
- *Can you use the same letter for more than one question?* (yes)
- *Can you answer the question with more than one letter?* (no)

Suggested underlining

Question: comment / tutor / each part

Options: **A** shorter **B** ideas / difficult to follow **C** information / added

❸ 🎧 To replicate exam conditions, play the recording once only. Students can then compare their answers with a partner. You can play the recording a second time for them to check.

Answers
1 C 2 B 3 A 4 B 5 C

Extension idea When students have finished, ask them to read the recording script on page 169 to see why each answer is correct.

❹ If students don't know all these words, tell them not to guess, but to match up the ones they do know first. This will narrow the choice for the words they don't know.

Extension idea Read out the following background information and ask students to write down the statistics as you read.

Desalination uses large amounts of energy and is very expensive. The largest plant in the world is in the UAE. This produces 300 million cubic metres of water per year. Worldwide there are 13,080 desalination plants and they produce 12 billion gallons of water per day.

> **Answers**
> **2** a **3** e **4** b **5** d

❺ Before students start, ask them what this flow chart shows (*answer*: the desalination process). Remind them they should always look at titles if supplied.

- Ask: *How many words can you write in each gap?* (*answer*: one or two)

- Ask: *Are all the Questions part of the flow chart?* (*answer*: no, 6 is separate)

Use the example: Ask:
– *How do you know it's a noun?* (*answer*: it comes between an article and the verb)
– *How do you know it's an animal?* (*answer*: throat) For some students, you may have to explain *throat*.

> **Answers**
> **6** noun / type of animal   **7** noun / place
> **8** adjective / describes process   **9** noun / something that can be harmed   **10** noun / a crop or type of land

❻ 🎧 As before, play the recording once, then again when students have compared answers. To check their answers, they can look at the recording script.

> **Answers**
> **6** seabird / sea(-) bird **7** plant **8** expensive **9** fish / marine life   **10** farmland / farm(-) land

Extension idea Ask students to look at the recording script and to underline words and phrases which introduce a new stage in the process which the student is describing.

- Write them on the board and ask students to copy them into their notebooks; they may be useful for describing processes in Writing Task 1 (*the first stage is…, the second stage, the next stage, the next point, after that*).

- Elicit other possible words and phrases for sequencing a process (e.g. *first, first of all, next, finally, lastly*).

❼ The disadvantages mentioned are that it's expensive and it is harmful to marine life. Other disadvantages might include the amounts of energy used to produce clean water, the need to construct underground pipes and plants and the damage this can cause to the environment, the problems that may result if a plant breaks down, etc. Parts of the world that have problems getting fresh water are those that receive little rainfall and have poor economies (e.g. many countries in Africa).

Reading
Matching headings; sentence completion; pick from a list

❶ *As a warmer* With books closed, ask students to work in pairs and say what they know about the reading test – you can write *number of parts, number of questions, time* on the board. When they have answered the questions in the book, ask them to check their answers by looking at the Exam overview on page 7.

> **Answers**
> **1** an hour   **2** three   **3** 20 minutes   **4** 40   **5** one
> **6** on the answer sheet   **7** spelling / number of words / grammar if a sentence

Extension idea *Ask students: What can you do, apart from course work, to prepare for the IELTS reading test?* (*suggestion*: students should read extensively as well as doing intensive IELTS-style reading practice. They can find scientific and academic articles on almost any subject on the internet, and should form a habit of reading them. Point out that IELTS reading topics include all the ones in this book, so building their knowledge of vocabulary and ideas related to these topics will help them understand the passages in the exam.)

❷ Ask students: *What do you think running water is?* (*answer*: a working water system in your house) *Where can people get water if they don't have running water in their houses?* (*answer*: from wells, rainwater, rivers, or by buying it).

> **Suggested answers**
> **1** the time and effort needed to go and fetch water
> **2** thirst, poor hygiene, disease

❸ *Alternative treatment* Ask students: *Apart from the title and subheading, what else should you look at before you read a passage?* (*answer*: any pictures or illustrations which accompany the passage).

- Tell students to look at the photograph and ask: *What does it show? What are the problems of having to fetch water in this way?*

- Tell them to use the photograph to help them decide what *burden* and *transformed* mean.

> **Answers**
> **1** *burden* has two meanings: something difficult or unpleasant that you have to deal with or worry about; and something heavy that you must carry. Both meanings are alluded to in the title. *transformed* = changed completely, usually an improvement.
> **2** b and d

Extension idea To perhaps further arouse your students' interest in the passage, ask:

– *Who has to bring the water? (answer:* women*)*

– *Why do you think women do this task?*

– *If they didn't have to do this, how do you think their societies would be transformed? Why?*

④ Give students two minutes to scan for and underline the words in the passage. Elicit that they should then read round the words to decide which is the correct definition – this will take longer.

Alternative treatment If you wish your students to deal with the reading passage and the exam-style tasks without pre-teaching vocabulary, you can do this exercise after Exercise 7.

> **Answers**
> They are all nouns.
> **1** c **2** f **3** a **4** d **5** b **6** e

⑤ Students did matching headings in Unit 3. This is the only IELTS reading task which is printed before the passage itself. Tell them that it's essential to read the headings carefully and understand them before they read the passage.

Alternative treatment Ask students to work in pairs and say what they think each heading means using their own words.

> **Suggested underlining**
> **i** plans / failed **ii** rural / urban / problem
> **iii** possible success **iv** new management style
> **v** statistics **vi** regular trip **vii** people / disease
> **viii** water / change / lives

Extension idea before reading the passage

• With books closed, ask students to work in pairs and remember the headings – they should note them down, but not worry about getting exactly the same words.

• When they've finished, ask them to compare their lists with another pair and then check in the book.

• Before they do the task, tell them that they should read the paragraphs one by one (i.e. read paragraph A and find the heading, read paragraph B and do the same, etc.). Tell them that to do this task, they should really read the passage carefully just once; in the exam they won't have time to do more.

• When students have finished, ask them to work in pairs or small groups and compare their answers. Where they disagree, they should refer back to the passage to justify their choices and try to reach a consensus.

• When you round up with the whole class, elicit why Paragraph A matches 'A regular trip for some people' (*answer: Alylito...has made this journey three times a day*), etc. Get students to explain why they chose the other answers.

> **Answers**
> **1** vi (*She has made this journey three times a day since she was a small child. So has every other woman in her village*)
>
> **2** v (*nearly 900 million people in the world have no access to clean water; 2.5 billion people have no safe way to get rid of human waste; lack of proper hygiene cause disease and kills 3.3 million people around the world annually*)
>
> **3** viii (*Communities where clean water becomes accessible and plentiful are transformed*)
>
> **4** i (*the biggest problem with water schemes is that about half of them break down*)
>
> **5** iv (*a UK-based international non-profit organization called WaterAid; Their approach; But the real innovation is*)
>
> **6** iii (*If all goes well, Aylito Binayo will have a tap with safe water just a three-minute walk from her front door.*)

⑥ Students did sentence completion in Unit 5.

• Ask them: *Will you have to answer the questions using your own words or words and numbers from the passage?* (words and numbers from the passage)

• Ask them: *Why is it important to underline the key ideas?* (*answer:* this will help them to scan the passage to find where the question is answered).

Alternative treatment When students have underlined the key ideas and decided what information is missing, give them two minutes to scan the passage and locate the parts they need to read more carefully to answer the questions.

> **Suggested underlining**
> **7** water levels / falling / because (noun – something that affects river levels) **8** globally / people who die (a number) **9** families / clean water / spend more time (noun – something people grow) **10** knowledge / equipment / dig (noun – something that is built) **11** WaterAid / dam / capture rainwater (noun – something used to make a dam)

> **Answers**
> **7** drought **8** 3.3 million **9** crops **10** wells
> **11** sand

7 Students did pick from a list in Unit 5.

- Remind them that they shouldn't read the whole passage again to answer the questions.

- When they've underlined, give them half a minute to find the right place in the passage (paragraph F). Elicit that they should do this by scanning for the name of the place – Orbesho. Tell them that names are always good to scan for if they occur in questions because they cannot be paraphrased, so they occur in the passage exactly as they are in the question.

- Give students the time they need to answer the questions correctly.

- When they have finished, ask them to compare their answers in pairs.

> **Suggested underlining**
> TWO activities / performed / villagers / Orbesho
> **Answers**
> **A** (*residents even constructed a road themselves*) and
> **C** (*They have … collected stones for the structures.*)

8 Encourage students to brainstorm other necessities for a poor village.

- Encourage them also to talk about people's experience in their country if, for example, people have moved recently from villages to cities.

- Get students to think about why they moved and what they gained, but also what things people have lost by leaving their villages (e.g. social ties, close family ties, a quiet life, etc.).

Spelling Some common mistakes

1 Tell students to copy these words correctly into their notebooks. Round up their answers by asking them to dictate the correct spelling to you, which you write on the board.

> **Answers**
> **2** furthermore **3** disease **4** business **5** experience
> **6** machines **7** available **8** believe **9** create
> **10** involve

2 *Alternative treatment* Dictate the words to your students, who write them down and then check the spelling in the passage.

Vocabulary
effect, benefit, advantage/disadvantage

1 *Extension idea* Ask students to work in small groups and look at sentences a and d. Ask them:

- *What advantages does village life have?*

- *What other disadvantages do modern cities have?*

When they have finished discussing, ask students to work alone and complete these sentences:

- *In my opinion the main advantage of village life is …*

- *The main disadvantage of city life is …*

They then compare their sentences with their group and round up by reading them to the whole class.

> **Answers**
> **2** have; on **3** of **4** for **5** has; on

2 Tell students these are words they will often have to use in the IELTS test and that they should take extra care when using them.

- When they have finished correcting the sentences, ask them: *What mistakes do students generally make with these words?* (they use the wrong verb or the wrong preposition). Elicit which verb and which preposition they should use.

> **Answers**
> **2** ~~for tourism~~ of tourism **3** ~~effect to~~ effect on
> **4** ✓ **5** ~~has not given~~ has not had
> **6** ~~advantage and disadvantage~~ in advantages and disadvantages of **7** ~~effect quality~~ effect on quality
> **8** ~~give a lot of advantages~~ offer/bring us a lot of advantages

Speaking Parts 2 and 3

1 *As a warmer* With books closed, tell students that they are going to work on Speaking Parts 2 and 3. Write on the board: *What happens in these parts of the test?*

- Ask students to work in pairs and answer the questions. When they have finished, ask them to compare their ideas with another pair. They can then check their answers by looking at the Exam overview on page 7.

> **Answers**
> **1** one minute **2** two **3** will **4** can **5** general
> **6** can

2 Students need to quickly decide what they're going to talk about and then make notes.

- Tell students always to choose a topic or activity to talk about which they think they are going to find easiest.

- Tell students that they can't change the topic but that it doesn't matter whether what they say is truthful or not. Sometimes they have to use their imagination. 'In or near water' is deliberately vague to give them scope for invention.

- Since this is near the end of the course, give students exactly one minute to make notes.

3 Students also worked on phrases to structure their talks in Unit 3, Exercise 7 on page 7. Ask students to look at the exercise to remind themselves.

When students have done this exercise, point out that by using these phrases, Carlos has:

- clearly structured his talk; the examiner will know what point Carlos is making at all times;
- used his own words, not merely repeated the task.

Remind students that they will get extra marks if they can do this and it is one of the things to consider during the minute they have to make notes.

Alternative treatment Tell students that Carlos is doing the Speaking task in Exercise 2. Ask them to look at the task and these phrases and predict what word will go in each gap. By doing this they should see that each phrase relates closely to one of the instructions in the task, but uses Carlos's own words (e.g. *describe – talk about*).

Answers
2 get   **3** places   **4** simple   **5** all

4

Answers
1 to introduce the talk   **2–4** to introduce each point
5 to finish the talk

5 Before they start, ask students to suggest phrases that they can use to introduce the different parts of their talks (you can write them on the board and students can copy them to their notebooks). Tell them that their phrases will probably be different because they will be talking about different subjects from Carlos.

Alternative treatment Before they start, ask students to think of good advice for candidates doing Part 2 (e.g. try to keep going for two minutes).

- Note on the board five or six good pieces of advice suggested by students.
- Ask the student who is listening to give feedback at the end based on the advice: which things did their partner do well and which could they do better?
- Round up useful feedback with the whole class. Then ask students to change roles and the student who was listening before should give their talk.
- Repeat the feedback process, then ask students to change partners and give their talks again.

Note: Now is a good moment to do the Pronunciation section on page 94, which is based on Carlos's answer.

6 Tell students that it helps if they can recognise what they are being asked to do in each question in Part 3 (compare, name, explain, etc.) so that they can answer with suitable language. Remind them they should always give a general answer; in this part they are not asked about themselves and their experiences.

Answers
1 a 2   **b** 1   **c** 3   **2** students' own answers

Extension idea For Question 1, ask students:

- *How many sports do you think you should name for question 1?* (at least four)
- *Should you just give a list of popular water sports, or should you explain a little about why they are popular, or say some things the sports have in common?* (explain a little)

For Question 2, elicit some aspects of the two sports which students can compare (e.g. danger, the amount of physical exercise, equipment, etc.).

For Question 3, think about people you know who don't like water sports. What are their reasons? Are they afraid of water? Can they swim? If you don't like water sports, use your own reasons but remember to speak generally.

7 Before they do the exercise, ask students to work in pairs and underline the different water sports which are mentioned and decide what each of them is (surfing, sailing, waterskiing, canoeing, rowing and swimming).

After they have done the exercise, ask them to check their spelling by looking at the script on page 170.

Alternative treatment Ask students to work in pairs and try to fill the gaps before they listen.

Answers
2 include   **3** Other   **4** easiest   **5** whereas   **6** more
7 cheaper   **8** depends   **9** reason   **10** possibility

Extension idea 1 Tell students: *The questions ask the candidate to name, compare and explain things.*

- *What things does Carlos name in A?* (surfing, sailing, waterskiing, canoeing, rowing, swimming)
- *What comparison does he make in B?* (between surfing and swimming)
- *What explanations does he give in C?* (reasons why some people don't like water sports)

Extension idea 2 Focus on the language Carlos uses. Ask the following questions, and with each answer, ask students to suggest their own sentences using the phrases focused on. Write good ones on the board and ask students to copy them into their notebooks.

- *What phrase does he use when he needs time to get his next idea? (let me think)*
- *Which word does he use to compare the idea 'surfers need a lot of waves' and 'swimmers usually prefer calm water'?* (whereas)
- *Which words does he use in B to introduce different items on his list? (For a start, also, lastly)*
- *What does he say in C to say different people have different reasons? (I think it depends on the person.)*
- *What phrase does he use to introduce a different possible reason? (Another possibility is that ...)*

❽ Students should work with a different partner from their partner in Exercise 5. Tell them to use the ideas they thought of when they did Exercise 5 – not just to repeat Carlos's answer.

❾ Ask students: *Which question asks you to ... ?*
- *name things*
- *compare two things*
- *explain something*

Alternative treatment Ask the students who are listening to give feedback on how their partners could answer the questions better. Get suggestions on this from the whole class. Then ask students to change partners and ask and answer the questions again.

Pronunciation Intonation 2

❶ 🎧 ***Alternative treatment*** Ask students to read the introductory information. Then ask: *Do you use intonation to show the same things in your language?*

❷

> **Answers**
>
> 1 For a start, you need a lot of waves to surf, whereas swimmers usually prefer calm water.
>
> 2 Yeah and lastly swimming's cheaper than surfing!
>
> 3 Even some people who can swim are afraid of water.
>
> 4 Another possibility is that these days the sea can be very polluted and they may be afraid of getting ill.

❸ 🎧 Tell students that there is no one correct intonation; it depends what they speaker is trying to indicate and that their answers where different may also sound natural.

❹ ***Extension idea*** Ask students, after they've practised, to read out sentences to the whole class. The class can say if they have used the intonation correctly or not.

❺ ***Extension idea*** Ask students to read out their answers to the whole class as well.

Writing Task 1

❶ ***As a warmer*** With books closed, tell students they are going to look at Writing Task 1. Ask them to work in small groups and try to remember as much as possible about what Task 1 involves. As prompts, you can write on the board: *number of words, time, instructions, type of information, things you must always include, number of marks.* When they have finished, round up with the whole class and then refer them to the Exam overview on page 7 to check their answers and for anything they've missed.

Tell students that sometimes in Task 1, they have to summarise a diagram showing how something works, or a process.

Before answering the questions:

- tell students to look at the diagram and its labels and decide what each of the following are (you can write them on the board): *lid, barrel* and *drum.*
- ask them to point out a pipe and a tap on the diagram.
- ask them to look at the instructions and underline the key ideas. (*system/ places without running water/ turns dirty water into clean water*)

> **Answers**
>
> 1 a (plastic) barrel, a (storage) drum, pipe and tap, plastic lid   2 sand, gravel and charcoal   3 It is poured into the top of the barrel   4 It comes out of the bottom of the drum   5 It passes the clean water from the bottom of the barrel into the drum.

❷ ***Alternative treatment*** Before they complete the plan, ask students to read the sample answer while looking at the diagram and to look at how the sample answer summarises the information in the diagram.

> **Answers**
>
> a list   b build   c operate   d overview

Extension idea 1 Ask students to work in small groups, look at the sample answer and the diagram and discuss what sort of language they have to produce in order to do the task. To get them started, ask:

- *Do you have to know the names of the parts of the device before you look at the diagram?* (no)
- *Do you have to express how they are placed?* (yes)
- *Do you have to express how the device works or is used?* (yes)

Extension idea 2 Ask students to underline the verbs in the answer and, where necessary, look up their definitions in a dictionary. Ask them to copy useful verbs into their notebooks (they should underline: *filtering, placed, linked, fixed, poured, goes, stored, comes out, shows, produce*).

Extension idea 3 Tell students that the writer of the sample answer used his own words where possible instead of copying the words from the instructions.

- Remind students that they will get higher marks if they can use their own words.
- Ask them to find words and phrases in the sample answer which mean the same as words and phrases in the instructions (*system – method; turns dirty water into clean water – filtering dirty water; clean water – drinking water*).

Note: Now is a good moment to do the Key grammar section on the passive on page 96.

❸ Elicit why it's important to use words and phrases to mark the order in which things happen (*answer*: so readers can follow the process easily).

Remind students that when they write, they must always ask themselves: *Is what I'm writing clear to the reader?* If the examiner cannot understand what they have written, they will lose marks.

> **Answers**
> **a** first   **b** finally   **c** when
> **d** next / after that / then

Extension idea 1 Ask students to copy the time markers into their notebooks and add others they can think of to their list. They then check the Language reference section on page 129 to complete their list.

Extension idea 2 If you did the extension idea in Listening Exercise 6, refer students to the phrases they noted down then. Tell them these can also be used in writing tasks. If you didn't do the extension idea, you can still refer students to the recording script and do it now.

❹ **Answers**
> **1** ~~The first~~ First/Firstly   **2** ~~Than~~ Then
> **3** ~~Finaly~~ Finally   **4** ~~At last~~ Finally / Lastly
> **5** ~~low, when low~~. When

❺ **Answers**
> **1 A** 1–2 metres **B** 50 metres
> **2 A** people **B** an ox or animal
> **3 A** basket and ropes **B** bucket, rollers and pulley
> **4 A** / **B** irrigation

Extension idea Ask students: *Which system uses a well?* (*answer*: B) *Where can water come from for the first system?* (*answer*: any source which is close to the surface).

❻ Tell the students who are listening to help their partner to describe where necessary. When they have finished, round up with the whole class so as to establish clearly how each system works.

❼ Ask students, while they are discussing, to make a plan. When they have finished, ask them to work with another pair and compare their plans.

> **Suggested answers**
> **1** There are two methods to compare; the similarities and differences can be highlighted as outlined in questions 1–4 in Exercise 4.
> **2** up to four paragraphs: an introduction (1), descriptions of each diagram / across the diagrams (2), a final comment + overview (4).
> **3** Begin with a statement about what the diagrams show and end by bringing out the main differences: the depth and location of the water and the collection methods (also the overview).

❽ This Writing task is probably best done for homework. Tell students that as this is nearly the end of the course, they should try to write their answer in 20 minutes. Candidates who spend too long on Task 1 do not have time to deal properly with Task 2 and so lose marks.

Extension idea 1 Give students a deadline for bringing their answers to class. When they bring them to class, ask them to exchange answers with a partner and compare what they have written. Partners should make suggestions for corrections and improvements before the finalised answers are handed in to you for correction.

Extension idea 2 Photocopy and hand out the sample answer below. Ask students to:

- compare the answer with the diagrams;
- say the purpose of each paragraph;
- compare the answer with their answers.

> **Sample answer**
> The diagrams show two traditional systems that can be used to collect water.
>
> The swing basket is used to collect ground water that is usually 1–2 metres deep. It consists of a bamboo or leather basket tied to ropes. First, two people hold the ropes and collect the water from the ground. Then they swing it over a hill and into irrigation channels where it flows to farmland.
>
> Unlike the swing basket, the rope and bucket are pulled by an ox. This animal is stronger than humans so it can be used to collect water from a 50-metre well. This method consists of a bucket and a pulley system. The ox is attached to the pulley and as it walks downhill, the bucket rises from the well. Water is then poured into irrigation channels.
>
> Clearly, both methods are easy to operate. However, they rely on different forms of power and collect water from different depths.

Key grammar The passive

❶ Go through the construction of passive verbs.

- Tell students the passive uses the verb *to be* in any tense, plus the past participle.
- Ask them to suggest other examples of the past participle with both regular and irregular verbs to ensure that they know what it is.
- When you work on when the passive is used (when we don't say who or what does/did something), point out that it is often used to describe processes. Ask: *Can you see who is pouring the water in the diagram in Writing exercise 1?* (*answer*: no) *So you will have to use the passive (i.e. Dirty water is poured ...) as you cannot invent information in this part of the Writing test.*

When students have done the exercise, go through the Language reference section on page 129.

> **Answers**
> 1 b and d   **2** b and d   **3** a and b are Present Simple; c and d are Past Simple

Extension idea Write the following sentences on the board:

- *Engineers install air conditioning in most public buildings.*

- *Scientists identified the whale from photographs.*

Ask students to work in pairs and write the sentences in the passive. If they need help, tell them to start with *Air conditioning* and *The whale*. They should also look at the tense of the original sentences and use this with the verb *to be* (*answer: Air conditioning is installed in most public buildings.; The whale was identified from photographs.*).

② **Answers**
> are placed, are linked, is made, is fixed, is poured, is stored, is turned on, can be used

Extension idea When students have finished, draw their attention to the last passive with *can* and ask them how the passive is formed with *can* (*can* + infinitive (*be*) + past participle).

- Elicit other sentences with *can* + passive and write them on the board. Ask students to correct any mistakes and to copy the corrected sentences into their notebooks.

- Ask: *What other words like 'can' can be used with 'be' + a past participle?* Students should be able to suggest *must, should, might, may* and other modal verbs. Ask them to suggest sentences as examples for each of these.

- You can write them on the board and ask students to copy them into their notebooks.

Note: correct copying into notebooks, apart from supplying students with a reference, is excellent practice at this level for several IELTS exam tasks.

③ ***Alternative treatment*** Use the example: elicit why the passive is used in this sentence (*answer:* the person/people who do this are not mentioned). For the second sentence ask: *What causes the water shortage?* (drought) *So, the thing which does the action is mentioned; should you use the active or the passive?* (active). Students can then do the other sentences in pairs, then compare answers.

> **Answers**
> 2 were dug   **3** have been involved
> 4 was constructed   **5** believes

④ **Answers**
> 2 ~~which shows~~ which is shown / shown
> 3 ~~did not affect~~ was not affected
> 4 ~~was occurred~~ occurred   **5** ~~should be provide~~ should be provided   **6** ~~is came~~ comes

Unit 9 photocopiable activity: Time for a shower!   Time: 40-50 minutes

> **Objectives**
> - To practise the passive when describing diagrams
> - To revise the use of time markers
> - To practise writing introductory sentences and overviews for Writing Task 1 questions
> - To recycle vocabulary for describing water systems

Before class

You will need to photocopy page 107 and cut it into two parts, so that half of the students have 'Student A' cards, and the other half have 'Student B' cards.

❶ Divide the class into two groups, A and B. Give a card to each student. Ask students to work in pairs with other members of their group to look at the diagrams and read through the descriptions on their card. Then ask them to work together to choose the correct form of the verbs (either active or passive) or the correct time marker. Explain that they will be able to check their answers later.

❷ Now ask students to find a different partner from the other group. They take turns to read their completed paragraph aloud and see if it matches the correct version on their partner's card.

❸ For the final phase, students stay in their A/B pairs and work together to complete the introductory sentence and final overview for both diagrams, in the relevant spaces on their card. When they have finished, elicit some possible versions from different pairs, before agreeing on the best one and writing it up on the board.

Student A

The diagrams show ....

The electric shower [1] *uses/is used* cold water from the mains. It [2] *consists/is consisted* of a simple shower unit which [3] *takes/is taken* electricity from a consumer unit. The supply of electricity [4] *can control/can be controlled* using a switch. [5] *First/The first*, the cold water [6] *takes/is taken* from the mains. [7] *Then/Than* it [8] *heats/is heated* directly in the shower unit. [9] *After that/After the* heated water [10] *arrives/is arrived* at the shower head.

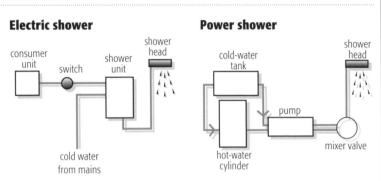

Unlike the electric shower, the power shower uses water which has already been heated in the central heating system. Firstly, hot water is taken from the hot water cylinder, while cold water arrives from the cold water tank. Then the hot and cold water is pumped into the shower by a special pump. Finally, the water is mixed by a valve before it comes out of the shower head.

Clearly, both systems ....

However, ...

Student B

The diagrams show ....

The electric shower uses cold water from the mains. It consists of a simple shower unit which takes electricity from a consumer unit. The supply of electricity can be controlled using a switch. First, the cold water is taken from the mains. Then it is heated directly in the shower unit. After that the heated water arrives at the shower head.

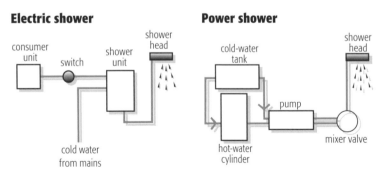

Unlike the electric shower, the power shower [1] *uses/is used* water which [2] *has already heated/ has already been heated* in the central heating system. [3] *Firstly/At first*, hot water [4] *takes/is taken* from the hot water cylinder, while cold water [5] *arrives/is arrived* from the cold water tank. [6] *When/Then* the hot and cold water [7] *is pumped/are pumped* into the shower by a special pump. [8] *At last/Finally*, the water [9] *mixes/is mixed* by a valve before it [10] *comes/is come out* of the shower head.

Clearly, both systems ....

However, ...

Vocabulary extension

Unit 9

Abbreviations: n/sln/pln = noun / single noun / plural noun; v = verb; adj = adjective; adv = adverb; p = phrase; pv = phrasal verb; T/I = transitive/intransitive; C/U = countable/uncountable

bottled water *n* [U] water which has been treated in order to make it very clean or which has come from a special place, and which is sold in bottles

cause damage *p* to harm or spoil something

control *v* [T] to order, limit or rule natural events such as the weather

drinkable *adj* clean and safe to drink

depth *n* [C/U] the distance from the top of something to the bottom

evaporate *v* [I/T] If a liquid evaporates or is evaporated, it changes into gas or vapour very small drops of water.

extreme weather *p* very severe or bad weather

faucet *n* [C] an object at the end of a pipe which you turn to control the flow of water

harbour *n* [C] an area of water near the coast where ships are kept and are safe from the sea

heatwave *n* [C] a period of time, usually a few days or weeks, when the weather is much hotter than usual

liquid *n* [C/U] a substance, for example water, that is not solid and that can be poured easily

mineral water *n* [C/U] water which is taken from the ground and contains chemicals that are good for your health

moisture *n* [U] very small drops of water in the air or on a surface

mudslide *n* [C] a mass of wet earth moving suddenly and quickly down a steep slope

pouring with rain *p* raining heavily, producing a lot of water

puddle *n* [C] a pool of liquid on the ground, usually from rain

recede *v* [I] to become further and further away

resource *n* [C] something that a country, person, or organisation has which they can use

shallow *adj* not deep

sewage *n* [U] waste water and waste from toilets

sink *v* [I/T] to go down or make something go down below the surface of water and not come back up

soaking wet *p* completely wet

stream *n* [C] a small river

tank *n* [C] a large container for storing liquid or gas

tide *n* [C] the regular rise and fall in the level of the sea

typhoon signal *n* [C] a warning that violent storm with very strong winds is about to happen

waterfall *n* [C] a stream of water that flows from a high place, often to a pool below

water shortage *n* [C/U] when there is not enough water

widespread (drought / floods) *adj* affecting or including a lot of places, people, etc.

Unit 10 Buildings

Unit objectives

- **Reading Section 3:** multiple-choice questions; matching sentence endings; Yes / No / Not Given
- **Listening Section 4:** note completion
- **Vocabulary:** adjectives to describe buildings *fun, impressive*, etc.; parts of buildings *structure, roof,* etc.; verb phrases *fit in, stand out*, etc.; deducing meanings from shape of word and context
- **Speaking Parts 2 and 3:** describing a building; answering Part 2 follow-up questions; linking ideas with *although, so* and *even though*; talking about different types of building
- **Pronunciation:** sentence stress to show contrast
- **Writing Task 2:** tasks with two viewpoints; analysing the question and brainstorming ideas; analysing a sample answer; correcting spelling and punctuation errors; using commas correctly
- **Grammar:** using linkers for contrast; modal verbs for possibility, certainty and obligation
- **Spelling:** correcting mistakes in a sample answer to a writing task

Starting off

❶ *As a warmer* With books closed, tell students to work in pairs. Tell them: *Think of a building in your town or city which you think visitors should see. What is its purpose and why is it interesting for visitors?*

To encourage student independence, don't help them with vocabulary. Tell them they should try to guess words and match the quotes in spite of not knowing all the words.

> **Suggested answers**
> a 4   b 6   c 2   d 1   e 5   f 3

Extension idea 1 Focus on vocabulary at this point.

- Write these words and phrases on the board: *escalator, stands out, falling down, fits in well with, surroundings.*
- Ask students to work in pairs or small groups and discuss what each of these words and phrases means (*answers: escalator* – moving stairs; *stand out* – to be very easy to see or notice; *fall down* – fall to the ground; *fit in with* – look pleasant together; *surroundings* – the place where someone or something is).

- Elicit other sentences from students using these words. Write correct sentences on the board and ask students to copy them to their notebooks.

Extension idea 2 Ask students to work in small groups and write down four other remarks they can make about the buildings, but without mentioning which building it is. Students then read out their remarks to the class, who have to say which building they are talking about.

❷ *Alternative treatment* Ask students to do this exercise in small groups. When they have finished discussing, ask one student to look at the answers on page 175 and tell them to the others.

Note: The Reading passage is about the Pompidou Centre. The answers on page 175 contain no information about it, as students will find out as they read.

> **Answers**
> 1 Exhibition hall   2 Apartment block   3 Library
> 4 Cultural Arts Centre   5 Hotel   6 Shop

❸ Tell students to use some of the language from the quotes in Exercise 1 to give reasons for their answers.

Reading 1
Multiple choice; matching sentence endings, Yes / No / Not Given

❶ *As a warmer* If appropriate, ask students: *Have any of you been to Paris and seen the Pompidou Centre? What's it like? What did you see there? Did you like it?*

Ask students: *What large, impressive buildings are there in your region/country? What is their purpose?*

Alternative treatment Help students by asking:

- *Who comes to see these buildings?* (*answer*: tourists, business people, visiting politicians, etc.)
- *Do companies or businesses like offices in impressive buildings? Why?* (*answer*: yes, because it gives a good impression of the company)
- *Who organises and pays for impressive buildings in your region/country?* (students' own answers)

> **Suggested answers**
> 1 they bring visitors into the city; they improve the status of a city; they have a special purpose (e.g. an arts centre)
> 2 local government / councils; national government; taxpayers

❷ The passage in this unit is approaching the level of difficulty of a Reading Section 3 passage in the live test. Reading Section 3 is the hardest part of the IELTS test and is normally aimed at students with a CEFR level of C1. Students studying this book are closer to B1 and will therefore find the passage hard. However, the exercises before they read and while they are reading are intended to give them the support and techniques to get to grips with the passage and the reading tasks as well as they can. Moreover, the simplified and shortened passages earlier in the book are all designed to bring students to the stage where they can realistically deal with full-length IELTS reading passages and maximise their scores on the tasks.

This exercise will give students an idea of the difficulty of the passage. They will see the logic of the quite long vocabulary section which follows this exercise before they do the exam-style Reading tasks. Remind students of the steps they should go through when approaching a Reading section.

1 Glance at the passage and the tasks which accompany it to see what they will have to do.

2 Read the title and subheading to give them an idea of what they're going to read.

3 Look at any accompanying illustrations which will help them understand the passage.

4 Skim the text quickly (in about three minutes) to get a general idea of what it's about, how it's structured and where they will locate information when they come to answer the questions.

Give them three to four minutes to answer the questions in this exercise, depending on your class.

Answers
1 over 30 years; built in the 1970s and opened in 1977
2 a competition
3 at first they didn't get any more work; later both became internationally successful and were given more important architectural projects

❸ Remind students that they should also decide what type of word they are looking at as they work through this exercise and Exercise 4.

Answers
1 c   2 a   3 c   4 b

❹ **Suggested answers**
1 to deal with and control a problem or feeling
2 made someone able to do something   3 able to be moved   4 designing a town or city
5 (buildings) that you can easily recognise
6 following a route that has a lot of bends

❺ Students did multiple-choice questions in Unit 4. Remind students that the first paragraph mentioned in Question 1 is not the subheading. When they do the IELTS test, they may be asked a question about a particular paragraph. They should count the first paragraph as the first one not in italics.

Alternative treatment 1 Elicit the reason for underlining the key ideas in the questions (so students know what the question is focusing on and to make it easier to find the relevant part of the passage). Ask:

– *Should you also underline the key ideas in each alternative?* (No, this will confuse – and anyway only one of them contains the key idea you need.)

– *What should you do after you have underlined the key ideas?* (Find the part of the passage which contains the answer and read that carefully.)

– *What should you do next?* (Once you've understood that section of the passage, read the alternatives and choose the one which matches the meaning expressed in the passage.)

– *Should you read the whole passage carefully before you start?* (No, time is short and you should concentrate on finding the answers to the questions. Some parts of the passage may not have a question, so reading those parts carefully wastes time.)

– *Can you answer a multiple-choice question from a general impression you have?* (No, you must find words in the passage to support your answer.)

Alternative treatment 2 Give your students an opportunity to try to tackle the questions. However, if the class runs into difficulty, reverse the process.

• Tell them the answers to the questions are 1 D, 2 A, 3 C and 4 C. Tell them to read the four paragraphs again and underline the key words.

• Ask students also to match synonyms between the correct answer and words in the passage (e.g. *hurry* and *scramble*).

Suggested underlining
2 writer say / second paragraph / construction
3 main purpose / third paragraph
4 what / architects' dream / fourth paragraph

Answers
1 D (*no-one was really aware of the significance of this unusual building*)
2 A (*a desperate last-minute scramble to finish the building*)
3 C (*But this was just a passing crisis ... with its success the critics swiftly changed their tune*)
4 C (*The architects had been driven by the desire for ultimate flexibility, for a building that would not limit the movement of its users.*)

❻ Matching sentence endings tests students' ability to scan the passage for words relating to each sentence beginning and then to understand in detail what is said before matching the idea or information with a paraphrased ending.

Point out to students that when they approach a second set of questions in a different type of task (e.g. matching here, where before they had multiple choice questions), they may have to go back to the beginning of the passage again to find the answers. NB. This is not the case with these particular sets of questions, which follow on one from the other.

Alternative treatment 1 So that students don't get confused dealing with relatively straightforward questions in a difficult passage, you can closely supervise how they deal with this task.

- Give students not more than 30 seconds to underline the key ideas. Then, round up what they have underlined with the whole class.

- Give them a minute to find the relevant parts of the passage for each question and round up again with the whole class. Ask students to point out exactly where the words in the questions coincide with words in the passage.

- Now give them time to read each part of the passage carefully and underline the words which gave them the answer. Do not help them with unknown vocabulary. Although there will be words they don't know, they should still be able to answer the questions themselves.

- Finally, ask students to quote the words from the passage which gave them the answers.

Alternative treatment 2 If, despite the supervision in Alternative treatment 1, your students still generally have difficulty getting the correct answers, you can reverse the process here too. Tell them what the answers are and ask them to quote the words from the passage which give these answers.

> **Answers**
> **1 5** escalators and lifts   **6** 1970s / pictures
>   **7** original plans / floors   **8** detailed structure
> **2 5** D (*With all the services at one end of the building, escalators and lifts at the other...*)
>   **6** B (*The image of the Pompidou pervaded popular culture in the 1970s, making appearances everywhere – on record album covers and a table lamp...*)   **7** F (*...floors that could also be adjusted up or down. This second feature did not in the end survive when the competition drawings were turned into a real building.*)   **8** A (*a superbly detailed structure. It was this quality which ... suggested that the Pompidou should be seen as closer to the 19th-century engineering tradition ...*)

Extension idea Go through the Exam advice and point out how they followed this process to do the task.

❼ Students have done Yes / No / Not Given, and True / False / Not Given tasks in Units 2 and 6.

Alternative treatment As with Exercise 4, you can closely supervise how your students do this task, so that they learn and gain confidence from doing it.

- Before they do the task, elicit how they should approach it (i.e. underline the key words in the questions, locate the relevant parts of the passage and read those carefully).

- Draw attention to the exam advice: there are words in the questions which will be clearly reflected in the passage to help them read the right part, even when the answer is NOT GIVEN.

- You can also ask them to read the Exam advice on pages 23 and 59.

- Once students have underlined the key ideas, give them two minutes to scan for the words reflected in the passage. Alternatively, you can do this with students step by step. Ask them to find a word which reflects *influenced* (*influential*), etc.

- Remind them that when names or dates occur in questions, this makes it much easier to scan the passage, as names and dates cannot be paraphrased.

> **Suggested underlining**
> **9** influenced / cities / designed
> **10** Guggenheim / more popular / Pompidou
> **11** building / better / construction
> **12** appearance / changed / since / opened
> **13** Nowadays / design / fails to shock
> **14** traditionalist view / changed
>
> **Answers**
> **9** YES (*Nevertheless, as a model for urban planning it has proved immensely influential.*)
> **10** NOT GIVEN (the passage mentions the Guggenheim but does not compare it to the Pompidou)
> **11** NO (*... this construction – it is hard to call it a building ...*
> **12** NO (*Today, the Pompidou Centre itself still looks much as it did when it opened.*)
> **13** NO (*The shock value of its colour-coded plumbing and its structure has not faded with the years.*)
> **14** YES (*But while traditionalists regarded it as an ugly attack on Paris when it was built, they now see it for what it is ...*)

❽ Give students a minute or two to think and make notes about what they want to say before they start.

Listening Note completion

❶ As a warmer Ask students: *What worries you about the listening test? Do you think it's the most difficult part of the exam? What can you do to prepare for it? What advice would you give to friends doing it?*

As general advice you can tell them:

- on *the day of the exam, do a short listening exercise before you go to the exam so that you are not listening to English for the first time that day.*

- *read the questions, underlining the key ideas.*

- *write the answers as you hear them, but remember, you have time to copy them onto the answer sheet at the end.*

- *if you don't understand something, don't panic or 'freeze'. Sit forward in your chair and concentrate.*

- *don't leave any questions without an answer. You don't lose marks for a wrong answer, so it's worth writing something – you might be right.*

Answers
1 T   2 F (You only hear the recording once.)
3 F (The questions follow the order of information in the recording.)   4 T   5 T   6 F (You write your answers onto the question paper and then have 10 minutes at the end of the test to transfer them onto the answer sheet.)   7 F (All answers must be spelled correctly.)

---

❷ Listening Part 4 is directed at students with a CEFR level of C1. It will, therefore, test items which are above the level of B1 students using this coursebook. However, to help students, this exercise pre-teaches vocabulary which will occur in this particular Listening section.

Before they answer the questions, ask students: *Where is Samoa? What do you think life is like there?*

Samoa is a country consisting of two main islands in the South Pacific, forming part of Polynesia. The climate in Samoa is equatorial; the average temperature is 26°c and there is a rainy season between November and April. The islands are volcanic, so the ground is fertile. The main products are dried coconut, cocoa beans and bananas. They also grow sugar cane and pineapples.

Suggested answers
1 thatched roof; floor; beams; posts; circular shape

---

❸ Students should use the picture in Exercise 2 to help them with vocabulary in these notes. Tell them, however, that this is a typical Listening Section 4 and that in the live exam they will not have this help. The Listening exam is graded so that Sections 1 and 2 are aimed at B1 level and this is where they should aim to maximise their marks. Sections 3 and 4 are aimed at a higher level.

- Tell them that in Listening Section 4, there is only one type of task (in this case, note completion) and that they hear the whole recording without a pause.

- Point out that they may need two words for the answers. If they think they need a noun, they may well need adjective + noun or a compound noun.

Suggested answers
1 adj / shape   2 noun / part of house that gives shelter   3 noun / something in or on the floor
4 adj / type of plant   5 adj / describes sides
6 noun / something that can go out of roof
7 noun / a place where wood can be found
8 noun / something linked to people
9 noun / person(s) or object that make(s) things
10 noun / way of attaching rope

---

❹ ⌒ Play the recording once. Then give students two or three minutes to complete their answers.

- They can then compare answers with a partner.
- Play the recording a second time so they can check.
- Ask students to read the recording script to check their answers and their spelling. You can play the recording again while they read.

Answers
1 oval (shaped)   2 blinds   3 (river) stones
4 sugar cane   5 steep   6 heat   7 forest(s)
8 status   9 old people   10 (complex) pattern

Extension idea When students have finished, talk about when to write one or two words.

- 'No more than two words' may mean that a lot of the questions have two-word answers or it may mean that only one does. Usually there are a few.

- If they think an answer is clear in one word (e.g. 'steep' or 'oval') they should not write any additional words. Similarly, if they think two words are essential (e.g. 'old people') they should write both words, even if they are unsure of the spelling of one of the words.

- However there may be times when they have to decide whether to write one or two words. If they know how to spell both words, as in 'river stones' they should write them both as this is clearly a more exact answer than 'stones'.

- On the other hand, if they are uncertain how to spell one of the words, they must decide how important they think each word is.
- For the answer to Question 10, 'complex pattern', both words might be hard to spell, but 'pattern' is the noun and is likely to be more important than 'complex', so they should choose to write just 'pattern'.

❺ *Extension idea* Ask:

- *What is the most unusual house you've seen or stayed in?*
- *Would you prefer to live in a modern house or a traditional house? Why?*

For stronger classes, you can ask: *Do you think traditional houses should be preserved, or should they be replaced by more modern buildings?*

Vocabulary Word choice

❶ Ask students to do this exercise in small groups. To get them started, ask: Is *there any difference in meaning?* (yes – see the suggested answer below) *Which sentence expresses the idea more exactly?*

Tell students they should not always use the first word they think of, or the easiest word, but think about which expresses the idea most exactly.

> **Suggested answer**
>
> The reader understands sentence b better. The word *traditional* explains more clearly what type of old house is being referred to. The word is often used to describe old buildings. The word *features* is also clearer than *parts*, which could refer to rooms, rather than building design.

❷
> **Answers**
> 1 d 2 i 3 h 4 c 5 f 6 b 7 j 8 k 9 a 10 e
> 11 l 12 g

Extension idea Ask students to think of other synonyms for *big, very important, busy* and *rich*. (Suggested answers: *big – large, huge, enormous*; *very important – key, main*; *busy – occupied*; *rich – well-off*)

❸
> **Answers**
> 2 flats – apartments / look – appearance
> 3 rich places – wealthy areas
> 4 wood – timber / build – construct
> 5 very important – essential / make – create
> 6 nice – attractive / fun – enjoyable

Extension idea Ask students to work in pairs and write two of their own sentences, each containing two words from the right-hand column of Exercise 2.

When they have finished, they compare their sentences in pairs. Round up by asking students to read some of their sentences aloud to the class.

Speaking Parts 2 and 3

❶ *As a warmer* With books closed, get students to think about how buildings affect them by asking:

- *What buildings make you feel good? Why?*
- *What buildings don't make you feel so good?*

If students don't come up with ideas, you can suggest things which might affect their feelings (e.g. colour, light, size of rooms, furniture, pictures and other decoration, *feng shui*). Write students' ideas on the board as reference for the task in this exercise.

- Before they do the task, elicit from the whole class possible buildings where they have enjoyed spending time. These could include their homes, friends' homes, a school, a sports centre, a swimming pool, a cinema, a restaurant, etc.
- Point out that to do the task, students needn't talk about architectural features or anything technical.

Alternative treatment If your students want exam practice at this stage in the course, give them a minute to prepare their talks alone and then pass directly to Exercise 2.

❷ As in previous units, ask the student who is listening to give feedback at the end of their partner's talk. If necessary, you can elicit criteria for the feedback before they start. When both students have finished and given feedback, ask them to change partners and do the exercise again.

❸ Elicit the meanings of *actually* and *really* (both are used when you are saying what is the truth of a situation).
> **Answers**
> 2 have / haven't   3 do / don't

❹
> **Answers**
> 1   their appearance: *ugly* versus *beautiful houses*
> 2   1 Although   2 so

Note: Now is a good moment to do the Pronunciation section on sentence stress on page 103.

❺ 🎧
> **Answers**
> **Jaeun:** 1 *even though*   2 traditional houses – amazing when they were built, versus old-fashioned now
> **Billy:** 1 *while*   2 new houses – great outside versus dull inside
> **Phillipe:** 1 *whereas*   2 traditional houses – interesting features versus very plain

6 With weaker classes, round up after each question and sort out difficulties. When they do questions 3 and 4, write their answers on the board and elicit any corrections necessary from the whole class.

> **Suggested answers**
>
> 1 starts with the main idea: *what they earn*
>
> 2 to show how strongly he feels that builders do a more important job
>
> 3 a Their jobs are different. Architects design buildings, whereas builders construct them.
>
> b Their places of work are different. While architects work in an office, builders work on a building site.
>
> c There are differences in status. Whereas architects can become famous for designing a building, no one knows who the builders were.

Extension idea After question 3, ask students in pairs to think of more contrasts between architects and builders. When they are ready, ask them to call them out to the whole class. Finally, ask them to think of contrasting ideas about buildings in cities and buildings in the country.

Ask students to write some of their ideas down as complete sentences for you to check.

7 **Extension idea** Write these questions on the board and ask students, without previous preparation, to work in pairs and ask and answer them.

– *How are airports different from train stations?*

– *Are modern school buildings basically the same as school buildings in the past?*

– *Which are more important to a town: shopping centres or sports stadiums?*

Pronunciation Sentence stress 3

1

> **Suggested underlining**
>
> some / amazing / built / most / old-fashioned
>
> She stresses words which contrast.

2 **Extension idea** Write on the board: *I live in a village, but my uncle lives in the city.* Ask students to predict which words should be stressed and to take turns saying the sentence (stress *I*, *village*, *uncle* and *city*).

3

> **Answers**
>
> 1 great / outside / inside / dull / boring
>
> 2 some / interesting / others / plain

4 Follow up by asking students to say the sentences to the whole class.

5 **Alternative treatment** For weaker classes, ask students to prepare answers in pairs and then change partners and take turns to ask the questions.

Writing Task 2

1 **As a warmer** Ask students to work in small groups and discuss: *What, for you, are the main problems with doing Writing Task 2?* When they have finished, round up with the whole class and discuss possible solutions.

• When they have done the exercise, ask them to look at the Exam overview on page 7.

> **Answers**
>
> 1 40 2 more 3 parts 4 notes 5 plan
>
> 6 punctuation

2 Check that students underline the key ideas as they are reading the task.

• The questions here should help students to think through the implications of the task. When they answer question 4, tell them that in tasks which say *Some people think* and *others believe* (or something similar) it's a good idea to think who might hold the different opinions and why.

• When students have finished discussing, ask them to change groups and compare their ideas.

> **Answers**
>
> There are two parts, expressing two views: buildings should be designed to last a long time vs accommodation should be built quickly and cheaply.

3 > **Answers**
>
> 1 second paragraph
>
> 2 third paragraph
>
> 3 first line of third paragraph: *Although I agree with this I also feel that poor people might not think it is fair* – and all of the last paragraph
>
> 4 Although I agree with this / I also feel that / I think that
>
> 5 second and third sentences of second paragraph
>
> 6 second paragraph: *Even though they were constructed..*; third paragraph: *Although I agree with this...*; Last paragraph: *While city accommodation ...*

4 In this unit, rather than a dedicated spelling section, students are asked to practise editing skills by finding spelling and punctuation mistakes which are commonly made by IELTS candidates at this level. Students need to know that making a lot of spelling mistakes or making mistakes that cause confusion for their reader can reduce their mark. Similarly, if they omit important punctuation, they can also lose marks.

Alternative treatment Before students look for the missing commas, go through the Language reference section on page 129 with them.

> **Answers**
>
> Most **governments** have to build housing for their citizens. As populations grow, more homes are needed, and sometimes the demand for accommodation increases rapidly. If people cannot find places to live, it is a huge worry for them. They do not care about the quality of their housing – they just need somewhere to live.
>
> In the past, many buildings were carefully designed, and people could see that **their** external appearance was important. In my **country**, some of the most beautiful houses are old ones because they have an interesting shape and the architecture is impressive. Even though they were constructed a long time ago, they are still used and can still cost a lot of **money** to buy. For this reason, some people **believe** that homes today should also be well built, using good materials.
>
> Although I agree with this, I also feel that poor people might not think it is fair. Some types of building material are much more expensive **than** others. Architects are also expensive if you use them. We have a lot of apartment blocks in the area where I live, and people want to live in them. They do not think about how much they cost to build. Unfortunately, these buildings may not last very long, and the occupants may have all sorts of **problems** with the building, **which** can mean that more homes have to be built.
>
> In conclusion, I think that both views are relevant. While city accommodation must be well built so that it does not start to fall down **too** soon, it should also be affordable and **available** for people who need it.

Note: Now is a good moment to do the Key grammar section on modal verbs.

5 *Extension idea* When students have finished discussing, ask them to change groups and compare their ideas. Then give them time to amend their plans.

6 Although this task can be done for homework, it's a good idea at some stage in the course and if time permits to ask students to do a writing task in class as if they were doing a mock exam. This gives them a feel for what the exam experience will be like and they may get a clearer idea of their level.

- Remind students that in the exam itself, they have about 40 minutes for this task and they should try to do this in that time.

- Point out that they do not have time to make a fair copy of their answer. When they notice they have made a mistake, they should cross it out and write their correction clearly above it. Remind them to leave space for corrections while they write.

> **Sample answer**
>
> Impressive city buildings are tourist attractions and governments like to spend money on them. However, people need hospitals and schools as well. Although they are less noticeable, this does not mean they are less important. I think governments should spend money on both types of building.
>
> When you visit any city centre, you notice the buildings that stand out. Buildings like the Pompidou Centre in Paris and the Burj Khalifa in Dubai, which is the tallest building in the world, bring many benefits to local citizens. Tourists want to see these buildings and they spend money in the country at the same time. The buildings are also used for important purposes, such as arts centres, and this makes them famous. I believe that governments have to spend money on city buildings if they want their country to be known around the world.
>
> However, governments must also make sure that their citizens are looked after. If there are not enough schools or the school buildings are old, children cannot be educated properly. Similarly, every society needs well-built hospitals and medical facilities. Where I live we have a very large, modern hospital but we also have a lot of elderly people who need care. Our government is planning to build a special centre for them and this will cost a lot of money.
>
> Overall, I believe governments should spend some of their money on city buildings because they need to look after the global status of their country. However, they should also ensure that they have modern school and hospital buildings for their people.

Extension idea As this is the last writing task in the course apart from the practice test at the end of the book, remind them of the stages they should go through in the writing test and suggested timings:

1 *Read the question, underlining the key ideas. (1 minute)*

2 *Analyse the question, think about their opinions, and make a brief plan. (3 minutes)*

3 *Write their answer. (34 minutes)*

4 *Check what they have written. (2 minutes)*

Key grammar Modal verbs

❶ When students have finished the exercise, go through the Language reference section on page 130 with them.

> **Answers**
> **a** must   **b** may/might   **c** can/could   **d** should

Extension idea If all your students speak the same first language, ask them how they would express each of these ideas in their own language.

❷ In order to reinforce the rules they have just studied, tell students to refer to the Language reference on page 130 while they do this exercise. When they finish, ask them why they chose each answer.

> **Answers**
> **2** don't have to   **3** should   **4** couldn't   **5** can
> **6** shouldn't

Extension idea Write these phrases on the board.

Tomorrow I must...   *My friends should...*

Next week I might...   *Last year I couldn't...*

My classmates mustn't...

- Ask students to work alone to complete them.
- When they have finished, ask them to compare their ideas with a partner.

❸ When students have finished, elicit that, apart from question 1, all the mistakes are using the wrong verb form after the modal.

Remind them that modals are always followed by an infinitive, usually without *to*. The only modal in this section which uses *to* is *have to*.

> **Answers**
> **2** ~~may are~~ may be   **3** ~~should to~~ had to   **4** ~~can't buying~~ can't/couldn't buy   **5** ~~cannot played~~ cannot play   **6** ~~have to saved~~ have to save   **7** ~~might stops~~ might stop   **8** ~~must uses~~ must use

Vocabulary and grammar review Unit 9

❶ **2** irrigation   **3** reservoirs   **4** diving   **5** wet   **6** tap
7 thirsty   **8** desalinate

❷ **2** were destroyed   **3** included   **4** designed   **5** is made
6 are created   **7** are classified   **8** comes
9 can be affected

❸ **2** consists of   **3** is located   **4** is needed   **5** is operated
6 switch on   **7** flows   **8** is heated   **9** reduces

Unit 10

❶ **2** landmark   **3** escalators   **4** exhibition   **5** flexibility
6 urban   **7** architects

❷ **2** feature   **3** materials   **4** inside   **5** surroundings
6 foundations   **7** outstanding   **8** appearance

❸ commas after: Spain, child, mother, artist, paper, Nowadays

❹ **2** touch   **3** don't have to   **4** shouldn't   **5** encourage
6 had to   **7** cannot   **8** couldn't

Unit 10 photocopiable activity: The architects Time: 40-50 minutes

> **Objectives**
> - To practise linkers for making contrasts
> - To practise speaking for extended periods
> - To recycle vocabulary related to architecture

Before class

You will need to photocopy page 117 and cut the first section into two parts, so that half of the class have 'A' cards, and the other half have 'B' cards.

❶ Tell students that they are going to prepare a presentation of the design of a new building. Divide the class into two groups, A and B. Then put students into pairs within each group. Give an A or a B card to each student.

- Ask each pair to decide who will be the architect and who will be the project manager. Go through the presentation points for each role and tell them that the presentation should last three minutes.

- You may wish to revise the phrases for beginning and ending talks from Unit 9, such as *I'm going to talk about* and *All in all*. Allow at least 10 minutes for preparation.

❷ When students are ready, ask each pair from the 'A' group to sit with a pair from a 'B' group and present their building. During the presentation phase, be sure to take notes on errors which you can address at the end of the class.

Unit 10 photocopiable activity
The architects

A The Skyline Development

❶ You are going to present the buildings in the picture to other students.

Speaker 1	Speaker 2
You are the project manager. Your job is to: • introduce the project • explain why you think people will like these buildings.	You are the architect. Your job is to: • describe the design of the buildings to the audience • explain how people can use the buildings.

❷ Listen to other peoples' presentations. Think of questions which you would like to ask. For example, *How can people move around? Are the buildings environmentally friendly?*

✂ ···

B The Greenview Development

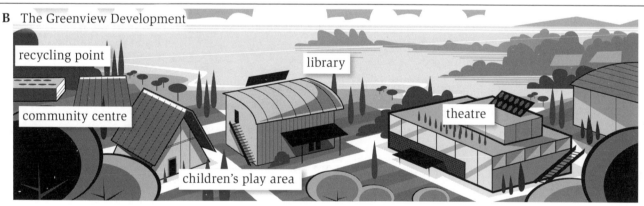

❶ You are going to present the buildings in the picture to other students.

Speaker 1	Speaker 2
You are the project manager. Your job is to: • introduce the project • explain why you think people will like these buildings.	You are the architect. Your job is to: • describe the design of the buildings to the audience • explain how people can use the buildings.

❷ Listen to other students' presentations. Think of questions which you would like to ask.
For example, *How can people move around? Are the buildings environmentally friendly?*

Vocabulary extension
Unit 10

Abbreviations: n/sln/pln = noun / single noun / plural noun; v = verb; adj = adjective; adv = adverb; p = phrase; pv = phrasal verb; T/I = transitive/intransitive; C/U = countable/uncountable

basement *n* [C] a room or set of rooms that is below ground level in a building

balcony *n* [C] a small area joined to the wall outside a room on a high level where you can stand or sit

cave *n* [C] a large hole in the side of a cliff straight, high rock next to the sea, mountain, or under the ground

collapse *v* [I/T] to fall down or towards the inside, or to make a structure or object fall down or towards its inside

community *n* [C] the people living in a particular area

date back to *p* to say how long ago something has existed or when it was made

demolish *v* [T] to destroy something such as a building

developer *n* [C] a person or company that buys land and builds houses, factories, shops, etc.

district *n* [C] a part of a city or country, either an official area or one that is known for having a particular characteristic or business

dominate the landscape *p* to be the largest, most important or most noticeable part of a place

engineering *n* [U] the work of an engineer, or the study of this work

ground floor *n* [C] the level of a building which is on the ground

insulation *n* [U] when you insulate something, or when something is insulated

layout *n* [C] the way that something is arranged

neighbourhood *n* [C] an area of a town or city that people live in

occupy a building *p* to move into a building and take control of it

(on the) outskirts *pln* the outer area of a city town, or village

private property *n* [C/U] a house or area that is only for the use of one person or group and not for everyone

renovate *v* [T] to repair and decorate a building that is old and in bad condition

x-storey building *p* [C] describes how many levels a building has

residential area *p* [C] a part of a town which has only private houses, not offices and factories

skyscraper *n* [C] a very tall building

sports stadium *n* [C] a large, open area with seats around it, used for playing and watching sports

terrace *n* [C] a row of houses that are joined together

terraced house *n* [C] one of a row of houses that are joined together

tile *n* [C] one of the flat, square pieces that are used for covering roofs, floors or walls

town planning *n* [U] the planning of the way in which towns and cities are built in order to make them pleasant to live in

vacant *adj* Somewhere that is vacant is available because it is not being used.

veranda(h) *n* [C] a room that is joined to the outside of a house and has a roof and a floor but no outside wall

❶ **Complete the paragraph with a word or phrase from the box. There are three words or phrases which you do not need to use.**

After	As	First of all	Finally	Where
At last	While	Then	However	

Different types of water pumps are suitable for different locations. **0** ....Where........ communities have no access to electrical power supplies, a solar water pump is ideal. A solar water pump works by four basic steps. **1** ...., a set of solar panels converts sunlight into electrical flow. **2** .... the electricity flows to a controller, which monitors the water level in the well and storage tank. **3** .... that, the electrical flow powers a pump, which moves water from the well to a storage tank. **4** ...., the water is distributed to water taps in individual homes. **5** .... other pumping systems can be expensive to operate, solar water pumps are relatively easy and cheap to run.

❷ **Match the beginnings of the sentences on the left with the endings of sentences on the right. There are three extra endings which you do not need to use.**

0 Desalination plants can be built	**A**	to store water for when it is needed.
1 Filters can be used	**B**	to help farmers water their crops.
2 Dams can be constructed	**C**	to force water out of the ground.
3 Irrigation systems can be set up	**D**	to find fresh water underground.
4 Reservoirs can be made	**E**	to carry water to people's houses.
5 Pipes can be installed	**F**	to make fresh water out of seawater.
	G	to hold back river water.
	H	to remove waste materials from water.
	I	to get drinking water out of taps.

❸ **Choose the correct word to complete each sentence.**

0 The region has been badly *affected* / ~~resulted~~ by drought this season.

1 Lack of water for farming is the main *cause* / *effect* of hunger in many of the world's poorest countries.

2 Installing a simple water pump in a village can *make* / *cause* people's lives so much easier.

3 Poor hygiene facilities can *affect* / *cause* many serious diseases.

4 Millions of people die every year as a *result* / *cause* of drinking polluted water.

5 Having access to clean water has a huge *effect* / *result* on people's health.

4 **Choose the best alternative (A, B or C) for each of these sentences.**

0 A person ....*can*........ learn to swim at any age.

Ⓐ can   **B** must   **C** should

1 Swimming is a cheap hobby because you .... buy any special equipment.

A couldn't   **B** don't have to   **C** mustn't

2 Everyone taking part in the diving course .... have a health check first.

A must   **B** could   **C** might

3 You .... go water-skiing unless you have had proper instruction.

A   don't have to   **B** shouldn't   **C** couldn't

4 I .... even stand up on my board when I began my windsurfing course.

A mustn't   **B** shouldn't   **C** couldn't

5 If you train hard, I think you .... be able to win the sailing competition.

A have to   **B** must   **C** might

5 **Complete these sentences with the correct form (active or passive) and tense of the verb in brackets.**

0 The pyramids *were constructed* around 4,000 years ago. (construct)

1 At the moment, archaeologists .... for the remains of a prehistoric city in South America. (look)

2 Even today, many fine examples of classical Greek architecture can .... in and around Athens. (see)

3 Nearly 2,000 years ago, the Romans .... a 120-kilometre wall across Britain. (build)

4 Historians believe that concrete .... as a building material in ancient Egypt. (use)

5 Some of the best quality marble comes from Carrara in Italy – it .... there since ancient times. (produce)

6 **Complete the paragraph by writing a word from the box in each gap. There are three words which you do not need to use.**

surroundings	occupant	interior	features	architect
appearance	shape	purposes	block	

The Lowry is an arts centre located next to a canal in a former industrial area of Salford, near Manchester, in NW England. It opened in 2000. Because it is situated on a narrow point of land with water on either side, the building is constructed in the **0** ....*shape*........ of a triangle. With its smooth, metallic walls and chimney-like tower, The Lowry has an **1** .... like a ship when viewed from the outside. The overall look of the building fits in perfectly with its maritime and industrial **2** .... This style continues into the **3** .... of the building too, with several **4** .... , such as the blue flooring criss-crossed with silver lines, that reflect the theme of sea travel. The space inside The Lowry is flexible, and can be used for a range of **5** .... such as concerts, exhibitions and conferences.

http://www.thelowry.com/about-the-lowry/the-lowry-building

Answers

Progress tests

PROGRESS TEST Units 1–2

❶ 1 cities **2** feet **3** children **4** women **5** lives

❷ 1 speak **2** I'm studying **3** is growing
4 rains **5** I'm spending

❸ 1 helpful **2** crowded **3** friendly
4 enjoyable **5** healthy

❹ 1 and **2** also **3** However **4** and **5** but

❺ 1 in **2** at **3** on **4** from **5** for

❻ 1 studied **2** met **3** wore **4** wrote **5** took

PROGRESS TEST Units 3–4

❶ 1 C **2** B **3** A **4** A **5** C

❷ 1 more convenient **2** less **3** worse
4 healthier **5** best

❸ 1 E **2** H **3** A **4** I **5** C

❹ 1 since **2** since **3** for **4** since **5** for

❺ 1 have/'ve ….. seen **2** has/'s gone **3** Have …. flown
4 has/'s … broken **5** have/'ve …. driven

❻ 1 data **2** object **3** influence **4** link **5** benefit

PROGRESS TEST Units 5–6

❶ 1 straight **2** cross **3** turn **4** follow **5** reach

❷ 1 Many **2** less **3** number **4** little **5** much

❸ 1 diet **2** predators **3** habitat **4** farmland **5** breed

❹ 1 think **2** look after **3** will disappear
4 reduce **5** you'll see

❺ 1 C **2** A **3** C
4 B **5** B

❻ 1 talented **2** successful **3** regularly
4 importance **5** ability

PROGRESS TEST Units 7–8

❶ 1 attend **2** participate **3** write **4** receive **5** give

❷ 1 risen **2** raise **3** rose **4** raised **5** rising

❸ 1 to **2** at **3** of **4** in **5** by

❹ 1 C **2** C **3** A **4** A **5** B

❺ 1 destination **2** resorts **3** accommodation
4 facilities **5** culture

❻ 1 impressive modern **2** lovely traditional
3 dull industrial **4** expensive new **5** friendly local

PROGRESS TEST Units 9–10

❶ 1 First of all **2** Then **3** After **4** Finally **5** While

❷ 1 H **2** G **3** B **4** A **5** E

❸ 1 cause **2** make **3** cause **4** result **5** effect

❹ 1 B **2** A **3** B
4 C **5** C

❺ 1 are looking **2** be seen **3** built **4** was used
5 has been produced

❻ 1 appearance **2** surroundings **3** interior
4 features **5** purposes

Speaking reference

Part 1 Questions

2 b 3 i 4 h 5 a 6 c 7 d 8 e 9 g

How are you rated?

1 b, e
2 d, g, h
3 a, i
4 c, f, j

Writing reference

Task 1

1 Pie charts

1 It shows which parts of the world tourists to Nepal came from in March 2008 and the percentages.
2 The high percentages are from Asia and Europe and the small percentage is from Australia.
3 It shows the additional numbers of tourists who went to Nepal in March 2008 and the overall percentage increase from March 2007.
4 the big increase in numbers from Europe and the Americas, the small increase in numbers from Asia, and the overall increase
5 the past simple
6 the first two sentences of the second paragraph; sentences 1, 2 and 4 in the third paragraph
7 Yes, they are accurate.
8 while; On the other hand; However; Whereas; However

2 Charts and graphs

1 the number of phones sold, in millions
2 Jun 07–Dec 10 (two years and three months). The data are presented in three-month periods, i.e. every quarter.
3 key points: a) the overall increase; b) the peak in Sep 08; c) the peak in Dec 10
4 By dividing the time into two sections: Jun 07–Sep 08 and Sep 08–Dec 10.
5 sales increased enormously; there was some fluctuation; rose from … to; fell back to; increased by; reached a peak of; steady drop in; began to rise again; a considerable increase to; a very slight decrease in; another big increase over; an upward trend in; over the period
6 The introduction is the first paragraph, and the overview is the last.

3 Tables

1 It rains in the cooler months at the beginning and end of the year, whereas it stops raining when it is hottest.
2 Suggested answer: the main contrast between amount of rainfall and sun
3 by summarising the table in the second paragraph and the graph in the third
4 The writer has included the figures that illustrate the key points.

4 Diagrams

1 the height and shape of the buildings; the building material; the foundations; the roofs; features such as the windows and sprinklers; the use of recycled material
2 examples: tall, high-rise, concrete, rectangular, flat, etc.
3 present tense and some passives
4 2nd paragraph: details of the shape, top and bottom of the buildings
   3rd paragraph: the walls
   4th paragraph: special features
   5th paragraph: the overview.
5 are built; are made of; are constructed; are also placed; is made of; is used; is related to
   The passive is used because the building deigns are more important than who constructed them.

Task 2

Advantages and disadvantages

1 travel to somewhere new and different / prefer familiar places
3 2 discover 3 new experiences 4 understanding
   5 stressful 6 travel arrangements 7 make mistakes
   8 trips
4 Paragraphs 2 and 3 are about the advantages, and paragraph 4 is about the disadvantages.
5 yes, in the final paragraph

To what extent do you agree?

2 possibly countries that have a lot of rainfall
3 main idea: link between water supply and weather supporting ideas: a lot of rain – no need to control supplies / little rain – must control supplies if possible / unexpected droughts – water use should be controlled
4 The writer's views are at the end of the first three paragraphs and the conclusion and in the third sentence of the fourth paragraph: *I think it depends on where you live. / In my view, it is not necessary to control water use in these countries. / There may be government controls about using water, for things like recreation or washing cars, but sometimes water is so*

hard to find or collect that controls are unnecessary. / I think these governments should tell people to use less water all through the year. While it is important to limit water use in some countries, it is impossible or not sensible to do this in others.

These views show that the writer clearly answers the question.

5 access to clean, running water / store / water supplies / rainfall / dry period / drought / conserve water / washing / collect

Two questions to answer

1 a) the destruction of animal habitats; b) the endangering of animals' lives
2 The brackets give more information about *animal species*. This is provided to help you – you do not have to write about these species in particular.
3 Paragraphs 2 and 3 answer the first question, and paragraphs 3 and 4 answer the second question.
4 *they* – animals; *them* – animals; *this* – hunting animals for reasons other than food or clothing; *their* – tigers and whales; *This/it* – cutting down forests and building roads and railways on farmland or grassland; *them* – hunters; *this* – cut down forests; *they* – the organisations; *there* – special animal sanctuaries; *this* – look after endangered animals

Practice test

Listening, Section 1

1 two/2 weeks
2 family room
3 Shriver
4 Scotland
5 0131 99/double 9 46 5723
6 (enjoy) swimming
7 (very) clean
8 too helpful
9 polite
10 bikes/bicycles

Narrator:	You will hear a woman talking on the phone to a hotel receptionist.
Man:	Good morning, Atlas Hotel, can I help you?
Woman:	Oh yes – a friend has told me about your hotel, and I'd like to book some rooms, please.
Man:	OK. When would you like to stay here?
Woman:	Well, we've booked flights on the 23rd of August.
Man:	OK … I'll just find that date.
(Pause)	
Man:	Good morning, Atlas Hotel, can I help you?

Woman:	Oh yes – a friend has told me about your hotel, and I'd like to book some rooms, please.
Man:	OK. When would you like to stay here?
Woman:	Well, we've booked flights on the 23rd of August.
Man:	OK … I'll just find that date. That seems to be fine – we have a few rooms available then.
Woman:	Oh, that's good. I was a bit worried – we've left things rather late.
Man:	Well, you're lucky – we had two cancellations last week.
Woman:	Oh!
Man:	Now, how long do you want to stay for?
Woman:	Well, last year we only stayed a week, and it wasn't long enough … so this time we thought two weeks, if it's possible.
Man:	Mmm, that looks fine … yes, you do need plenty of time here to really relax … it'll be getting towards the end of the tourist season as well, so it won't be quite so hot then.
Woman:	Oh good. Um … we've got two children, and I was wondering if you have any rooms that are next to each other?
Man:	Mmm. Let's see … I'm afraid that isn't possible, but we do have what we call a family room, which is a lot bigger than a double room and can take two adults and two children.
Woman:	Oh, that sounds perfect.
Man:	OK – I'll book you in for that. So, can I have your name and address, please?
Woman:	Yes, it's Mr and Mrs Shriver.
Man:	Can you spell that for me?
Woman:	Yes, it's S-H-R-I-V-E-R.
Man:	Thank you. And you said two children, didn't you?
Woman:	Yes, they're two boys of 10 and 12.
Man:	Fine – and can I have your home address?
Woman:	Yes, we live at flat 29, Tower Heights.
Man:	OK – is that England?
Woman:	No, it's Scotland, actually. We're from Dunbar. The postcode's EH41 2GK.
Man:	OK. Great – that's a country I'd really like to visit!
Woman:	You'd have to bring a lot of warm clothes!
Man:	I know … And can I have a contact telephone number?
Woman:	Sure – our home number is 0-1-3-1 double 9-4-6-5-7-2-3.

Man:	7-2-3. Thank you. I hope you don't mind, but we always ask our guests what the purpose of their trip is. I'm guessing yours is a holiday?
Woman:	Yes – we're really looking forward to it!
(Pause)	
Man:	As you've been here before, I wonder if you'd mind answering a few short questions for our tourist board?
Woman:	No, not at all.
Man:	They collect information from tourists, so that they can try to improve the tourism industry here.
Woman:	That's a good idea.
Man:	OK – um, so what type of holiday activity do you like best?
Woman:	Well, I like a lot of things … I like shopping and sightseeing … but I think as a family, we all enjoy swimming the most.
Man:	OK … and do you go to the beaches to do that?
Woman:	Well, sometimes we do. We also like to sit around the pool at the hotel.
Man:	When you go to the beaches, what do you think of them?
Woman:	Well, they're a bit crowded …
Man:	I know.
Woman:	But then you expect that in the holidays. The main thing is that they're very clean. That's why we come back here.
Man:	I'm glad to hear that. And you said you like shopping …?
Woman:	Yes – it's fun.
Man:	How are the shop staff? Are they—
Woman:	Well, I don't want to criticise, but sometimes … well, they're a bit too helpful.
Man:	… trying to sell you souvenirs.
Woman:	Yes – I prefer to choose things myself.
Man:	Uh-huh … What about eating … and the service in the restaurants?
Woman:	Oh, the food is delicious – always. And the waiters – well, they're polite and so fast … Nothing takes very long.
Man:	That's good news. Sometimes people complain, but …
Woman:	Well, I haven't been to every restaurant – there are rude waiters everywhere, I suppose.
Man:	Well, we like to avoid it if we can. Do you have suggestions for things which might improve your holiday experience here?

Woman:	Um – not really. Let me think … Oh yes – I did notice last time I was there that there are local buses, but you don't seem to have any bikes.
Man:	No, we don't – most people have cars.
Woman:	Mmm – it's just nice to hire one and get some exercise … go at a slower pace so that you can really see the landscape.
Man:	OK – I'll note that down. Well, thank you very much …

Section 2

11 welcome
12 70 species
13 (hand-)feed
14 farm(-)yard / farmyard
15 exercise run
16 B
17 G
18 E
19 C
20 H

Good morning, everyone. I'm a keeper here at Orana Wildlife Park, and that means that my job is to look after some of the animals that we have here. First, let me tell you a bit about us. Um, the word 'Orana' means 'welcome' in the local Maori language, and we are very pleased to see you all here.

As you probably know, we're run by a charity and we specialise in endangered species of animals, birds and reptiles. The park grounds cover 80 hectares of land, and we have 400 animals altogether from 70 different species. So that you can see the animals in their natural environment, we've built streams and banks to separate you from the animals and make sure your trip around the park is safe.

Our animals come mainly from here – New Zealand – and from Australia, Africa and South America. There are a lot of animals to see and quite a number of things you can do here, so let me tell you about a few of the exciting encounters before you decide where to go.

One of our most popular animals is a type of giraffe called a Rothschild. It's easy to spot – it has three horns, rather than the usual two. Giraffes are amazing animals close up, and you have an opportunity to hand-feed them here at the park at twelve noon or three in the afternoon. This is one of the most popular activities and will be one that you'll never forget.

In fact, we believe hands-on education is very important. So, you can touch or pat a variety of friendly animals, such as cows and goats at the farmyard. This experience goes on all day and is designed to help children take an interest in animals and their environment. I can assure you it's not at all dangerous.

Another exciting activity for visitors is watching some of our big cats reach speeds of up to 70 kilometres per hour during their exercise run. The cheetah is the fastest land mammal, and this 'event' takes place at 3.40 every day. You can watch them go down their paddock in under 30 seconds.

(*Pause*)

So here's a plan of the park. As you can see, we're here at the main entrance, and there's an information centre and to your right.

Now – it's quite easy to get around the park. We have daily guided walkabout tours, which let you get up close to the animals. Or if you prefer to be at a distance, you can take the safari bus and drive around with a wildlife expert.

If you decide to take the walkabout tour, it leaves at 10.45 – that's in just under an hour – from the meerkats enclosure next to us. From there, the walk passes the adventure playground, and the otters in the first enclosure and then arrives at the New Zealand birds area in the next enclosure just in time to see them being fed. Then you go on to the reptile house and the tigers and the rest of the animals!

Alternatively, you can wait until the afternoon walk. There are plenty of other things to see in the morning. One of these is the African Village. Just turn to your right from the main entrance, walk past the first bus stop and it's just before the African wild dogs enclosure. It's a wonderful, colourful experience.

You can also go to the shop and buy your souvenirs there. We have beautiful soft toys – giraffe and zebra for children and a whole range of T-shirts, hats and skin-care products with an African theme. After that, why not have lunch in the picnic area on the far eastern side of the park? I'd recommend this because, while you're eating, you might catch sight of the ostriches on one side of you or buffalo on the other.

For the afternoon walkabout tour, you'll need to find your own way to the African lion habitat, which is on the west side of the park, just past the Conservation Centre. To join the tour, you actually go past the lion habitat. You'll see two bus stops … keep walking, and the meeting place is about half a kilometre after the second one. If you've gone past the zebra, you've gone too far!

For those of you who would prefer to travel on the safari bus, this runs from 10.30 to 4 p.m. There are stations throughout the park, but the first one is at Jomo's Café, which is directly opposite where we're standing – go straight ahead and it's just in front of the giraffes. There are various feeding times for the animals, and the bus stops in time for all of these. So, let me just give you some safety guidelines …

Section 3

21 C
22 B
23 A
24 A
25 B
26 C
27 B
28 lectures
29 diagram
30 (wide) margin

Narrator:	You will hear two students giving the results of a survey they conducted.
Tutor:	Right – now it's time for Sylvie and Daniel to give us the results of their survey into the study-skills course that some of you did last term.
Sylvie:	Thanks, Mr Driver. Um – shall I start Daniel?
Daniel:	Sure, go ahead.
Sylvie:	OK. Well, as you know, some students in our year did the study-skills course run by the English department last term.
Daniel:	Um, it was interesting because it was completely voluntary … it wasn't a compulsory component of the exam course or anything that we need in that way … but Mr Driver thought it would be a good idea … that it would help with our other work.
Sylvie:	Yeah, so after the course finished, Daniel and I decided to review it … ask students what they thought about it … as part of our education assignment.
Daniel:	Yeah.
Sylvie:	So … this is how we did it … our study method. At first, we thought about interviewing students face to face. But we have so much other work and we knew it'd be quicker to use email and just send out a questionnaire.
Daniel:	Though we also had to write that!
Sylvie:	Yes, and this method does rely on students filling it in and sending it back … but the response rate was pretty good.
Daniel:	Yeah – 70 percent, I think.
Sylvie:	OK – so, first of all, 33 students signed up for the course.
Daniel:	And we did 12 sessions over the term, and they took place every Monday morning.
Sylvie:	A good start to the week, I thought.
Daniel:	Yeah – and the rest of the week, we could put things into practice.
Sylvie:	Mmm. So what did we expect?

Daniel:	For me … I expected it to be useful for all my subjects … things like philosophy –
Sylvie:	Yeah – that's what Mr Driver had said.
Daniel:	– and I was right … I feel more able to deal with difficult texts now – you know, like the ones we have in economics.
Sylvie:	You feel you can do it. I think other people found that it actually made them want to read more frequently … and read books outside the course list.
Daniel:	If you've got time! Um – as for our teacher on the course – Jenny – everyone felt she was really good. We learned a lot from her. Not because she set a lot of homework or anything like that …
Sylvie:	… the thing people said was that she gave us fascinating articles and ideas to work with … some of them … well, we were quite happy to carry on looking at them at home.
Daniel:	Yeah – that's so important. It's really easy to get bored in class, but that didn't happen.
(Pause)	
Daniel:	OK – so, we've done a couple of charts … let's have a look at the findings. I'll put up the first chart …
Sylvie:	This is your overall view of the usefulness of the course.
Daniel:	… and as you can see, only a small percentage of students didn't feel it was useful.
Sylvie:	Which is good …
Daniel:	Yeah – everyone else had a positive view of the course, and more than half of us – that's about 60 percent – thought it was very useful.
Sylvie:	Which … well, as this is the first time the course has been run, I guess this is a strong recommendation for it to take place again next year.
Daniel:	The next chart shows how useful you felt each part of the course was.
Sylvie:	So just to remind you … there was the speed-reading component – that came out top.
Daniel:	No surprise there, really.
Sylvie:	Mmm. On the other hand, giving talks was … well, we all like talking, but it's not something we have to do that often.
Daniel:	Yeah – so that was the least useful.
Sylvie:	Then the <u>note-taking</u> component you found to be quite useful – and you had a lot of comments about that.

Sylvie:	Ok, so let's have a look at some of your comments. You said a lot about the activities, but the main comment seemed to be that the techniques we learned on the note-taking course helped us focus more in lectures.
Daniel:	Several people said that they daydream much less.
Sylvie:	Yeah … have a longer attention span.
Daniel:	So that's the first benefit. The second is that students said they really appreciated the instruction on when to use a diagram to take notes.
Sylvie:	Mmm, like many people, I'd never thought of this technique, but now I find it really helpful.
Daniel:	… and it's much more fun!
Sylvie:	Yeah. And then the last comment we wanted to mention was about the type of paper that we used in the note-taking sessions.
Daniel:	It seems obvious now that a wide margin down the side of the paper provides another area where you can add points that you've missed.
Sylivie:	And that makes it a lot easier to read the notes afterwards.
Daniel:	OK, so now we'll look at the results …

Section 4

31 bus station
32 city
33 mass tourism
34 international business
35 (first) impression
36 (open) areas
37 stress
38 roof
39 (shaded) garden(s)
40 energy (use)

Narrator:	You will hear a lecture about airport design.

Good morning, everyone. Well – last week, we looked at some of the architectural features of modern house design and today we're going to move on to look at airport design and how this has changed over the years.

So, if we start by going back to … um … the 1960s and 70s, when there were a lot fewer airports than there are today … well, check-in desks, customs and waiting areas were all very basic. They were rather like a bus station – er, designed to allow air traffic in and out of the terminal, but not very welcoming for passengers. Even though passengers spent a lot of time there, the important features were related to the flights, rather than the people who took them … or indeed the places where the airports were built.

But that all changed in the next few decades, and if you look at any big airport now, it's more like a mini city. It combines a transport centre with a mall full of shops and facilities designed to make passengers feel more comfortable. So, airports have been transformed. And as with any city building, their design now takes into account features outside the airport terminal as well.

So why did this change happen? Well, there are two main reasons. The first was the huge increase in passenger numbers … in the number of people travelling by plane. And this was a direct result of mass tourism, with things like, um, cheap holiday packages and low-cost airlines … with the construction of high-rise hotels and hotel complexes. And then people started travelling more regularly from one country to another for things like meetings, and so the growth in international business also pushed numbers up. In fact, passenger growth has been so significant over the past 30 years that it's estimated that some 21st-century airports will need to handle up to 50 million passengers a year by 2020.

The second reason for the change is – and this is a key aspect of airport design – people have realised that the airport is the first place you see when you visit another country. This means it forms your first impression of that country and that impression has to be good. Airports are now called 'gateways' to the cities they serve, and that raises visitor expectations.

Now, what are the changes that have taken place in airport design? Well, the interior design – the inside of most airports – is now completely different. First, the dark, enclosed airports of the past have been replaced by large, open areas that look out onto the surroundings. Look at this picture of Beijing airport – there's a huge amount of space and light, and this is typical of many airports today.

Second … well, in the past, you had to go outside the airport to get trains to terminals, but now these are integrated into the design. Also, airport walkways are wide and can cope with the large volume of people … people who want to feel calm and relaxed – who want to get around the airport easily. In this way, the stress of modern travel has been minimised.

Outside, the buildings have changed, too. Airports were once ugly buildings with large towers and concrete boxes around them. Now they're designed to fit into their surroundings. Look at this picture of the Arctic Circle airport in Norway. The airport itself is surrounded by mountains. So, as you can see, the roof of the airport has been designed so that it's shaped like a range of mountains. There are peaks at the top and then steep sides that touch the ground.

In the same way, these airports in Thailand and India have beautiful shaded gardens all around them that reflect the landscape of the country. They also provide a connection with local tradition and art … another feature that is important inside airports, too.

And there's one final but very important issue. It's been said that airports are a 'new building type'. They're often light, steel structures with what looks to the passenger like a lot of glass. But this is special glass that can maximise daylight and comfort and cut down on energy use. Bangkok's main airport is flooded with controlled daylight in a tropical climate … and this is achieved through the use of new materials and modern technology, which have also allowed engineers to come up with methods of reducing costs. So let's take a closer look at some of these …

Reading

Section 1

1 (basic) physics
2 (small) model
3 scrap yards / scrapyards
4 (bath) pipe
5 tractor fan
6 FALSE
7 FALSE
8 NOT GIVEN
9 TRUE
10 TRUE
11 39 feet
12 kerosene
13 science

Section 2

14 C
15 G
16 A
17 H
18 E
19 A or D
20 D or A
21 D or E
22 E or D
23 explorers
24 summer (season)
25 ice rink
26 (melting) glaciers

Section 3

27 B   28 D   29 C   30 D   31 A   32 Not Given   33 Yes
34 Yes   35 No   36 No   37 D   38 F   39 A   40 E

Writing

Task 1

Sample answer

The chart shows how many hybrid vehicles were sold in Japan, the US and the rest of the world from 2006 to 2009. During this time, total sales more than doubled from 360,000 to 740,000. However, the trends in the US and Japan were very different.

According to the data, sales were high in the US, but the pattern fluctuated. While they rose by 100,000 from 2006 to 2007, they peaked in 2007 at 350,000. After that, there was a steady fall to 280,000 in 2009. On the other hand, sales in Japan were much lower at the start. They rose gradually to 90,000 in 2008, but then they jumped to 330,000 in 2009. Sales in the rest of the world increased steadily from 50,000 to 120,000 during the four-year period.

Overall, the data show that more hybrid vehicles were bought in the US than in any other country. However, in 2009, Japan overtook the US and became the country where most vehicles were sold.

(166 words)

Task 2

Sample answer

Inventors are creative people who develop new ideas and products, whereas doctors are specialists who make us feel better when we are ill. I believe that both types of people are important to society, but in different ways.

Inventors have had an enormous impact on our lives. In the past, they developed things like electricity, television and aeroplanes. These transformed people's home lives and working conditions and enabled them to travel more quickly to other countries. More recently, inventors have created computers, the World Wide Web and many other technological products that we now rely on completely. For these reasons, most people would agree that inventors are important people.

Doctors, on the other hand, save lives. They train for many years and they develop knowledge and skills that ordinary people do not have. If we get ill, we need someone who knows what is wrong and can tell us what medicine to take. If we go to hospital, we expect doctors to look after us. Everyone depends on doctors in this way all through their life.

Although we cannot live without doctors, it is also true that we cannot live without inventors. In fact, they also depend on each other. Doctors use inventions to help them in their work, and inventors get ill and need doctors to cure them.

To conclude, I think doctors and inventors are equally important. Like many people in society, they play an important part in human progress. So it is impossible to say who is more important.

(252 words)